新视域普通高等教育
大学英语规划教材

透过电影看文化

陈红 ◎ 主编
徐丽华 马友 ◎ 副主编

Culture
Through Movies

人民邮电出版社
北京

图书在版编目（CIP）数据

透过电影看文化 / 陈红主编. -- 北京：人民邮电出版社，2013.9（2019.1重印）
新视域普通高等教育大学英语规划教材
ISBN 978-7-115-32831-1

Ⅰ. ①透… Ⅱ. ①陈… Ⅲ. ①英语－阅读教学－高等学校－教材 Ⅳ. ①H319.4

中国版本图书馆CIP数据核字(2013)第200815号

内 容 提 要

本书适合普通高等院校完成基础阶段英语学习的各类非英语专业学生进行文化素质拓展教育的培养，也适用于英语专业学生了解英美文化。全书共包括走马观花看英美、英伦王室、驴象庄园、美国梦、假日佳日、爱字从心、什锦色拉、曾经时刻、文学经典的影像脚注和一路光芒10个单元。每个单元由"给力起步"、"光影星荟萃"和"美文品读"三部分构成。每单元第一部分通过Notes对相关的文化背景知识做了详尽的解释说明；第二部分由"好片抢先知"、"星光闪烁"、"余音绕梁"、"文化反光镜"和"八卦一下"介绍电影并讲解相关的文化知识；第三部分选取相关文章并通过"解文说词"、"文化大本营"和"写作秘笈"对其中的语言点、重要的文化背景知识和写作技巧进行讲解。

◆ 主　　编　陈　红
　　副 主 编　徐丽华　马　友
　　责任编辑　李海涛
　　责任印制　彭志环　杨林杰

◆ 人民邮电出版社出版发行　北京市丰台区成寿寺路11号
　　邮编　100164　电子邮件　315@ptpress.com.cn
　　网址　http://www.ptpress.com.cn
　　北京天宇星印刷厂印刷

◆ 开本：787×1092　1/16
　　印张：13　　　　　　　　　2013年9月第1版
　　字数：335千字　　　　　　2019年1月北京第4次印刷

定价：39.80元

读者服务热线：(010)81055256　印装质量热线：(010)81055316
反盗版热线：(010)81055315

前　言

随着全球化的发展和跨文化交流的日益加强，高校学生在提高自身英语水平的同时，还应深入了解英语国家的社会与文化概貌。本书旨在培养高校学生文化素质拓展教育，帮助学生熟悉西方礼仪、风土民情及英美国家的价值观、思维方式和心理结构，从而从整体了解西方文化，开拓视野，提高跨文化交流能力。

本书摒弃了传统的课文解读英美文化的模式，通过电影、美文的方式了解文化，将电影作为一个平台，着眼点在于文化，同时兼顾语言的视听说和应用，使学生在一种轻松、愉悦的环境下更容易接受教授的知识。

本书具有如下主要特点。

一、简明扼要、脉络清晰：将英美文化融为一体，以文化为切入点，尤其注重文化的平衡和对比，培养学生对文化的敏感度，增强对不同文化的理解。

二、主线明确、选题典型：每单元围绕一个相关的文化主题展开，选择的影片风格多样，兼顾不同风格。

三、有限篇章、无限知识：不仅分析电影，还通过电影所反映的时代背景，分析了西方社会的政治经济和历史文化，更多地将电影当作一种社会文化文本，为人们了解西方文化提供了一种影像解读的窗口。除此之外，在每单元之后增加扩充篇，补充同类文化背景的电影作品，以弥补篇幅及课时之限。

四、双语教材、双语读物：本教材为双语教材和双语读物，选取英文原版电影，语言地道、语境真实，英语讲述文化点，并配以汉语阐释，使学生更易理解。

五、学习欣赏、美文点睛：有别于一般视听说教材，本书侧重于在欣赏电影的同时，提供英美文化知识的切入角度和学习方法，为此在每单元特增加相关文化背景的美文供学生品读，加深学生对英美文化的理解深度，并对美文进行解读，在了解文化的同时，学习一些写作技巧。

六、精彩电影、趣味文化：本教材摒弃了传统的课文解读英美文化的模式，通过电影、美文的方式了解文化，学生在一种轻松、愉悦的环境下更容易接受教授的知识。

PREFACE

　　本书为西安邮电大学战略发展项目中"大学英语教学改革"的主要配套教材，是项目核心"课程体系建设"四大模块之一——"知识文化类"的重要教材，为非英语专业学生的英语文化知识拓展而编写，可用于已完成基础阶段英语学习的各类非英语专业学生的文化素质拓展教育，具有广泛的社会意义和社会效益。

　　本书由陈红（编写11万字）任主编，参加编写工作的还有徐丽华（编写11万字）、马友（编写11万字）。本书在编写过程中参阅了有关材料，力求达到通俗、易懂、全面、实用，虽经精心编写，但因水平等条件有限，书中或有不妥与疏漏之处，敬请读者不吝赐教。

　　本书在出版过程中得到西安邮电大学外国语学院的袁小陆和陈德院长及人民邮电出版社的大力协助，谨在此表示感谢。

编　者

2013年4月

目 录

Unit 1

**Unit 1　Now for Britain and America
走马观花看英美　　　　　　　　1**

United Kingdom of Great Britain and Northern Ireland
大不列颠及北爱尔兰联合王国　　　2
The United States of America　美利坚合众国　　12

Unit 2

**Unit 2　British Monarchy: Love It or Loathe It?
英伦王室：英国人的纠结　　　　21**

Part Ⅰ. Get-go　给力起步　　　　22
Part Ⅱ. cineWatch　光影星荟萃　　25
The Queen　《女王》　　　　　　25
Part Ⅲ. Extra Credit　美文品读　　29
Royal Wedding: Savior of the British Monarchy?
王室大婚：谁能拯救温莎王朝?　　29

Unit 3

Unit 3　For The Donkey or The Elephant?
驴象庄园：这个地方有点乱　　　　　　　34

Part Ⅰ. Get-go　给力起步　　　　　　　35
Part Ⅱ. cineWatch　光影星荟萃　　　　38
All the President's Men　《总统班底》　38
Part Ⅲ. Extra Credit　美文品读　　　　43
Imagine the thoughts in Blagojevich's veins
布拉戈耶维奇：你手上的青筋已经告诉了我　　43

Unit 4

Unit 4　This is American Dream
梦想与现实　　　　　　　　　　　　　49

Part Ⅰ. Get-go　给力起步　　　　　　　50
Part Ⅱ. cineWatch　光影星荟萃　　　　54
Forrest Gump　《阿甘正传》　　　　　54
Part Ⅲ. Extra Credit　美文品读　　　　58
Wake up to American Dream
还做美国梦吗？该醒醒了！　　　　　　58

Unit 5 Come Together for Holidays
假日佳日：节日欢歌　　　　　　　　　　66

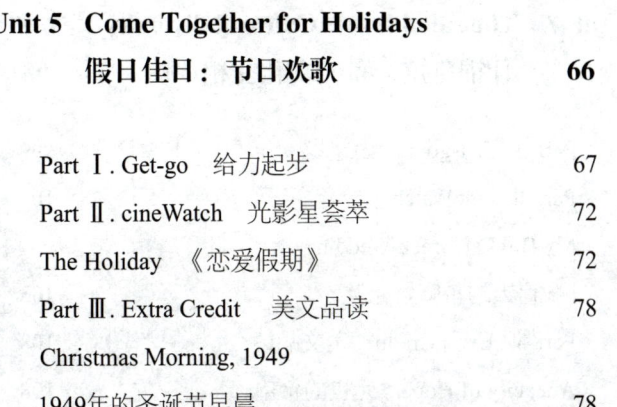

Part Ⅰ. Get-go　给力起步　　　　　　　67

Part Ⅱ. cineWatch　光影星荟萃　　　　72
The Holiday　《恋爱假期》　　　　　　72

Part Ⅲ. Extra Credit　美文品读　　　　78
Christmas Morning, 1949
1949年的圣诞节早晨　　　　　　　　　78

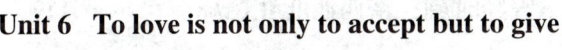

Unit 6 To love is not only to accept but to give
爱字从心：这是心的接受和给予　　　　82

Part Ⅰ. Get-go　给力起步　　　　　　　83

Part Ⅱ. cineWatch　光影星荟萃　　　　88
Stepmom　《继母》　　　　　　　　　　88

Part Ⅲ. Extra Credit　美文品读　　　　93
College girl stops home for a spray tan
我的小潮女，爸爸就爱你!　　　　　　93

Unit 7

Unit 7   The salad bowl: Cultural diversity
　　　　　什锦色拉：多元文化交相辉映　　　　98

　　　Part Ⅰ. Get-go   给力起步　　　　　　　99
　　　Part Ⅱ. cineWatch   光影星荟萃　　　　103
　　　My Big Fat Greek Wedding
　　　《我盛大的希腊婚礼》　　　　　　　　　103
　　　Part Ⅲ. Extra Credit   美文品读　　　　108
　　　Audacity of Hope   无畏的希望　　　　　108

Unit 8

Unit 8   Something racial: I still have a dream
　　　　　曾经时刻：密西西北在燃烧　　　　117

　　　Part Ⅰ. Get-go   给力起步　　　　　　　118
　　　Part Ⅱ. cineWatch   光影星荟萃　　　　125
　　　The Help   《女仆》　　　　　　　　　　125
　　　Part Ⅲ. Extra Credit   美文品读　　　　133
　　　I Have a Dream   我有一个梦想　　　　　133

Unit 9

Unit 9 Literature's marriage to Movies: Yes, I Do!
电影：文学经典的影像脚注　　　　　140

    Part Ⅰ. Get-go　给力起步　　　　　141
    Part Ⅱ. cineWatch　光影星荟萃　　　146
    Gone With the Wind　《乱世佳人》　　146
    Part Ⅲ. Extra Credit　美文品读　　　150
    When the ordinary becomes universal
    当平凡成为真理　　　　　　　　　　150

Unit 10

Unit 10 Not of an Age, but All Time
一路光芒：英雄与时间同在　　　　156

    Part Ⅰ. Get-go　给力起步　　　　　157
    Part Ⅱ. cineWatch　光影星荟萃　　　186
    Lincoln　《林肯》　　　　　　　　186
    Part Ⅲ. Extra Credit　美文品读　　　192
    Charismatic Leader Dies　永别了，南美硬汉！　192

参考文献　　　　　　　　　　　　　　198

Unit 1

Now for Britain and America

走马观花看英美

United Kingdom of Great Britain and Northern Ireland

大不列颠及北爱尔兰联合王国

Geography 地理篇

The total area of the United Kingdom is approximately 243,610 square kilometres. The country occupies the major part of the British Isles archipelago and includes the island of Great Britain, the north-eastern one-sixth of the island of Ireland and some smaller surrounding islands. It lies between the North Atlantic Ocean and the North Sea with the south-east coast coming within 35 kilometres of the coast of northern France, from which it is separated by the English Channel. As of 1993 10% of the UK was forested, 46% used for pastures and 25% used for agriculture.

大不列颠及北爱尔兰联合王国（简称英国），是由英格兰、苏格兰、威尔士和北爱尔兰组成的联合王国。英国是位于欧洲西部的岛国，由大不列颠群岛、爱尔兰东北部和一些小岛组成，隔北海、多佛尔海峡、英吉利海峡与欧洲大陆相望。

Royal House 皇室篇

The United Kingdom is a unitary state under a constitutional monarchy. Queen Elizabeth II is the head of the state of the UK as well as of fifteen other independent Commonwealth countries. The monarch itself is symbolic rather than political, and only has "the right to be consulted, the right to encourage, and the right to warn".

英国的政体为君主立宪制。女王伊丽莎白二世是英国和其他15个英联邦成员国的国家元首。作为宪法意义上的国家元首，君主仍然保留了重要的象征意义。

Government 政府篇

The UK has a parliamentary government based on the Westminster system that has been emulated around the world—a legacy of the British Empire. The parliament of the United Kingdom that meets in the Palace of Westminster has two houses: an elected House of Commons and an appointed House of Lords. Any bill passed requires Royal Assent to become law.

> 英国的议会政体被称为"威斯敏斯特体系",该法令系统被世界很多国家采用。英国议会分为选举产生的下议院(平民院)和指定产生的上议院(贵族院),所有通过的法案草案须由英国君主批准后方可成为法律。

Economy 经济篇

The UK has a partially regulated market economy. Based on market exchange rates the UK is today the sixth-largest economy in the world and the third-largest in Europe after Germany and France, having fallen behind France for the first time in over a decade in 2008.

> 英国作为一个重要的贸易实体、经济强国以及金融中心,是世界第六大经济体,也是全球最富裕、经济最发达和生活水平最高的国家之一。

Education 教育篇

Education in Britain is the responsibility of the Secretary of State for Education, though the day-to-day administration and funding of state schools is the responsibility of local authorities. Education is now mandatory from ages five to sixteen. The majority of children are educated in state-sector schools, only a small proportion of which select on the grounds of academic ability. State schools which are allowed to select pupils according to intelligence and academic ability can achieve comparable results to the most selective private schools.

英格兰、威尔士和苏格兰实行5~16岁义务教育制度,北爱尔兰地区实行4~16岁义务教育制度。义务教育归地方政府主管,高等教育则由中央政府负责。英国公立学校学生免交学费。私立学校收费高,但师资条件与教学设备都较好,学生多为富家子弟。

Religion 宗教篇

Forms of Christianity have dominated religious life in what is now the United Kingdom for over 1,400 years. Although a majority of citizens still identify with Christianity in many surveys, regular church attendance has fallen dramatically since the middle of the 20th century, while immigration and demographic change have contributed to the growth of other faiths, most notably Islam. This has led some commentators to variously describe the UK as a multi-faith, secularised, or post-Christian society. In the 2001 census 71.6% of all respondents indicated that they were Christians, with the next largest faiths (by number of adherents) being Islam (2.8%), Hinduism (1.0%), Sikhism (0.6%), Judaism (0.5%), Buddhism (0.3%) and all other religions (0.3%). 15% of respondents stated that they had no religion, with a further 7% not stating a religious preference.

在英国,每个人都享有宗教自由。因此,在英国各中心地区也形成了多种不同的宗教信仰蓬勃发展的局面。绝大多数的英国人都信奉基督教,穆斯林是英国国内最大的非基督教团体。此外,印度教、锡克教、犹太教和佛教也拥有大量的信徒。

Culture 文化篇

The culture of the United Kingdom has been influenced by many factors including: the nation's island status; its history as a western liberal democracy and a major power; as well as being a political union of four countries with each preserving elements of distinctive traditions, customs and symbolism. As a result of the British Empire, British influence can be observed in the language, culture and legal systems of many of its former colonies, including Australia, Canada, India, South Africa and the United States.

英国的生活方式融合了世界各地的文化背景及当代思维模式，由一种强烈的认同感及传统维系在一起。

(Revised from *A Guide to English-Speaking Countries*)

England《英格兰》

地处欧洲大陆边陲的小小岛国，曾孕育出大英帝国，横跨英格兰的神奇历史之旅开始了。

Storyline 好片抢先知

Sitting at the edge of continental Europe, England is a tiny island nation, which gave birth to an empire that once ruled half of the world. The traveler in this film embarks on an historic journey across England, exploring its rich past still remembered and alive today.

Culture inside 文化反光镜

Battle of Hastings: a battle occurred on 14 October 1066 during the Norman conquest of England, between the Norman-French army of Duke William II of Normandy and the English army under King Harold II. It took place at Senlac Hill.

黑斯廷斯战役：公元1066年，诺曼人在征服者威廉的率领下，横渡英吉利海峡，在哈斯丁登陆（位于伦敦东南87公里的港口）。战役中击溃了盎格鲁-撒克逊军队，英王哈罗德战

死，英国被征服。史称此战役为"黑斯廷斯战役"，亦称哈斯丁战役，或"诺曼征服"（the Norman Conquest）。从此，英国结束了分裂状态，置于中央集权的封建制度统治之下。

William the Conqueror (1028 –1087): also known as William I, was the first Norman King of England from Christmas 1066 until his death. He was also Duke of Normandy from 3 July 1035 until his death.

征服者威廉：威廉一世，英格兰诺曼王朝第一任国王，绰号"征服者威廉"。他一生只做了一件大事，这件事后来被称为"诺曼征服"，他对英国乃至世界的历史进程产生了重要影响。

King Harold II (1022 –1066): the last Anglo-Saxon King of England. Harold reigned from 6 January 1066 until his death at the Battle of Hastings, fighting the Norman invaders led by William the Conqueror during the Norman conquest of England.

哈罗德二世即哈罗德·葛温森，盎格鲁-萨克逊王朝之韦塞克斯王国最后君主（1066年在位），在黑斯廷斯战役中战死。

Chainmail: a type of armour consisting of small metal rings linked together in a pattern to form a mesh.

锁子甲：古代战争中使用的一种金属铠甲，由于其材质构造与外观的奇异，可以说是真正意义上的"铁布衫"。

Normandy: a geographical region corresponding to the former Duchy of Normandy. The continental territory covers 30,627 km² and forms the preponderant part of Normandy and roughly 5% of the territory of France.

诺曼底：法国一地区，北滨英吉利海峡。

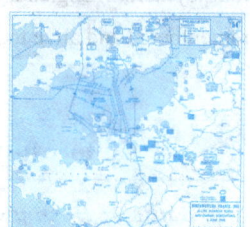

Saxons: the Germanic people whose homeland was in the north German coastal plain, especially between the rivers Elbe and Wester. Saxons participated in the Germanic settlement of Britain during and after the fifth century.

撒克逊人：日耳曼民族的一支，最早居住于波罗的海沿岸和石勒苏益格地区，公元5世纪早期开始在德意志北部以及沿高卢和不列颠的海岸迅速扩张，成为最早定居英国的日耳曼民族。

Beachy Head: a chalk headland in the United Kingdom. The cliff there is the highest chalk sea cliff in Britain, rising to 162 m (530 ft) above sea level. Its height has also made it one of the most notorious suicide spots in the world.

俾赤岬位于英格兰东萨塞克斯郡西南的英吉利海岸边，为一处白垩组成的海岸悬崖。悬崖高达162米，是英国最高的海岸悬崖，为著名的旅游胜地。

Brighton: the major part of the city of Brighton and Hove in East Sussex, England on the south coast of Great Britain. It emerged as a health resort featuring sea bathing during the 18th century and became a destination for day-trippers from London after the arrival of the railway in 1841.

布莱顿：英格兰南部海滨城市，标志性建筑是英皇阁（Royal Pavilion），以其密布鹅卵石的海滩而著称。

King George IV (1762–1830): the King of the United Kingdom of Great Britain and Ireland and also of Hanover from the death of his father, George III, on 29 January 1820 until his own death ten years later.

乔治四世：英国汉诺威王朝第四任君主，自1812年开始实际掌权18年。他是历任君主中最有才华的一个，对文学、艺术、建筑都有很深的造诣；但他同时又是历任君主中最懒惰和不负责的一个，最终在一片骂声中去世。

London: the capital of Great Britain, also one of the world's capitals of finance, fashion, arts and entertainment. The city has a recorded history dating back to Roman times and encompassing the lives of such illustrious political figures as William the Conqueror, Queen Elizabeth I, as well as those of William Shakespeare, John Milton, and the other authors who created one of the world's great bodies of literature. In the twentieth century, the city enters a new century reinvigorated by a booming economy, as well as the inauguration of a new form of local government.

伦敦：英国首都，欧洲第一大城市，世界顶级的国际大都市和全球最繁华的城市之一。伦敦因其在政治、经济、人文、娱乐、科技发明等领域上的卓越成就，是英国政治、经济和文化中心。

Big Ben: the nickname for the great bell of the clock at the north end of the Palace of Westminster in London. It is the largest four-faced chiming clock and the third-tallest free-standing clock tower in the world. It celebrated its 150th anniversary on 31 May 2009, during which celebratory events took place.

大本钟，英国著名古钟，是威斯敏特宫的报时钟，位于英国国会会议厅附属的钟楼上，建于1859年，是伦敦的传统地标性建筑。至2009年5月31日已启用150年。

British Parliament: the supreme legislative body in the United Kingdom, British Crown dependencies and British overseas territories, located in London. Parliament alone possesses legislative supremacy and thereby ultimate power over all other political bodies in the UK and its territories. At its head is the Sovereign, Queen Elizabeth II.

英国议会：议会是英国政治的中心舞台，是英国的最高立法机关。政府从议会中产生，并对其负责。议会为两院制，由上院和下院组成。自有议会以来，议会成员通常在伦敦的一座古老的建筑——威斯敏斯特宫（议会大厦）举行会议。

Samuel Johnson(1709 –1784): an English author who made lasting contributions to English literature as a poet, essayist, moralist, literary critic, biographer, editor and lexicographer.

塞缪尔·约翰逊：英国诗人、文学批评家、传记作家、词汇学家。英国历史上首部《英语大辞典》的编著者，因此也被尊称为"字典约翰逊"。

Tower of London: a historic castle on the north bank of the River Thames in central London. It was founded towards the end of 1066 as part of the Norman Conquest of England.

伦敦塔：位于泰晤士河北岸的历史城堡，也是英国王室权利的象征。其官方名称是"女王陛下的宫殿与城堡，伦敦塔"。1066年底建成，历史上曾是堡垒、军械库、国库、铸币厂、宫殿、天文台、避难所和监狱，曾特别用于关押上层阶级的囚犯。

Thames River: the longest river entirely in England and the second longest in the United Kingdom. It is best known because its lower reaches flow through central London.

泰晤士河：英国著名的"母亲"河，发源于英格兰西南部，注入北海，全长402公里，横贯英国首都伦敦与沿河的10多座城市，流域面积13000平方公里，是英格兰最长，英国第二长的河。泰晤士河以流经首都伦敦的中心而出名。

East End: the area of London. It was synonymous with poverty, overcrowding, disease and criminality. Now the East End is undergoing further change, but some parts continue to contain some of the worst poverty in Britain.

伦敦东区：位于伦敦东部、港口附近的地区，为伦敦传统工业区，曾是一个拥挤的贫民区：街道狭窄、房屋稠密，多为19世纪中期建筑。第二次世界大战中，大部分遭轰炸破坏，后重建。2012年奥运会主会场建于此。

Jack the Ripper: the best-known name given to an unidentified serial killer who was active in the largely impoverished areas in and around the White chapel district of London in 1888. The name originated in a letter, written by someone claiming to be the murderer, that was disseminated in the media.

开膛手杰克：1888年8月7日到11月9日间，于伦敦东区的白教堂一带以残忍手法连续杀害至少五名妓女的凶手的代称。犯案期间，凶手多次写信至相关部门挑衅，却始终未落入法网。其犯案手法大胆，经媒体一再渲染引起当时英国社会的恐慌。至今他依然是欧美文化中最恶名昭彰的杀手之一。

Charles Dickens (1812 –1870): an English novelist, generally considered the greatest of the Victorian period. He remains popular, having been responsible for some of English literature's most iconic novels and characters.

查尔斯狄更斯：19世纪英国批判现实主义小说家，为英国批判现实主义文学的开拓和发展做出了卓越的贡献。他的作品至今依然盛行且影响深远。其主要作品有《远大前程》、《匹克威克外传》、《雾都孤儿》、《老古玩店》、《艰难时世》等。

Yorkshire: a historic county of Northern England and the largest in the United Kingdom. Because of its great size in comparison to other English counties, functions have been increasingly undertaken over time by its subdivisions, which have also been subject to periodic reform.

约克郡：英格兰东北部的一个郡，也是英国最大、最著名的郡。

Emily Bronte (1818 –1848): an English novelist and poet, best remembered for her only novel, Wuthering Heights, now considered a classic of English literature.

艾米莉·勃朗特：19世纪英国小说家、诗人，英国文学史上著名的"勃朗特三姐妹"之一。她唯一的一部小说《呼啸山庄》奠定了她在英国文学史以及世界文学史上的地位。

Captain Cook (1728 –1779): a British explorer, navigator and cartographer who ultimately rose to the rank of captain in the Royal Navy.

库克船长：一位因进行了三次探险航行而闻名于世的伟大探险家。他给人们关于大洋——特别是太平洋的地理学知识增添了新的内容。他改善船员的饮食——包括增加水果和蔬菜等，因此被认为在预防长期航行中出现的坏血病方面也有所贡献。

Whitby Abbey: a ruined Benedictine abbey overlooking the North Sea on the East Cliff above Whitby in North Yorkshire, England. It was disestablished during the Dissolution of the Monasteries under the auspices of Henry VIII.

惠特比修道院：一个被毁了的本笃会修道院，建在悬崖绝壁之上，俯瞰北海。需踏199级台阶而上，方可达此修道院。

British Railways: the operator of most of the rail transport in Great Britain between 1948 and 1997. It was formed from the nationalisation of the "Big Four" British railway companies and lasted until the gradual privatisation of British Rail, in stages between 1994 and 1997.

英国铁路公司：英国国有运输公司，1947年在原有的英国四大铁路公司的基础之上成立起来。它在1947年至1997年间管理着英国绝大多数的铁路运输系统。1997年英国铁路系统由原来的国有制转向私人经营，英国铁路公司也随之解散。

Liverpool: a city and metropolitan borough of Merseyside, England, along the eastern side of the Mersey Estuary. It was founded as a borough in 1207 and was granted city status in 1880.

利物浦：英格兰西北部的一个著名港口城市，英国第四大城市。

Beatles: an English rock band, active throughout the 1960s and one of the most commercially successful and critically acclaimed acts in the history of popular music.

甲壳虫乐队：也叫披头士乐队，是一支成立于1960年的英国利物浦的摇滚乐队，在流行音乐史的商业和艺术上都取得了巨大成功。乐队灵魂为约翰·列侬（John Lennon），是摇滚史上最伟大的音乐家之一；成员保罗·麦卡特尼（Paul McCartney）被认为是20世纪顶级的音乐标志，被吉尼斯世界纪录列为史上最成功的作曲人；其他成员是吉他手和主唱之一的乔治·哈里森（George Harrison）以及林戈·斯塔尔（Ringo Starr）。

Queen Victoria (1819 –1901): the monarch of the United Kingdom of Great Britain and Ireland from 20 June 1837 until her death. From 1 May 1876, she used the additional title of Empress of India.

维多利亚女王：英国历史上在位时间最长的君主，在位时间长达64年，她是第一个以"大不列颠和爱尔兰联合王国女王和印度女皇"名号称呼的英国君主。她在位期间是英国最强盛的所谓"日不落帝国"时期。女王统治时期，在英国历史上被称为"维多利亚时代"。

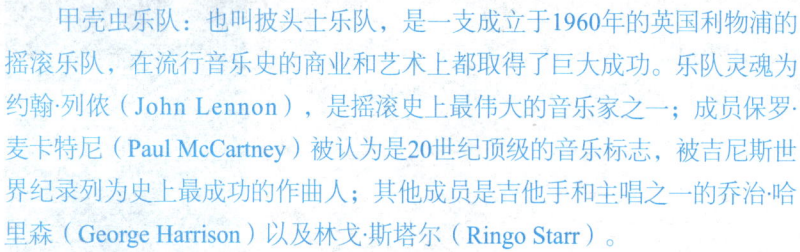
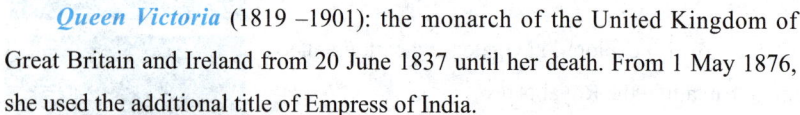

Stonehenge: a prehistoric monument located in the English county of Wiltshire. Stonehenge is composed of a circular setting of large standing stones set within earthworks. It is at the centre of the most dense complex of Neolithic and Bronze Age monuments in England, including several hundred burial mounds.

巨石阵：也叫斯通亨治，是欧洲著名的史前时代文化神庙遗址。它位于英格兰威尔特郡索尔兹伯里平原，约建于公元前4000～2000年。

Glastonbury: a small town in Somerset, England, situated at a dry point on the low lying Somerset Levels.

格拉斯顿堡：位于英国萨默赛特的一个历史小镇。

King Arthur: a legendary British leader of the late 5th and early 6th centuries, who, according to Medieval histories and romances, led the defence of Britain against Saxon invaders in the early 6th century.

亚瑟王：传说中古不列颠最富有传奇色彩的伟大国王。传说他是圆桌骑士（Knights of the Round Table）的首领，是一位近乎神话般的传奇人物。

Neo-Druidism: a form of modern spirituality or religion that generally promotes harmony and worship of nature, and respect for all beings, including the environment.

新德鲁伊教派：一精神教派，崇尚和谐，崇拜自然。

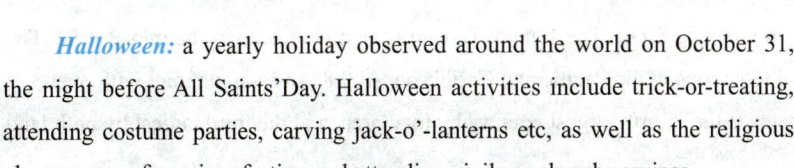

Halloween: a yearly holiday observed around the world on October 31, the night before All Saints' Day. Halloween activities include trick-or-treating, attending costume parties, carving jack-o'-lanterns etc, as well as the religious observances of praying, fasting and attending vigils or church services.

万圣节：西方传统节日，庆祝活动主要是在每年的10月31日晚上。节日源自古代凯尔特民族的新年节庆。此日也是祭祀亡魂的日子，在避免恶灵干扰的同时，也以食物祭拜祖灵及善灵以祈平安渡过严冬。

Guy Fawkes Day: an annual commemoration observed on 5 November, primarily in England. Its history begins with the events of 5 November 1605, when Guy Fawkes, a member of the Gunpowder Plot, was arrested while guarding explosives the plotters had placed beneath the House of Lords.

盖伊福克斯日：每年11月5日，英国人在此日纪念成功破获1605年盖伊福克斯试图用20桶火药炸掉国会大厦的阴谋。人们自己制作"盖伊"——一个用旧衣服填充做成的假人，再把它放到篝火上焚烧。最后，绚丽的焰火燃放起来，代表多年前的那场爆炸根本没有发生过。

Tar barrel: Ottery St Mary typically stages annual events around Guy Fawkes Night when, in a tradition dating from the 17th century, barrels soaked in tar are set alight and carried aloft through parts of the town by residents.

焦油桶：这是在盖伊福克斯日的一项活动。当地人将浸满焦油的桶点燃，扛到市中心去燃烧，引来无数的旁观者。

The United States of America
美利坚合众国

Geography 地理篇

The United States of America is a federal constitutional republic comprising fifty states and a federal district. The country is situated mostly in central North America, where its forty-eight contiguous states and Washington, D.C., the capital district, lie between the Pacific and Atlantic Oceans, bordered by Canada to the north and Mexico to the south. The state of Alaska is in the northwest of the continent, with Canada to the east

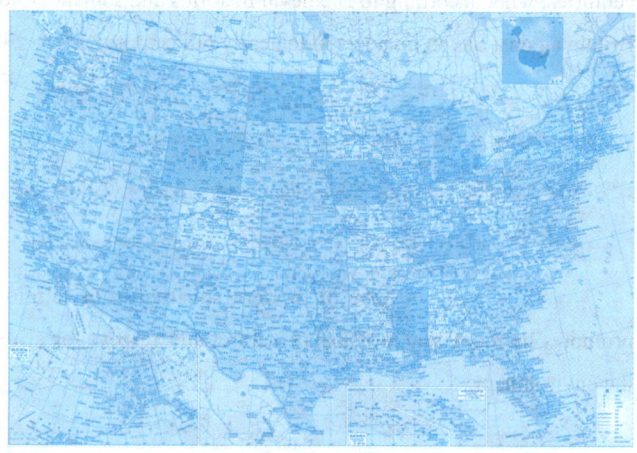

and Russia to the west across the Bering Strait. The state of Hawaii is an archipelago in the mid-Pacific. The country also possesses several territories in the Pacific and Caribbean. At 9.83 million km^2 and with over 312 million people, the United States is the fourth largest country by total area, and the third largest by both land area and population.

美利坚合众国位于北美中部，西邻太平洋，东濒大西洋，是一个由五十个州和一个联邦直辖特区组成的宪政联邦共和制国家。美国北面是加拿大，南部与墨西哥及墨西哥湾接壤。除阿拉斯加州和夏威夷州之外的48个州都位于美国本土，阿拉斯加州位于北美大陆西北方，东部为加拿大，西临白令海峡，夏威夷州则是太平洋中部的群岛。此外，美国在加勒比海和太平洋还拥有多处领土和岛屿地区。

The United States is a constitutional republic and representative democracy. The government is regulated by a system of checks and balances defined by the U.S. Constitution, which serves as the country's supreme legal document. In the American federalist system, citizens are usually subject to three levels of government, federal, state, and local; the local government's duties are commonly split between county and municipal governments.

> 美国的政治体制为相互监督和制衡的民主共和制，联邦、州、地方构成三级政府。

Parties 政党篇

The United States has operated under a two-party system for most of its history. For elective offices at most levels, state-administered primary elections choose the major party nominees for subsequent general elections. Since the general election of 1856, the major parties have been the Democratic Party, founded in 1824, and the Republican Party, founded in 1854.

> 美国实行共和党和民主党两党制。民主党于1824年建党，当时由部分种植园主、农民和某些与南方奴隶主有联系的资本家组成。共和党成立于1854年，当时主要由反对扩大奴隶制的北方工商业的资本家组成。共和党主张小政府、大社会，它反对扩大政府在经济和社会事物方面的预算开支，但却主张扩大国防预算开支；而民主党赞成政府采取更积极的行动来推动社会福利事业和控制企业活动。

Economy 经济篇

The United States has a capitalist mixed economy, which is fueled by abundant natural resources, a well-developed infrastructure, and high productivity. The U.S. economy is the world's largest national economy.

> 美国有高度发达的现代市场经济，其国内生产总值和对外贸易额均居世界首位。

Education 教育篇

American public education is operated by state and local governments, regulated by the United States Department of Education through restrictions on federal grants. Children are required in most states to attend school from the age of six or seven until they turn eighteen; some states allow students to leave school at sixteen or seventeen. About 12% of children are enrolled in parochial or nonsectarian private schools. Just over 2% of children are homeschooled. The United States has many competitive private and public institutions of higher education. According to prominent international rankings, 13 or 15 American colleges and universities are ranked among the top 20 in the world.

在美国，教育管理是州或地方政府的责任，而非联邦政府。不过，联邦政府教育部可以通过控制教育基金来施加一定程度的影响。学生有法定义务在公立学校接受从幼儿园到12年级的教育；通常，18岁才可以毕业。美国的平均教育水平极高，联合国的经济指数调查中将美国的教育水平列为世界第一。

Religion 宗教篇

The United States is officially a secular nation; the First Amendment of the U.S. Constitution guarantees the free exercise of religion and forbids the establishment of any religious governance. The study categorizes white evangelicals, 26.3% of the population, as the country's largest religious cohort; another study estimates evangelicals of all races at 30%–35%. The total reporting non-Christian religions in 2007 was 4.7%, up from 3.3% in 1990. The leading non-Christian faiths were Judaism (1.7%), Buddhism (0.7%), Islam (0.6%), Hinduism (0.4%), and Unitarian Universalism (0.3%). The survey also reported that 16.1% of Americans described themselves as agnostic, atheist, or simply having no religion, up from 8.2% in 1990.

美国保障宗教自由的权利，政府实行政教分离制度，不支持也不反对任何一种宗教。但是，基督新教势力在美国政治选举中有相当的影响力。

Culture 文化篇

The United States is a multicultural nation, home to a wide variety of ethnic groups, traditions, and values. Aside from the now small Native American and Native Hawaiian populations, nearly all Americans or their ancestors immigrated within the past five centuries. Mainstream American culture is a Western culture largely derived from the traditions of European immigrants with influences from many other sources, such as traditions brought by slaves from Africa. More recent immigration from Asia and especially Latin America has added to a cultural mix that has been described as both a homogenizing melting pot, and a heterogeneous salad bowl in which immigrants and their descendants retain distinctive cultural characteristics.

American culture is considered the most individualistic in the world. Though the American Dream, or the perception that Americans enjoy high social mobility, plays a key role in attracting immigrants. While the mainstream culture holds that the United States is a classless society, scholars identify significant differences between the country's social classes, affecting socialization, language, and values.

> 美国文化根植于英属殖民地时期，随着当地的环境发展出独立而独特的文化。描述美国文化的一个典型用词是"色拉碗"：移民带来的文化会保持一些自己独立的文化特征，而非完全融入原有的美国文化，但他们所带来的文化也会成为美国文化的一部分。

(Revised from *A Guide to English-Speaking Countries*)

Washington D.C.《华盛顿》

波多马克河畔的华盛顿，集政治、文化、建筑之大家风范为一体，值得品游。

Storyline 好片抢先知

Washington DC is one of the most famous cities in the world, but its local culture is relatively unknown. The traveler in this film goes beyond the myths and mystique to get at the real DC and the real Washingtonians. She also discovers the history of the first settlers and the founding of the nation.

Culture inside 文化反光镜

Washington, D.C.: the capital of the United States. On July 16, 1790, the United States Congress approved the creation of a federal district to become the national capital as permitted by the U.S. Constitution. The District is therefore not a part of any U.S. state. It was formed from land along the Potomac River donated by the states of Maryland and Virginia; however, the Virginia portion was returned by Congress in 1846.

华盛顿：美国首都，位于哥伦比亚特区，是为纪念美国开国元勋乔治·华盛顿和发现美洲新大陆的哥伦布而命名的，是美国政治、文化中心。

US Capitol: the meeting place of the United States Congress, the legislature of the federal government of the United States. Located in Washington, D.C., it sits atop Capitol Hill at the eastern end of the National Mall. Though it has never been the geographic center of the federal district, the Capitol is the origin by which both the quadrants of the District are divided and the city was planned. Officially, both the east and west sides of the Capitol are referred to as "fronts."

国会大厦：指作为美国联邦政府的立法机构——美国国会办公机构的国会建筑。由于它坐落在一处海拔83英尺的高地之上，故常称为"国会山"。美国人把它看做是民有、民治、民享政权的最高象征。

James Town: the first permanent English settlement in what is now the United States. Today, Jamestown is one of three locations comprising the Historic Triangle of Colonial Virginia, along with Williamsburg and Yorktown, with two primary heritage sites. Historic Jamestowne, the archaeological site on Jamestown Island, is a cooperative effort by Jamestown National Historic Site.

詹姆斯敦：美国殖民地遗址，是英国在北美的第一个永久居住地。1607年5月14日，105名英国人来到美国弗吉利亚州，建立詹姆斯敦，从此开始了美国的历史。

Williamsburg: the private foundation representing the historic district of the city of Williamsburg, Virginia, USA. The district includes buildings dating from 1699 to 1780 which made colonial Virginia's capital. The site has been used for conferences by world leaders and heads of state, including U.S. Presidents.

威廉斯堡：位于弗吉尼亚州，是美国历史名城。它始建于1632年，曾是殖民地时期弗吉尼亚的首府，也是美国独立战争的发祥地。

Thomas Jefferson (1743–1826): the principal author of the United States Declaration of Independence (1776) and the Statute of Virginia for Religious Freedom (1777), the third President of the United States (1801–1809) and founder of the University of Virginia (1819). He was an influential Founding Father and an exponent of Jeffersonian democracy.

托马斯·杰斐逊：美国开国元勋，第三任总统，美国"独立宣言"的主要起草者。美国历史上的杰出总统之一，与华盛顿、林肯、罗斯福等总统齐名。

York Town: most famous as the site of the siege and subsequent surrender of General Cornwallis to General George Washington during the American Revolutionary War on October 19, 1781. Yorktown also figured prominently in the American Civil War (1861–1865), serving as a major port to supply both northern and southern towns, depending upon who held Yorktown at the time.

约克镇：美国独立战争中的重镇之一。1781年，华盛顿率领大陆军将康华利将军所率领的英军包围在此，取得约克镇大捷，康华利将军率英军向美军投降，这标志着独立战争中北美战场上战争的结束。

Arlington National Cemetery: a military cemetery in the United States of America, established during the American Civil War on the grounds of Arlington House, formerly the estate of the family of Confederate general Robert E. Lee's wife Mary Anna (Custis) Lee, a great grand-daughter of Martha Washington. The cemetery is situated directly across the Potomac River from the Lincoln Memorial in Washington, D.C. It is famous for Eternal Flame, a flame or torch that burns day and night for an indefinite period, commemorating U.S. President John F. Kennedy following his assassination in 1963.

阿灵顿国家公墓：美国最著名的国家公墓，埋葬着士兵、政要、在岗位上殉职的国家公务人员等。这里的一个重要标志就是肯尼迪总统墓前的"永恒的烈火"。

George Town: a historic neighborhood, commercial, and entertainment district located in northwest Washington, D.C. Founded in 1751, the port of Georgetown predated the establishment of the federal district and the City of Washington by 40 years. Georgetown remained a separate municipality until 1871, when the United States Congress created a new consolidated government for the whole District of Columbia.

乔治敦：位于华盛顿特区的西北部，为美国历史名城。

John Fitzgerald Kennedy (1917–1963): often referred to by his initials JFK, was the 35th President of the United States, serving from 1961 until his assassination in 1963.

约翰·菲茨杰拉德·肯尼迪：美国第35任总统，在美国历史上具有巨大的影响力。

Jefferson Memorial: a presidential memorial in Washington, D.C. that is dedicated to Thomas Jefferson. Construction began in 1939, the building was completed in 1943, and the bronze statue of Jefferson was added in 1947.

托马斯·杰斐逊纪念堂：一座罗马神殿式圆顶建筑风格的纪念堂。它坐落在首都华盛顿，是为纪念杰斐逊总统而建，1943年建成。杰斐逊的铜像于1947年在此落成。

Franklin Delano Roosevelt (1882–1945): also known by his initials, FDR, was the 32nd President of the United States (1933–1945), leading the United States during a time of worldwide economic crisis and world war. The only American president elected to more than two terms, he facilitated a durable coalition that realigned American politics for decades.

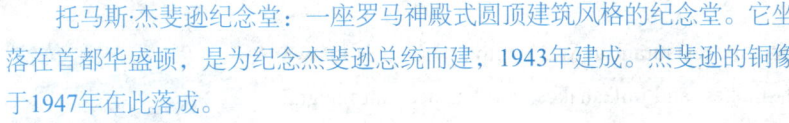
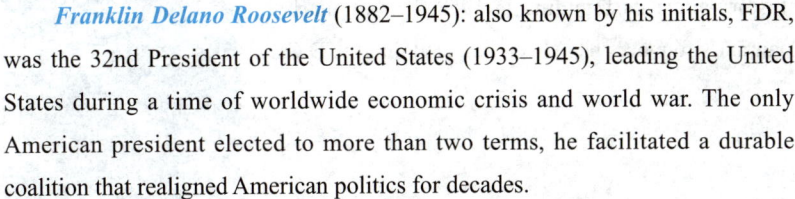

富兰克林·罗斯福：美国历史上唯一蝉联四届的总统。罗斯福在20世纪的经济大萧条和第二次世界大战中扮演了重要的角色，被一致认为是美国最伟大的三位总统之一，同华盛顿和林肯齐名。

Lincoln Memorial: an American memorial built to honor the 16th President of the United States, Abraham Lincoln. It is located on the National Mall in Washington, D.C. The building is in the form of a Greek Doric temple and contains a large seated sculpture of Abraham Lincoln and inscriptions of two well-known speeches by Lincoln, The Gettysburg Address and his Second Inaugural Address.

林肯纪念堂：华盛顿市标志，为纪念美国第十六届总统亚伯拉罕·林肯而建。纪念堂位于华盛顿的国家大草坪西端，与东端的国会大厦遥遥相望，是一座用通体洁白的花岗岩和大理石建造的古希腊神殿式纪念堂。此纪念堂里的林肯大理石坐像极富盛名。

Martin Luther King, Jr. (1929–1968): an American clergyman, activist, and prominent leader in the African-American Civil Rights Movement. He is best known for being an iconic figure in the advancement of civil rights in the United States and around the world, using nonviolent methods following the teachings of Mahatma Gandhi. King has become a national icon in the history of modern American liberalism.

马丁·路德·金：美国著名的民权领袖，诺贝尔和平奖获得者，其演讲《我有一个梦想》享誉全世界。

Mount Vernon: located near Alexandria, Virginia, was the plantation home of the first President of the United States, George Washington. The mansion is built of wood in neoclassical Georgian architectural style, and the estate is located on the banks of the Potomac River.

芒特弗农：位于美国弗吉尼亚州北部，首都华盛顿南21公里处的古迹名胜，是乔治·华盛顿总统的家乡和坟墓所在地。

Lincoln Theatre: located on "Washington's Black Broadway", served the city's African American community when segregation kept them out of other venues. The Lincoln Theatre included a movie house and ballroom, and hosted jazz and big band performers such as Duke Ellington.

林肯剧院：位于华盛顿的"华盛顿黑人百老汇"，在种族隔离时期，是黑人看戏的地方。

Ben's Chili Bowl: a landmark restaurant in Washington, D.C. It is known locally for its chili dogs, half-smokes, and milkshakes, and has been an integral part of the neighborhood's history since its founding in 1958. It is regularly visited by celebrities. The restaurant's founders have been inducted into the D.C. Hall of Fame.

宾士红辣碗餐厅：华盛顿一餐厅。这里的辣热狗在华盛顿地区享有盛名，也是奥巴马总统钟爱的餐厅之一。

Anacostia: the most famous neighborhood in the Southeast quadrant of Washington, located east of the Anacostia River, after which the neighborhood is named. Like the other quadrants of Washington, D.C. Southeast encompasses a large number of named neighborhoods, of which Anacostia and Capitol Hill are the most well known.

阿纳科斯蒂亚：华盛顿一社区，距离白宫不到8公里。

Virginia: a U.S. state on the Atlantic Coast of the Southern United States. Virginia is nicknamed the "Old Dominion" and sometimes the "Mother of Presidents" after the eight U.S. presidents born there.

弗吉尼亚州：美国东部大西洋沿岸的一个州，美国最初的13州之一。该州为美国历史最悠久的州之一。1607年英国在沿海的詹姆斯敦建立起北美第一块定居点，所以该州有"老自治领州"的别名。取名"弗吉尼亚"（Virginia），是为纪念英国伊丽莎白女王一世对开拓英国殖民事业的贡献终身未嫁，因此被称为"童贞女王"（Virgin Queen）。本州被誉为"总统之母"，有8位美国总统生于本州。

Civil War (1861–1865): in response to the election of Abraham Lincoln as President of the United States, 11 southern slave states declared their secession from the United States and formed the Confederate States of America ("the Confederacy"); the other 25 states supported the federal government ("the Union"). After four years of warfare, mostly within the Southern states, the Confederacy surrendered and slavery was outlawed everywhere in the nation

美国内战：又称南北战争，是美国历史上一场大规模的内战，参战双方为"联邦"政府和美利坚联盟国（简称"邦联"）。这场战争的起因是美国南部十一州以亚伯拉罕·林肯于1861年就任总统为由而陆续退出联邦，另立政府。战争最终以北方的胜利而告终。此战不但改变当时美国的政经情势，导致奴隶制度在美国南方被最终废除，也对日后美国的民间社会产生巨大的影响。

Battle of Cedar Creek: one of the final, and most decisive, battles in the Valley Campaigns of 1864 during the American Civil War. The final Confederate invasion of the North was effectively ended. The Confederacy was never again able to threaten Washington, D.C., through the Shenandoah Valley, nor protect the economic base. This victory aided the reelection of Abraham Lincoln and Union Army Maj. Gen. Philip Sheridan won lasting fame.

雪松溪战役：美国南北战争中最后也是最具决定性的战役。

The National Museum of American History: preserves and displays the heritage of the United States in the areas of social, political, cultural, scientific and military history. Among the items on display are the original Star-Spangled Banner and Archie Bunker's chair. The museum is part of the Smithsonian Institution and located in Washington, D.C., on the National Mall.

美国国家历史博物馆：于1964年对公众免费开放，是一座长方形的五层楼高白色大理石建筑，里面收藏了许多美国历史上非常重要的文物。

Smithsonian: an educational and research institute and associated museum complex, administered and funded by the government of the United States. Most of its 19 museums, its zoo, and its nine research centers facilities are located in Washington, D.C.

史密森尼博物馆：世界上最大的博物馆与美术馆联合会，拥有全球数量最多、规模最大的博物馆群落。藏品总数现已有1.4亿多件。

Wizard of OZ: a 1939 American musical fantasy film produced by Metro-Goldwyn-Mayer. Notable for its use of special effects, Technicolor, fantasy storytelling and unusual characters, it has become, over the years, one of the best known of all films and part of American popular culture.

《绿野仙踪》：1939年米高梅出品的音乐剧，以其特有的电影特效、彩色电影、神奇的故事和人物 成为美国电影史上的经典和美国文化的象征。

The National Air and Space Museum (NASM) of the Smithsonian Institution: a museum that holds the largest collection of historic aircraft and spacecraft in the world. It was established in 1976. It is a center for research into the history and science of aviation and spaceflight, as well as planetary science and terrestrial geology and geophysics. Almost all space and aircraft on display are originals or backups to the originals.

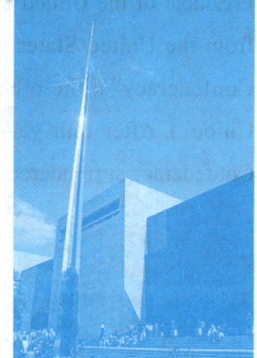

国家太空博物馆：于1976年7月开馆，是全世界首屈一指的有关飞行的专题博物馆。

Apollo 11: the spaceflight which landed the first humans, Neil Armstrong and Edwin "Buzz" Aldrin, Jr, on Earth's Moon on July 20, 1969. The United States mission is considered the major accomplishment in the history of space exploration.

阿波罗11号：执行美国国家航空航天局（NASA）的阿波罗计划中的第五次载人任务时使用的宇宙飞船。此次是人类第一次实现登月任务。1969年7月20日，阿姆斯特朗与奥尔德林成为了首次踏上月球的人。

Charles Lindberg (1902-1974): an American aviator, made the first solo nonstop flight across the Atlantic Ocean on May 20-21, 1927. Other pilots had crossed the Atlantic before him. But Lindbergh was the first person to do it alone nonstop.

查尔斯·林德伯格：美国飞行员，首个进行单人不着陆的跨大西洋飞行的人。

Unit 2

British Monarchy: Love It or Loathe It?
英伦王室：英国人的纠结

Part I. Get-go
给力起步

When British people talk about the royal family they usually mean the present Queen and her family: her husband, Prince Philip and their children. The present royal house is the House of Windsor, popularly known as "The Windsors". Elizabeth II is descended from William I (1066 – 1087).

> 英国当朝王室为温莎王朝，伊丽莎白二世是征服者威廉一世的后裔。

The role of the monarchy

The monarch or sovereign originally had sole power. Over time, the sovereign's powers have been reduced and, though the present Queen is still head of state and commander-in-chief of the armed forces, she "acts on the advice of her ministers", and Britain is in practice governed by "Her Majesty's Government". The Queen has various duties connected with government, such as formally opening a new session of parliament and giving the royal assent to new laws. She is also Supreme Governor of the Church of England.

The main role of the Queen is as a representative of Britain and the British people. She is a symbol of the unity of the nation beyond party politics. She is also head of the Commonwealth and works to strengthen the links between member countries.

> 君主曾经独揽大权，而今虽说君主仍是国家元首，并且连首相执掌的政府也称为"女王陛下的政府"，但事实上，君主更多的只是一个国家的象征，用老百姓的话来说就叫"面上的事"。

Changing public attitudes

During World War II, when London was bombed, *George VI* and his queen (the present *Queen Mother*) won great public admiration by staying in London throughout the war. The present Queen has also been much respected and her concern for the Commonwealth has strengthened the monarchy.

For many years, people expected the royal family to have high moral standards and to display all the ideals of family life. Until recently, the public rarely saw the royal family except on formal occasions. They remained aloof and dignified, and any family problems were kept private. Alongside a hunger for yet more revelations, traditional respect for the royal family began to decline.

All this caused people to question the role of the monarchy. Many people began to think that the royal family was out of touch with modern attitudes. Some felt that they should be more open about their problems and not try to be different. Others thought that the royal family should express the nation's feelings, that in effect they should become a people's monarchy. Many people liked the combination of glamour and human concern that Princess Diana brought to the royal family and did not want this human touch to be lost.

In response to the criticism the royal family is trying to be more open and the Queen wants to meet a wider range of people. The royal family had already established its own *Way* Ahead *group* to consider the monarchy's future. It also has its own Internet site. Since 1993, the Queen has paid income tax on her private wealth and on the part of the *Privy Purse* used for personal expenses.

> 随着时代的变迁，君主的角色也在悄然变化，王室得到的传统尊重也在递减。女王领导的王室在兼顾传统与跟随时代步伐上找平衡，实为明智之举。

The Future of the monarchy

The constitutional position of the monarchy has also suffered. It has been suggested that the monarchy is undemocratic and unnecessary. Legal experts argue that getting rid of the monarchy would create serious constitutional difficulties. Defenders of the monarchy claim that the royal family pays for itself because it attracts tourists and business to Britain. Others say it is an expensive luxury. Many people have no strong feelings. They are used to the present system and, though they might like some aspects of the monarchy to be more modern, they would be reluctant to see any radical change.

Love them or loathe them, British Monarchy has for hundreds of years the signature dish of the Great Britain, anyway.

> 英伦王室，虽说有点像是奢华的摆设，可要废黜它，英国人的心里恐怕还难下这个狠心。管你是爱它，还是怨它，王室总是大不列颠的一道招牌菜，难道不是吗？这道菜都上了几百年了。

(Revised from *Oxford Guide to British and American Culture*)

NOTES

Royal house: also called royal family, royal line, royalty, referring to royal persons collectively.

王室：王室成员的集体称谓，王室或皇室是指在君主制国家运用皇权或王权进行统治的家族集团。

The House of Windsor: the current royal house of the Commonwealth realms. It was founded by King George V by royal proclamation on the 17 July 1917, when he changed the name of his family from the German *Saxe-Coburg and Gotha* to the English *Windsor*, due to the anti-German sentiment in the United Kingdom during World War I.

Currently, the most prominent member of the House of Windsor is Elizabeth II, the reigning monarch of the Commonwealth realms.

温莎王朝：自1917年统治英国和其海外领地的王室家族，其前身为萨克森-科堡-哥达王朝。第一次世界大战时为安抚民心改为温莎以去德国化。温莎一名来自温莎堡，它是英国最古老的王宫之一。

Royal assent: (in Britain refers to) the formal signing of an act of Parliament by the sovereign, by which it becomes law.

御准：在英国，经下议院、上议院一致同意（或者依照法律可以不经上议院同意）的议案须呈交君主御准。君主如给予正式的同意，议案则因此成为法案。

Supreme Governor of the Church of England: a title held by the British monarchs which signifies their titular leadership over the Church of England. Even though the monarch's authority over the Church of England is not strong, the position is still very relevant to the church and is mostly observed in a symbolic capacity. The Supreme Governor formally appoints high-ranking members of the church on the advice of the Prime Minister of the United Kingdom, who is in turn advised by church leaders.

英国国教：指英国在宗教改革中建立的民族教会。在英王亨利八世时脱离了罗马教皇的统治，从此英国国王或女王成为英国国教的最高统治者。在当今英国，一般由英国首相提名，然后由英国女王伊丽莎白二世任命两位英国大主教和所有主教。

Commonwealth: a traditional English term for a political community founded for the common good. Historically, it has sometimes been synonymous with "republic". More recently it has been used for fraternal associations of some sovereign nations. Most notably, the Commonwealth of Nations, an association primarily of former members of the British Empire, is often referred to as simply "the Commonwealth". The head of the commonwealth is Queen Elizabeth II.

英联邦：一个以英国为主导的国家联合体，由50多个主权国家（含属地）组成，成员大多为前大英帝国的殖民地或附属国。该组织元首为英国女王伊丽莎白二世，她同时身兼英联邦王国内部分成员国的国家元首。

George VI (1895–1952): King of the United Kingdom and the Dominions of the British Commonwealth from 11 December 1936 until his death. Father of the present Queen Elizabeth II.

乔治六世：全名艾伯特·弗雷德里克·阿瑟·乔治·温莎（Albert Frederick Arthur George Windsor），英国国王，1936年12月11日至1952年2月6日在位，当今女王伊丽莎白二世的父亲。电影《国王的演讲》就是关于乔治六世的故事。

Queen Mother: (1900 – 2002) queen consort of George VI and mother of Elizabeth II.

伊丽莎白皇太后：当今英国女王的母亲，也是英国历史上最长寿、最受人尊敬的王室成员。她是一个不同凡响的女性，几乎经历了20世纪发生的所有重大事件。她的一生充满了传奇色彩：20世纪30年代，英国国王爱德华八世"不爱江山爱美人"，作为弟媳的她敢于当面向辛普森夫人表示不敬；"二战"中，她因临危不惧而被希特勒称为"欧洲最危险的女人"。她在丈夫乔治六世去世、长女登基成为女王之后，便早早隐退，但仍以王太后的身份继续为国效力。

Way Ahead Group: the Windsors' committee was launched in 1994 by the Lord Chamberlain, the Earl of Airlie, and it includes the Queen, Prince Philip, Prince Charles and their private secretaries, as well as Princess Anne and Princes Andrew and Edward. Its mandate revolves around constitutional issues surrounding the monarchy. But increasingly, it has become obsessed with the larger question of the monarchy's survival after Elizabeth II's death.

前瞻小组：1994年成立的由王室宫务大臣牵头、女王携菲利普亲王及四个子女（包括他们的私人秘书）为成员的小组，其任务是处理与王室相关的宪法问题、前瞻王室的未来。

Privy Purse: (in Britain) an allowance voted by Parliament for the private expenses of the monarch.

私用金：女王的固定收入之一，是政府每年拨给君主专用的资金，与王室俸禄是分开的。2010年至2011年财政年度,女王领到私用金1328万英镑。

Part II. cineWatch
光影星荟萃

The Queen 《女王》

"端着"的日子不好过，"放下"才是硬道理。别看九五至尊你，是人谁都不例外。

Storyline 好片抢先知

The Queen depicts the events following the death of Diana Princess of Wales in 1997. Against a backdrop of a public mourning the death of "the People's Princess", the film looks at the relationships between the Queen and her family, the newly popular Prime Minister and the British people.

1997年，戴安娜王妃车祸身亡，举国悲痛欲绝，但是英国王室人员却对此采取了逃避疏离的态度。这种漠不关心激怒了很多英国民众。民众反王室的情绪相当高涨，紧急形势让王室陷入了严重的危机。但是伊莉莎白二世（海伦·米伦Helen Mirren 饰）并没有出来稳定民心，而是携家人躲到了度假行宫。托尼·布莱尔（麦克·辛Michael Sheen 饰）此时刚出任首相，面对此刻棘手的情势，他必须尽快找到平衡各方利益的措施，让王室摆脱信任危机，使女王重新修好与国民的关系，同时让自己也在当中树立权威。

Cast 星光闪烁

Stephen Frears … Director 奥斯卡最佳导演提名

Helen Mirren … the Queen 奥斯卡影后，获三次金球奖、四次艾美奖、两次戛纳奖

Michael Sheen … Tony Blair 英国电影学院奖最佳男演员提名

Alex Jennings … Prince Charles 多次获英国奥利弗戏剧奖

Memorable quotes 余音绕梁

HM Queen Elizabeth II: I prefer to keep my feelings to myself, and foolishly, I believed that was what people wanted from their Queen — not to make a fuss, nor wear one's heart on one's sleeve. Duty first, self second. That's how I was brought up. That's all I've ever known.

Tony Blair: But... well, my advisors... have been taking the temperature among people on the streets... and, well, the information I'm getting is that the mood is quite delicate.

HM Queen Elizabeth II: I doubt there is anyone who knows the British people more than I do, Mr. Blair, nor who has greater faith in their wisdom and judgment.

HM Queen Elizabeth II: Something's happened. There's been a change, some shift in values. When you no longer understand your people, mummy, maybe it is time to hand it over to the next generation.

Robin Janvrin: The Prime Minister is on his way, ma'am.

HM Queen Elizabeth II: To be, Robin, Prime Minister to be. I haven't asked him yet.

Prince Charles: She's mother to your grandchildren!

HM The Queen Mother: If there is a photographer out there, he could be the first kill of the day.

Portrait Artist: You may not be allowed to vote, ma'am, but it is your government.

HM Queen Elizabeth II: Yes. I suppose that is some consolation.

Prince Philip: It's not right, you know.

HM Queen Elizabeth II: No, but further discussion is no longer helpful, either.

Prince Philip: Something about Diana managing to be even more annoying dead than alive.

Tony Blaire: Will someone please save these people from themselves!

Tony Blaire: That woman has given her whole life in service to her people. Fifty years doing a job she never wanted! A job she watched kill her father. She's executed it with honor, dignity, and, as far as I can tell, without a single blemish, and now we're all baying for her blood! All because she's struggling to lead the world in mourning for someone who... who threw everything she offered back in her face. And who, for the last few years, seemed committed 24/7 to destroying everything she holds most dear!

HM Queen Elizabeth II: I've never been hated like that before.

Tony Blaire: She was the people's princess and that's how she will… stay, how she will remain… in our hearts and in our memories… forever.

Culture inside 文化反光镜

Queen Elizabeth II: the Queen is Head of State of the UK and 15 other Commonwealth realms. The elder daughter of King George VI and Queen Elizabeth, she was born in 1926 and became Queen at the age of 25, and has reigned through more than five decades of enormous social change and development. The Queen is married to Prince Philip, Duke of Edinburgh and has four children and eight grandchildren.

女王伊丽莎白二世：英国温莎王朝第四代君主、英王乔治六世的长女。她是现任英国君主，英国、英联邦及部分成员国国家元首，国教会最高首领。伊丽莎白二世1952年加冕，2012年6月举行了登基六十周年大庆，是英国史上最年长的君主，先后有十三位首相为其效命。

Parties and Prime Minister: there are basically two major parties in Britain: the Labor Party and the Conservative Party. The party which wins sufficient seats at a General election will command a majority in the Government. The leader of the majority party is appointed Prime Minister. PM is the head of Her Majesty's Government in UK.

英国政党和首相：英国主要有两个党派：工党和保守党。一般情况下议会下议院的多数党党魁或执政联盟的首领自动成为首相人选，该人选须经国王/女王确认并任命后才正式成为首相。

Tony Blair (1953–):former British Labour Party politician who served as the Prime Minister of the United Kingdom from 2 May 1997 to 27 June 2007.

托尼·布莱尔：英国前首相，1953年生于英国北部的苏格兰首府爱丁堡，毕业于牛津大学法律系。布莱尔自1994年起任工党党魁，1997年至2007年任英国首相。他是工党历史上在任时间最长的英国首相，也是该党唯一一位带领工党连续3次赢得大选的首相。

Buckingham Palace: served as the official London residence of Britain's sovereigns since 1837 and today is the administrative headquarters of the Monarch.

白金汉宫：英国的王宫。建造在威斯敏斯特城内，位于伦敦詹姆士公园（St. James'Park）的西边。1703年为白金汉公爵所建，因而得名，1837年正式成为王宫。白金汉宫既是英王生活和工作的地方，也是王室权力的象征。

Balmoral Castle: on the Balmoral Estate in Aberdeenshire, Scotland is the private residence of The Queen. Beloved by Queen Victoria and Prince Albert, Balmoral Castle has remained a favourite residence for The Queen and her family during the summer holiday period in August and September. The Castle is located on the large Balmoral Estate, a working estate which aims to protect the environment while contributing to the local economy.

巴莫拉尔城堡：位于苏格兰的巴莫拉尔城堡是维多利亚女王购置的地产，如今仍是英国王室最喜爱的避暑胜地。

Trooping the Color: a ceremony performed by regiments of the British and the Commonwealth armies. It has been a tradition of British infantry regiments since the 17th century. Since 1748, Trooping the Colour has also marked the official birthday of the British Sovereign. It is held in London annually on the second Saturday in June on Horse Guards Parade by St. James's Park, and coincides with the publication of the Birthday Honor List. Among the audience are the Royal Family, invited guests, ticketholders and the general public. The colorful ceremony, also known as "The Queen's Birthday Parade", is broadcast live by the BBC.

自1959年起，英国女王的官方生日定在每年6月的第二个星期六庆祝。这一天皇室近卫军的骑兵卫队要举行游行，这就是所谓的"行军旗致敬礼分列式"，简称"军旗分列式"。这一传统起源于古老的军事活动，目的是展示各团队的旗帜，以便各部队能认清自己的旗帜，在激战时作为集合处的标志。最初把这一活动和君主的生日合并举行是在1748年11月30日。后来，这逐渐演变成了每年一度的盛大庆典，参加者包括800名部队的士兵，来自步卫队的5大兵团的乐手、118名骑兵、51名骑兵乐手、169匹皇室骑兵团的军马、6门野战炮、60名炮兵，还有皇家骑兵炮队。

Trivia 八卦一下

Helen Mirren's performance received a five minute standing ovation at the film's premiere at the Venice Film Festival.

在威尼斯电影节举行的电影《女王》的首映式上，全场观众起立五分钟为海伦·米伦的精彩表演鼓掌。

Helen Mirren says transforming herself into the Queen came almost naturally after the wig and glasses, especially since she shares a default facial expression, a slightly down turned mouth, with the monarch.

海伦·米伦说当她带上假发和眼镜时，她立刻就找到了女王的感觉，原因是她和女王本人的脸型相似，嘴角也微微下垂。

Large parts of the film are real life; it includes several of Diana's real press conferences, scenes from outside Buckingham Palace after the death of Diana (including those of flowers, and the hysterical population taking interviews), and scenes from her funeral.

本片中很多片段都来自真实的纪录片，如戴安娜王妃的记者招待会、戴安娜王妃去世后白金汉宫外的悼念鲜花和仪式以及戴安娜王妃的葬礼等。

The five corgis that portray the Queen's dogs won the 2007 London Film Festival's first-ever Fido award for dogs in movies.

片中女王所牵的五条威尔士矮脚狗在2007年伦敦电影节上首次获得电影节所颁发的爱犬奖。

The real Queen Elizabeth II refuses to watch this film, as she does not wish to relive "one of the worst weeks of her life."

女王伊丽莎白二世拒绝看此电影，她说她不愿意回想自己一生中最糟糕的几个星期。

 **Part III. Extra Credit**
美文品读

Royal Wedding: Savior of the British Monarchy?
王室大婚：谁能拯救温莎王朝？

As Kate and her family dine together tonight in a London hotel on the eve of wedding, the air will be full of the dress, the hairstyle, the walk up the aisle. Few would be unkind enough to worry the bride with thoughts on her vital role in saving the British Monarchy.

But that's what this wedding, to be watched by an estimated two billion worldwide, is all about. The House of Windsor is dying from lack of interest. The crowds turn out to greet the Queen on her tours home and abroad, yes. That's more of a habit. There is little to attract the next generation when this year's flag-wavers have passed on.

Certainly the Queen will be rapturously received for her Diamond Jubilee celebrations next year – but huge events like this are stage-managed. Speak to teenagers today, even the brightest, and they are bemused by the House of Windsor. They know the Queen is very old but silent. They've heard she's done a good job but they're not interested in her. She is outdated. Can you blame them? After all, we are all inclined to remember the downsides of the famous, not their better moments. Hence we recall Oliver Cromwell sprouted facial warts but forget he executed a king. We recall Catholic fanatic Mary Tudor as Bloody Mary but forget how she won this notoriety.

Thus, Prince Charles today is remembered not for his success of his Prince's Trust that has helped countless young people set up in business, but as the peevish man we know to sulk when thwarted. We also feel he was tragically weak when he allowed himself to be bullied into marrying the unfortunate Diana.

Prince Philip, 90 in June, has nothing to offer these days. The Princess Royal is known for her rudeness rather than her international equestrian success. Her brother, Andrew, has made headlines for free-loading, his dubious friends, and his corblimey wife. As for Edward, who is he?

But Kate and William. They're different. For all their good fortune and cushioned lives, they can both capture the huge interest and affection bestowed on Diana, who glorified in her self-perceived victimhood. With no such emotional problems, tomorrow's newlyweds can strike an entirely new note.

We want some laughter-makers among the Windsors, good-looking young people still in touch with their future subjects. But their first job must be to blow away many Palace cobwebs and outdated traditions.

We want Williams and Kate to be seen at the cinema when a talked-about new film opens – not whisked up in a limo and past the crowd who've waited for hours to see them.

We want to see William buying Kate one of those monster Malteser buckets and having a song as the lights go down.

She must avoid at all cost the danger of falling into the hands of the fashionistas, those strange and misguided people who truly believe they have a serious job as arbiters of British taste.

They have a place among the very wealthy certainly, among the newly-moneyed. But they must never achieve the influence over Kate that Diana's designers exercised over her.

The new bride, don't forget, scored multiple brownie points in her courtship's early days when she'd trot round in Jigsaw clothes – remember that polka-dotted dress copied throughout the world? We'd like Kate all dolled-up for Royal cash on £20,000 frocks and £5,000 handbags.

Feeling spurned by Charles and determined to show him what he was missing, Diana spent hours daily planning her fabulous wardrobe. It passed time for a lonely woman with little intellectual interests in the arts or world affairs.

Kate is totally different. She'll not be lonely. Her good education and degree has opened her mind. She is receptive. She asks questions. She reads. She doesn't need the prop of extravagantly expensive clobber. If she wants to be loved, let her slip unannounced into the Oxford Street M&S, buy herself a couple of suits and dresses, then wear them on her next Royal outing.

Better still, let her not spend a fortune on designer labels for her Canadian tour in June. She has the glorious figure to show off ready-mades, thereby waving the flag for British fashion in a simple and telling export drive.

That would be enough for Kate and William for the first few months of married life.

(From Birmingham Mail, Apr.28, 2011)

Making Sense 解文说词

① the air will be full of the dress, the hairstyle, the walk up the aisle (Para. 1)

大家的话题都是关于婚纱、发型以及步入教堂的时刻。

This is a metaphor and "the air" is used to refer to everybody present at the diner.

② …when this year's flag-wavers have passed on (para. 2)

……那些王室的当前拥趸们离开之后

"flag-waver" originally refers to one who is intensely and conspicuously patriotic and here it refers to those very much supporting of the Monarchy.

③ After all, we are all inclined to remember the downsides of the famous, not their better moments (para. 3)

的确，我们都习惯性地记着名人倒霉的时刻，而他们的辉煌之时早已被我们抛到脑后了。

④ For all their good fortune and cushioned lives, they can both capture the huge interest and affection bestowed on Diana, who glorified in her self-perceived victimhood. With no such emotional problems, tomorrow's newlyweds can strike an entirely new note. (para. 6)

威廉和凯特富有且生活安逸无忧，他们天然地继承了人们对因悲情而名声盖世的戴妃的爱和痴迷。明天的这对新婚夫妇并没有戴妃所遭受的情感困惑，因此他们未来的生活一定会是一路凯歌。

⑤ The new bride, don't forget, scored multiple brownie points in her courtship's early days when she'd trot round in Jigsaw clothes – remember that polka-dotted dress copied throughout the world? (para. 12)

别忘了，在和王子恋爱初期新娘所穿的Jigsaw时装就给她加够了印象分，还记得那件曾经风靡世界圆点花上衣的吧？

Brownie points in modern usage are a hypothetical social currency, which can be accrued by doing good deeds or earning favor in the eyes of another, often one's superior.（印象分）

 Background 文化大本营

Diamond Jubilee: a celebration held to mark a 60th anniversary in the case of a person (e.g. wedding anniversary, length of time a monarch has reigned as King or Queen, etc.). Elizabeth II is scheduled to have her Diamond Jubilee on June 2 to 5 of 2012 when she will also celebrate her 86th birthday. Her Majesty's Government in the United Kingdom has announced a significant celebration during this time and an extra bank holiday（法定节假日）.

2012年6月2日至5日，英国耗资13亿英镑，举办了一系列"英女王钻禧庆典"官方活动，纪念伊丽莎白二世登基60周年。在为期4天的时间里，举办了埃普瑟姆赛马会、开曼岛放生海龟、千艘游艇巡游泰晤士河、伦敦大本钟更名、全新女王蜡像的揭幕仪式等庆祝活动。钻禧庆典活动在6月5日达到高潮，英女王在圣保罗大教堂举行感恩仪式。英女王由此被冠以"钻禧女王（DIAMOND QUEEN）"的美誉。

Oliver Cromwell (1599 – 1658): an English military and political leader who overthrew the English monarchy and temporarily turned England into a republican Commonwealth, and ruled as Lord Protector（护国公）of England, Scotland and Ireland from 1653 until his death at 1658.

克伦威尔：英国政治家、军事家、宗教领袖。17世纪英国资产阶级革命中，资产阶级——新贵族集团的代表人物、独立派的首领。1649年，他处死国王查理一世，宣布成立共和国。1653年，克伦威尔建立军事独裁统治，自任"护国公"。

Bloody Mary(1516 –1558): Mary I was Queen regnant（在位女王）of England and Ireland from July 1553 until her death. She was the eldest daughter of Henry VIII and only surviving child of Catherine of Aragon. As the fourth crowned monarch of the Tudor dynasty（都铎王朝）, she is remembered for restoring England to Roman Catholicism after succeeding her short-lived Protestant half brother, Edward VI. In the process, she had almost 300 religious dissenters burned at the stake in the Marian Persecutions（玛丽一世在英国用来镇压宗教改革者新教徒的一次迫害运动）, earning her the sobriquet （外号）of "Bloody Mary". Her re-establishment of Roman Catholicism was reversed by her successor and half-sister, Elizabeth I.

血腥玛丽：英格兰和爱尔兰女王，1553年7月至1558年11月在位。她是都铎王朝的第四任君主，极其虔诚的天主教徒。她一生致力于把英国从新教恢复到罗马天主教。为此，她曾处决了差不多三百个反对者，因而被称为"血腥玛丽"。从此以后，Bloody Mary在英语中就成了"女巫"的同义词。但是，她的宗教政策在很大程度上，被她的继任者、她的妹妹伊丽莎白一世所颠覆。

Prince's Trust: a charity in the UK founded in 1976 by Charles Prince of Wales to help young people. They run a range of training programs, provide mentoring support and offer financial grants to build the confidence and motivation of disadvantaged young people.

威尔士亲王信托基金：由威尔士亲王——王储查尔斯在1976年设立的，旨在培训和资助贫困的年轻人以帮助其树立自信和理想。

The Princess Royal(1950 –): Anne Elizabeth Alice Louise, born on 15 August 1950, is the only daughter of Elizabeth II and Prince Philip, Duke of Edinburgh. Anne is known for her charitable work, being the patron of over 200 organizations, and she carries out about 700 royal engagements and public appearances per year. She is also known for equestrian（马术）talents; she won two silver and one gold medal at the European Eventing Championships, and is the only member of the British Royal Family to have competed in the Olympic Games. Currently married to Vice-Admiral Timothy Laurence, she has two children from her previous marriage to Mark Phillips and one granddaughter.

安妮长公主：全名安妮·伊丽莎白·爱莉斯·路易斯·劳伦斯，生于1950年8月15日，是英国女王伊丽莎白二世的长女，也是其唯一的女儿。英国王室第十位继承人。安妮公主是著名的慈善工作者。她还是参加国际奥委会的英国代表团团长和伦敦奥运会组委会成员，也是王室中唯一参加过奥运会比赛的成员。

Malteser: a confectionery product manufactured by Mars, Incorporated. Maltesers consist of a roughly spherical malt honeycomb centre, surrounded by Milk chocolate. They are most popular in the UK, Australia, Ireland, Canada, Poland, France and Portugal.

麦提莎巧克力：世界最大的休闲食品制造商美国玛氏麾下的一种巧克力豆，内有麦芽、麦精、蜂蜜等，外面包裹巧克力。麦提莎巧克力球被称为"能量小球"，风靡世界多国。

Marks and Spencer plc (also known as M&S): a British retailer headquartered in the City of Westminster, London, with over 700 stores in the United Kingdom and over 300 stores spread across more than 40 countries. It specializes in the selling of clothing and luxury food products.

玛莎百货公司：创立至今已经有126年的历史，是英国最大的跨国商业零售集团。玛莎百货在英国本土开设了600家分店，遍布英国各个城市和地区，在全球40个国家和地区共开设了285家分店。2008年，玛莎百货在上海开设了在中国大陆的第一家分店。

Writing Tips 写作秘笈

在这篇分析性的新闻特写中，作者首先用了一个急转弯的开头紧紧抓住读者的注意力，第一句的轻松还没有让人停留片刻就转向严肃重大的任务。为什么凯特嫁给王室任重而道远呢，作者用实例呈现了他的观点和结论。首先是王室的过气急需新的兴奋点，随后7、8、9段均以"We want"开头，有力的排比，有力的转折，巨大的期望。

Unit 3

For The Donkey or The Elephant?

驴象庄园:这个地方有点乱

Part I. Get-go
给力起步

Choosing the Nation's President
总统是这样选出来的

Selecting the candidates

Every four years, Americans participate in a unique and exciting ritual — selecting the nation's president and vice president. Beginning early in a presidential election year, people who would like to "run" for the office of president try to win delegates to their party's national political convention. Delegates are chosen from each state. Some are selected at state caucuses and others by party conventions. But most are chosen by primary elections.

> 每四年，美国人都要重新选举自己的总统和副总统。选举从预选开始，民主、共和两大政党分别在全国各州选出参加本党全国代表大会的代表。

The summer before the election, each of the two major political parties — the Democrats and the Republicans — holds a national convention lasting about four days. At these conventions, delegates select the people who will be candidates for president and vice president. The number of delegates from each state is determined by its population and its support for that party in previous elections.

Convention business usually begins with the creation and acceptance of the party's platform. The next order of business is the nomination of prospective presidential candidates. A speaker nominates each nominee, telling that person's strengths and accomplishments. Each nominating speech is followed by a long, noisy demonstration. Bands play, and thousands of delegates wave flags and signs, sing, yell and clap.

After the nominations, the delegates get down to the serious work of choosing their party's presidential candidate. What the delegates consider the most important quality of the candidate is the ability to win the election and also a nominee's integrity, philosophy, and talent for leadership. After the presidential candidate is selected, his/her running mate is chosen. At the convention, the two candidates are formally nominated, elected as the party's candidates, and cheered greatly before and after they give their acceptance speeches.

> 预选结束后，民主、共和两党分别要召开为期四天的全国代表大会。会上先讨论通过本党竞选纲领，然后提名并最终确定本党总统和副总统候选人。

The campaign

Campaigning for the general election traditionally begins on Labor Day in early September. From that time until Election Day, in early November, voters are bombarded from all sides — by radio, television, newspapers, and personal communications — with political materials. Each candidate tries to convince a majority of the American voters that he is best qualified to lead the country for the next 4 years. Since the candidate has only 2 months in which to do this, he must campaign very hard, day and night.

Campaigning is extremely expensive, and a candidate must receive a majority of the electoral votes to be elected; therefore, only the candidates of the two major parties can expect to win.

> 竞选活动始于九月初的劳工节，至全国投票日结束。这是世界上最奢华、最烧钱的竞选活动，两党总统候选人为争取更多的选票，要跑遍全国。

The election

On the Tuesday following the first Monday in November, voters cast their ballots for president and vice president, who are voted as a team. The entire House of Representatives, one-third of the Senate, and many state and local officials are also elected. Thanks to the voting machines and computers, Americans usually know most the winners by late evening.

The President and Vice president are not actually chosen by how many people vote for them; instead, they are chosen by electoral votes. Altogether, there are 538 electoral votes; it takes 270 to win. When citizens cast votes for presidential candidates, they are selecting their state's electors, who, as a group, are called the Electoral College. The number of electors for each state is equal to the total number of representatives and senators who represent that state in Congress.

> 全国选民投票在选举年11月第一个星期一的次日举行，这一天被称为"大选日"。选民投票时，不仅要在总统候选人当中选择，而且要选出代表50个州和华盛顿特区的538名选举人，以组成选举人团。赢得270张或以上选举人票的总统候选人即获得选举胜利。因此，根据各州选举人票的归属情况，通常大选日当晚就能决出选举获胜者。

(Revised from *Ethel Tiersky & Martin Tiersky*《美国制度与文化》)

NOTES

State caucuses: a meeting of the local members of a political party especially to select delegates to a convention or register preferences for candidates running for office.

各州政党基层会议：主要指美国民主和共和两党召开的基层会议，旨在选举参加全国代表大会的会议代表并表明对总统候选人的倾向。

Primary elections: one of the first steps in the process of electing the US President. They provide a method for U.S. Political parties to nominate and unite behind one popularly chosen candidate for the Presidency.

初选就是用个人投票选举或政党基层会议这两种形式选举出将要代表本政党参加大选的总统候选人。

Platform: (also known as Manifesto), list of the principles which a political party supports in order to appeal to the general public for the purpose of having said party's candidates voted into office.

政纲：某一政党为了将其所推选的总统候选人送到白宫所制订的一系列政治纲领。

Labor Day: national holiday observed in the US on the first Monday in September in honor of working people.

（美国的）劳工节：相当于中国的"五一"劳动节，是劳动者的节日，只是它在九月的第一个星期一庆祝。这天一般都会有大型的游行活动。

Election Day: in the United States is the day set by law for the general elections of public officials. It occurs on the Tuesday after the first Monday in November, which is usually also the first Tuesday in November. The earliest possible date is November 2 and the latest possible date is November 8.

选举日：四年一次的总统选举投票日叫做"选举日"。由于定在大选年的十一月的第一个星期一后的星期二，所以也叫"超级星期二"（Super Tuesday）。

Electoral votes, vote by the Electoral College（选举团） that chooses the President and Vice President of the US at the conclusion of each presidential election.

选举团：指的是一批"选举人"，他们由各州的政治活动家和政党成员提名。在选举日，这些保证支持某一位总统候选人的选举人经普选产生。在总统选举后的12月，当选的选举人于各自所在州的首府投票选举总统与副总统。由于美国国会有100名参议员、435名众议员，加上华盛顿哥伦比亚特区的3票，总统选举人票总共538票。因此，获得超过270张选举人票者方可当选。

The US House of Representatives: one of the two Houses of the United States Congress, the bicameral legislature which also includes the Senate. The major power of the House is to pass federal legislation that affects the entire country. Each state receives representation in the House in proportion to its population but is entitled to at least one representative. Each representative serves for a two-year term. The Constitution grants the House several exclusive powers: the power to initiate revenue bills, to impeach officials, and to elect the President in case of an Electoral College deadlock.

众议院：美国国会的两院之一。依照美国宪法第一条，众议院席位的分配以各州人口数作为基础，以每十年举行一次的人口普查为依据。但是，各州至少要有一名代表。众议员一任两年，众议员总数的法定名额为435名。众议院议场在华盛顿特区的国会山南翼。

The Senate: the upper house of the bicameral legislature of the United States, and together with the United States House of Representatives comprises the United States Congress. Each U.S. state is represented by two senators, regardless of population. Senators serve staggered six-year terms. The Senate has several exclusive powers not granted to the House, including consenting to treaties as a precondition to their ratification and consenting or confirming appointments of Cabinet secretaries, federal judges, other federal executive officials, military officers, regulatory officials, ambassadors, and other federal uniformed officers, as well as trial of federal officials impeached by the House.

参议院：美国国会两院之一，另一院为上述的众议院。按照美国法律，各州在众议院中的代表权以人口为基础，但在参议院中是均等代表权，即每个州都是两个参议员，共100名。宪法规定，法律制定须经两院通过。参议院所单独拥有的权力较众议院所单独拥有的权力更为重要。参议员一任六年，可连任。参议院议场在华盛顿特区的国会山北翼。

Electoral College (in US): a set of electors who are selected to elect the President and Vice President. The Electoral College was established by the founding fathers as a compromise between election of the president by Congress and election by popular vote.

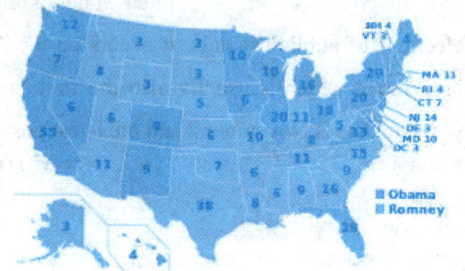

选举团：美国的选举团制度于1788年开始实行。根据此制度，选民投票时，不仅要在总统候选人当中选择，而且要选出代表50个州和首都华盛顿哥伦比亚特区（简称华盛顿）的538名选举人，以组成选举团。总统候选人获得超过半数的选举人票（270张或以上）即可当选总统。

 Part II. cineWatch
光影星荟萃

All the President's Men 《总统班底》

紧密的打字声爆出历史的真相，宣告了尼克松总统的辞职。

Storyline 好片抢先知

This is the story of the process of discovery of the political scandal known as Watergate by two Washington reporters, covering the years from 1972 to 1974. It all begins rather simply with the report of a 1972 break-in at the Democratic Party headquarters in the Watergate complex. Through a series of interviews of potential informants, we watch the reporters as they get closer and closer to the truth

about and behind the break-in. The Watergate scandal ultimately led to the resignation of President Richard Nixon.

该片是根据水门事件揭发人Carl Bernstein和Bob Woodward所写自传改编的电影。二人是《华盛顿邮报》的记者，在水门事件里，他们历尽艰辛揭开政治黑幕，人物和事件一同成为美国一段家喻户晓的历史。故事由五名盗贼开始，他们潜入水门大肆行窃。本来是一桩不甚重大的刑事案件，却在Bernstein（达斯汀·霍夫曼Dustin Hoffman 饰）和Woodward（罗伯特·雷德福Robert Redford 饰）的追查下，最终撕开了一条大裂缝，矛头直指总统尼克松。从1972年到1974年，从尼克松竞选总统到尼克松连任上台，华盛顿邮报受到的压力越来越大，甚至被威胁。主编本·布莱德利站在了新闻自由和相信自己记者的这边，Bernstein和Woodward得以继续追寻事件真相，并得到了重要线人"深喉"的帮助。经历了难以想象的曲折艰辛后，"水门事件"最终导致尼克松总统下台。

Cast 星光闪烁

Alan J. Pakula … Director 奥斯卡最佳导演提名

Robert Redford … Bob Woodward 奥斯卡最佳导演、演员、终生成就奖

Dustin Hoffman … Carl Bernstein 两届奥斯卡最佳男演员奖，美国电影协会终生成就奖

Memorable quotes 余音绕梁

The Deep Throat: Follow the money.
Bob Woodward: What do you mean? Where?
Deep Throat: Oh, I can't tell you that.
Bob Woodward: But you could tell me that.
Deep Throat: No, I have to do this my way. You tell me what you know, and I'll confirm. I'll keep you

in the right direction if I can, but that's all. Just... follow the money.

Bob Woodward: I don't mind what you did; I mind how you did it.

Deep Throat: It leads everywhere. Get out your notebook. There's more.

Bob Woodward: How do you think your check got into the bank account of a Watergate burglar?

Kenneth H. Dahlberg: I'm, uh, a proper citizen. What I do is proper.

Bob Woodward: Well, I - I understand.

Kenneth H. Dahlberg: I've just been through a terrible ordeal. My neighbor's wife has been kidnapped!

Clark MacGregor: I don't know. You're implying that I should know. If you print that, our relationship will be terminated.

Bob Woodward: Sir, we don't have a relationship!

Ben Bradlee: How much can you tell me about Deep Throat?

Bob Woodward: How much do you need to know?

Ben Bradlee: Do you trust him?

Bob Woodward: Yeah.

Ben Bradlee: I can't do the reporting for my reporters, which means I have to trust them. And I hate trusting anybody. Run that baby.

Harry Rosenfeld: Bernstein, why don't you finish one story before trying to get on another?

Carl Bernstein: I finished it.

Harry Rosenfeld: The Virginia legislature story?

Carl Bernstein: I finished it.

Harry Rosenfeld: All right, give it to me.

Carl Bernstein: I'm just polishing it.

Bob Woodward: Excuse me, what is your name? I'm Bob Woodward, of the Washington Post.

Markham: Markham.

Bob Woodward: Markham. Mr. Markham, are you here in connection with the Watergate burglary?

Markham: I'm not here.

Ben Bradlee: Where's the goddamn story?

Bob Woodward: The money's the key to whatever this is.

Ben Bradlee: Says who?

Howard Simons: Deep Throat.

Ben Bradlee: Who?

Howard Simons: Oh, that's Woodward's garage freak; his source in the executive department.

Ben Bradlee: Garage Freak? Jesus, what kind of a crazy fucking story is this? Who did you say?

Howard Simons: He's on deep background, I call him deep... throat.

Deep Throat: You'll have to figure that on your own.

Bob Woodward: Look, I'm tired of your chicken shit games! I don't want hints! I need to know what you know!

Deep Throat: The Watergate burglary... it was a Haldeman operation. The whole business was run by Haldeman, the money... everything. It won't be easy getting at him. He was insulated somehow, you'll have to find out how. Mitchell started doing covert stuff before anyone else. The list of the people involved is longer than anyone can imagine. It involves the entire U.S. Intelligence Community. FBI... CIA... Justice... it's incredible. The cover-up had little to do with the Watergate foul-up. It was mainly to protect the covert operations. It leads everywhere. Get out your notebook. There's more. I think your lives are in danger.

Judge: Your names, please, and state your professions.

Barker: Bernard Barker, anti-communist.

Judge: Anti-communist? That, sir, is not your average profession.

McCord: James McCord, security consultant.

Judge: With?

McCord: Government, uh, recently, uh, retired.

Judge: Where in the government?

McCord: Central Intelligence Agency.

Culture inside 文化反光镜

Political parties in the US: a two-party system has been dominant in the US, the Democratic Party as the now-president Barack Obama's party and the Republican Party as the former-president George W. Bush's party. Normally speaking, the Democratic Party is more liberal; while the Republican Party is more conservative.

美国的党派：美国有两个主要政党，民主党（现总统奥巴马所属党派）和共和党（前总统布什所属党派）。一般来讲，民主党温和、开放一些，而共和党更保守一些。

Richard Nixon (1913 –1994): the 37th President of the United States, serving from 1969 to 1974, the only president to resign the office. Internationally, although Nixon initially escalated the war in Vietnam, he subsequently ended US involvement in 1973. Nixon's visit to China in 1972 opened diplomatic relations between the two nations, and he initiated détente and the Anti-Ballistic Missile Treaty with the Soviet Union the same year. Domestically, his administration generally embraced policies that transferred power from Washington to the states. Among other things, he initiated wars on cancer and drugs, imposed wage and price controls, enforced desegregation of Southern schools and established the Environmental Protection Agency. Although resigned by the Watergate Scandal, Nixon was recorded as one of the top US presidents.

理查德·尼克松：美国第37位总统。1972年2月尼克松访华，打开了两国关系的大门，成为访问新中国的第一位美国总统。尼克松因1972年6月17日发生的"水门事件"被迫辞职。

Bod Woodward (1943–): an American investigative journalist and non-fiction author. He has worked for *The Washington Post* since 1971 as a reporter, and is currently an associate editor of the Post. While a young reporter for *The Washington Post* in 1972, Woodward was teamed up with Carl Bernstein; the two did much of the original news reporting on the Watergate scandal. These scandals led to numerous government investigations and the eventual resignation of President Richard Nixon.

鲍勃·伍德沃德：美国记者，是揭穿"水门事件"丑闻的两名《华盛顿邮报》记者之一。他1970年退役后进入《华盛顿邮报》成为了一名实习记者，从而开始了记者生涯。1972年，鲍勃·伍德沃德与另一名记者卡尔·伯恩斯坦通过其内线"深喉"的情报及协助，率先披露了"水门事件"丑闻，从而迫使总统尼克松下台，名噪新闻界。两人也因此获得了1973年的普利策新闻奖，随后他们把事件经过合集成书——《总统班底》（*All the President's Men*）。该书在1974年出版。

Carl Bernstein (1944 –): an American investigative journalist who, at *The Washington Post*, teamed up with Bob Woodward; the two did the majority of the most important news reporting on the Watergate scandal. These scandals led to numerous government investigations, the indictment of a vast number of White House Officials such as H.R. Haldeman, John Ehrlichman, Charles Colson, and John Mitchell, and the eventual resignation of President Richard Nixon. For his role in breaking the scandal, Bernstein received many awards; his work helped earn the *Post* a Pulitzer Prize for Public Service in 1973.

卡尔·伯恩斯坦：《华盛顿邮报》前记者，1972年美国"水门事件"主要调查者，普利策奖获得者。"水门事件"后，他于1976年退出华盛顿邮报。伯恩斯坦后来成为《名利场》杂志编辑。

The Watergate scandal: a political scandal during the 1970s in the United States resulting from the break-in of the Democratic National Committee headquarters at the Watergate office complex in Washington, D.C. Effects of the scandal eventually led to the resignation of the President of the United States, Richard Nixon, on August 9, 1974, the only resignation of any U.S. President. It also resulted in the indictment, trial, conviction and incarceration of several Nixon administration officials.

水门事件：指美国共和党政府在1972年总统竞选运动中的非法活动暴露后的政治丑闻。水门是华盛顿的一座综合大厦。1972年6月17日有五个人因潜入位于华盛顿特区的美国民主党总部——水门大厦而被捕。随后的调查表明，尼克松政府为破坏选举的进程采取了一系列的行动，闯入水门只是其中之一。该事件的结果导致政府的几个官员锒铛入狱以及美国历史上第一次出现的总统辞职。

Deep Throat: the pseudonym given to the secret informant who provided information to Bob Woodward of *The Washington Post* in 1972 about the involvement of United States President Nixon's administration in what came to be known as the Watergate scandal. Thirty-one years after Nixon's resignation, Deep Throat was revealed to be former Federal Bureau of Investigation Associate Director Mark Felt.

深喉：在水门事件中为记者提供重要资料的人。1972年，美国《华盛顿邮报》记者鲍勃·伍德沃德和卡尔·伯恩斯坦依据线人"深喉"的消息，捅开"水门事件"的内幕，导致当时的美国总统尼克松辞职下台。事后,这两名记者一直拒绝透露当时线人的身份,但是《华盛顿邮报》的总编辑西蒙斯引用了当时一部知名色情电影《深喉》的片名,作为告密者的化名。2005年5月31日,美国联邦调查局前副局长马克·费尔特承认自己就是"水门事件"中那个曾被称为"深喉"的人。随后,《华盛顿邮报》和费尔特的家人均确认,"深喉"就是时年91岁的费尔特。

 Trivia 八卦一下

Frank Wills, the security guard who discovered the break-in at the Watergate complex, plays himself.
在水门事件中第一个发现有人晚上潜入民主党总部的保安叫弗兰克·威尔斯,在电影中他饰演他自己。

This was the first film Jimmy Carter watched during his presidential tenure.
这是卡特总统在他的总统任期内看的第一部电影。

The telephone number that Robert Redford dials for the White House is the real number of the White House Switchboard: 456-1414.
电影中罗伯特·雷德福拨的白宫的号码就是白宫真正的号码:456-1414。

On 31 May 2005, ninety-one-year-old W. Mark Felt acknowledged publicly for the first time that he was in fact "Deep Throat," a fact corroborated by Bob Woodward and the Washington Post. At the time of the Watergate break-in, Mr. Felt was second in command at the F.B.I.
2005年5月31日,91岁的W·马克·菲尔特首次公开承认他就是真正的"深喉","水门事件"时,他任联邦调查局的副局长。

The movie was not shot in The Washington Post newsroom. Instead, a $450,000 replica was built in Los Angeles. Trash, papers, and desks from the Post offices were shipped to California to make it feel more real.
电影拍摄中的《华盛顿邮报》的新闻编辑室是耗资45万美元在洛杉矶搭建的。为了使编辑室更加真实,编辑室内的桌椅纸张包括垃圾都是从华盛顿邮报的编辑室运到洛杉矶的。

 **Part III. Extra Credit**
美文品读

Imagine the thoughts in Blagojevich's veins
布拉戈耶维奇:你手上的青筋已经告诉了我

A blue vein ran along the back of Rod Blagojevich's left hand, snaking back from the base of index finger as the former governor of Illinois took that beating in federal court on June 27.

Sliding across the flat of the hand, that vein turned back toward the thumb, splitting, raised, and then finally running to hide inside the cuff of that fine blue suit worn by Dead Meat.

He was still, hardly moving, only a few feet away as the beating rained down on him. Even with that, and all that prison time coming, the back of his suit was perfectly flat. There was not even one wrinkle in it.

He was mute, perhaps numb, but that vein of his did all the talking.

His wife, Patti, wearing a white suit , was sobbing in her brother's arms, shaking her head "no" as she sat in the seat in front of me, as the clerk read out the 17 guilty criminal verdicts: "With respect to count 12 in the indictment, we the jury find the defendant guilty…"

There was meter to the chant of his guilt, and it went on like that for some time, with the clerk tolling off the counts as if in liturgy, and Rod finally still, except for that vein pulsing away in the forgotten hand.

At last, he'd finally stopped acting. Dead Meat didn't have to play a part anymore. There was nobody to charm, nobody to convince. All he had to do was sit there and take it.

And I wonder if Dead Meat had time then to consider the arc of his life as the perfect Chicago political cautionary tale.

The desperate kid who wanted to be liked, the boy who married the ward boss' daughter, and kid who ingratiated his way into the 5th Congressional District, and who, with the help of patronage armies of knuckle draggers, was finally elected governor as a self-professed reformer.

It all began to fall apart for him around Christmas of 2004, when Blagojevich and his father-in-law, Chicago Alderman Richard Mell, had a very public falling out over an in-law's role in a Will county landfill.

It got ugly, then it got uglier, and when it became public, drawing the attention of FBI, Blagojevich was becoming Dead Meat.

Mell accused Blagojevich of trading public-sector jobs for campaign donations. He said publicly that he had been replaced in Dead Meat's inner circle by his son-in-law's friend, contractor Christopher Kelly.

Chris Kelly killed himself in September of 2009, after he'd been netted in the case called Operation Board Games. Kelly couldn't take the pressure.

Operation Board Games has exposed what I've been calling the bipartisan Illinois Combine, in which powerful Democrats work with powerful Republicans to gorge from the public trough and call it legal.

Once Blagojevich and Mell fell out, once they began fighting and blaming each other and air the family's dirty laundry, once Mell publicly accused his son-in-law of corruption, it was over for Blagojevich.

Without Mell guarding his flank, Illinois House Speaker Michael Madigan had no qualms about cutting Dead Meat to size. And that was just the politics.

The FBI also picked up on the family feud, which spiraled into a federal investigation, which led to the guilty verdicts, which led to that blue vein pulsing in Blagojevich's left hand.

And after the guilty counts had been read, Rod turned to Patti and touched his lips as the jury filed out. "All rise," said the bailiff, and everyone stood, even Rod. The only ones who kept their seats in the court room were Patti and her brother. Moments later, Rod kissed her. As he put his chin over her right shoulder, you could see that his eyes were wet.

"Patti and I obviously are very disappointed in the outcome," Dead Meat told reporters in courthouse lobby. "I, frankly, am stunned."

Perhaps he was the only one.

(By John Kass, Chicago Tribune, from "*21st Century,* June 6, 2011")

Making Sense 解文说词

① A blue vein ran along the back of Rod Blagojevich's left hand, snaking back from the base of index finger as the former governor of Illinois took that beating in federal court on June 27. (para. 1)

伊利诺斯州前州长布拉戈耶维奇6月27日在联邦法庭败诉的时候，他左手背上的一条青筋蜿蜒而下，又从食指底部迂回向上。

Here " to take a beating" is an idiom meaning "to be defeated or lose a lot of money." Also notice the verbing of the noun "snake", meaning "to move with a sinuous motion" , a very vivid description.

② Sliding across the flat of the hand, that vein turned back toward the thumb, splitting , raised, and then finally running to hide inside the cuff of that fine blue suit worn by Dead Meat.（para.2）

青筋在手背上纵横而过之后，从大拇指折回、分叉、突起，最终钻进了"倒霉的家伙"的极其考究的蓝色西服袖口里。

Here "Dead Meat" is a nickname given to Blagojevich by Chicago Tribune columnist John Kass, indicating that Blagojevich's everything, even his life is doomed to be ruined.

③ …only a few feet away as the beating rained down on him. (para. 3) ……

宣判他败诉的法官离他只有几尺之遥。

Here " the beating rained down on him" means that when the judge pronounced his judgement (of Blagojevich being defeated)。

④ He was mute, perhaps numb, but that vein of his did all the talking. (para. 4)

他一直缄默，也许早已麻木，但是他手上的青筋告诉了人们一切。

Here "do all the talking" means "to show everything".

⑤ There was meter to the chant of his guilt, and it went on like that for some time, with the clerk tolling off the counts as if in liturgy, and Rod finally still, except for that vein pulsing away in the forgotten hand. （para. 6）

宣判的声音带有某种节奏，书记员像做礼拜一样一字一句地念着他的罪状；布拉戈耶维奇始终是一动不动，可他那只不被人注意的手上的青筋在不停地悸动。

⑥ …to consider the arc of his life as the perfect Chicago political cautionary tale.（para. 8）

……是否有想到他人生的轨迹竟然是一个绝佳的芝加哥政坛警示录。

⑦ Operation Board Games has exposed what I've been calling the bipartisan Illinois Combine, in which powerful Democrats work with powerful Republicans to gorge from the public trough and call it legal.（para. 14）

我把经营局调查所暴露的问题称之为"伊利诺斯两党大联合"，即有权势的民主和共和两党联合起来打着"合法"的幌子侵吞公共财产。

⑧ "air the family's dirty laundry"（para. 15）also can be phrased to air your dirty laundry in public , meaning "to talk about the things (usually a problem or dispute) that should be kept private."

把家丑抖出来

⑨ Without Mell guarding his flank, Illinois House Speaker Michael Madigan had no qualms about cutting Dead Meat to size. And that was just the politics. (para. 16)

布拉戈耶维奇失去了梅尔的保护，伊利诺斯州议院议长迈克尔·麦迪根就可以毫无顾忌地向他开刀了。这就叫政治。

Background 文化大本营

Rod Blagojevich (1956 –): an American politician who served as the 40th Governor of Illinois from 2003 to 2009. On December 9, 2008, Blagojevich was arrested on federal corruption charges including conspiracy to commit mail and wire fraud and solicitation of bribery. As a result, on January 9, 2009, the Illinois House of Representatives voted by a 114–1 vote to impeach Blagojevich for corruption and misconduct in office, the first time such an action has been taken against a governor of Illinois, making him the second state official in Illinois history to be impeached. The Illinois State Senate 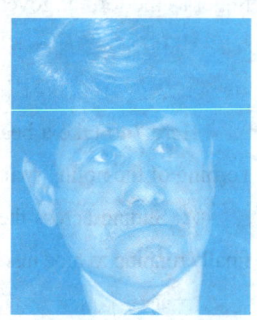 unanimously found him guilty of the charges of impeachment, and he was removed from office on January 29, 2009. In a separate also unanimous vote, Blagojevich was banned for life from holding public office in the State of Illinois. On August 17, 2010, Blagojevich was found guilty of lying to the FBI; on June 27, 2011, Blagojevich was found guilty on 17 of 20 counts presented during his retrial. On Thursday, September 29, 2011, it was announced that in mid-August, administrators for the Illinois Attorney Registration and Disciplinary Commission（伊利诺斯州律师登记和纪律委员会）asked the Illinois Supreme Court（伊利诺斯州最高法院）to suspend the former attorney's law license, in a likely prelude to the further disgrace of disbarment. On December 7, 2011, Blagojevich was sentenced to 14 years in federal prison.（from www.wikipedia.com）

罗德·布拉戈耶维奇：美国伊利诺伊州前州长，是南斯拉夫移民后代，出身于芝加哥草根阶层家庭，靠擦鞋和送外卖赚钱读大学，从法律学院毕业后最终成为一名律师。1997年布拉戈耶维奇当选为国会众议员，2002年当选伊利诺伊州州长，2006年获得连任，任期至2011年。2009年他因涉嫌卖官、受贿、敲诈勒索等罪名成为伊利诺斯州第一个被弹劾的州长，2011年被判在联邦监狱服刑14年。

5th Congressional District: refers to the 5th Congressional District of Illinois. A congressional district is a geographical division of a state from which one member of the House of Representatives is elected. It is made up of three main components, a representative, constituents（选民）, and the specific land area that both the representative and the constituents live in.

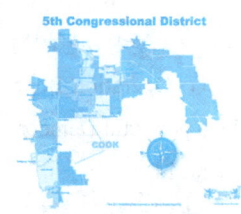

第五国会选区：美国国会选区按一个州的地理区域划分，每个区可选一个国会议员。

Ward: The City of Chicago is divided into fifty legislative districts or wards. Each district is represented by an alderman who is elected by their constituency to serve a four year term. In addition to representing the interests of their ward residents, together the fifty aldermen comprise the Chicago City Council, which serves as the legislative branch of government of the City of Chicago. The legislative powers of the City Council are granted by the state legislature and by home rule provisions of the Illinois constitution. Within specified limits, the City Council has the general authority to exercise any power and perform any function pertaining to its government and affairs including, but not limited to, the power to regulate for the protection of the public health, safety, morals and welfare; to license; to tax; and to incur debt.

地方选区：地方选举的选区叫做"地方选区"，也叫"立法选区"，或"大选区"，简称LD。联邦众议员的选区叫"国会选区"，简称CD。一个州有多少个CD，取决于州的人口数。每个地区根据人数可包括很多大选区，如芝加哥共有50个大选区。每个区可选一个联邦议员，任期为四年。此选区的议员将代表本区的选民和本区选民的利益。所有的立法选区的议员就构成了本地区（如芝加哥）的市议会。

Richard Mell (1938 –): an American politician and long-time member of the Chicago City Council(芝加哥市议会). He is a Democrat. Mell is the chairman of the Rules Committee（法规委员会）.

理查德·梅尔：美国著名政治家，芝加哥市议会资深委员，芝加哥市议会法规委员会主席，第33选区区长，民主党党员。

The Federal Bureau of Investigation(*FBI*) is an agency of the United States Department of Justice（美国司法部）that serves as both a federal criminal investigative body and an internal intelligence agency. Its motto is a backronym（逆向首字母缩拼词）of FBI, "Fidelity（忠诚），Bravery（勇敢），Integrity（正直）". The FBI's headquarters, the J. Edgar Hoover Building, is located in Washington. Fifty-six field offices are located in major cities throughout the United States, and there are over 400 resident agencies in smaller cities and towns across the country. More than 50 international offices called "legal attachés" are in U.S. embassies and consulates general worldwide.

联邦调查局：美国最重要的情报机构之一，隶属于美国司法部。美国联邦调查局根据其职能和授权，广泛参与国内外重大特工调查案件，它现有的调查司法权已经超过200种联邦罪行。

Christopher Kelly (1958 – 2009): a commercial roofing contractor and former chief fundraiser for ousted Illinois Gov. Rod Blagojevich. Kelly raised millions of dollars for Blagojevich's campaigns and was among his closest advisers. He was found died (suicide) on Sept 15,2009, just days before he was to begin serving at least eight years in federal prison for fraud that included using his company's money to pay gambling debts and claiming it as a business expense.

克里斯多夫·凯利：美国屋顶承包商，伊利诺斯州前州长布拉戈耶维奇的主要顾问和筹款人。2009年9月15日就在他将要在联邦监狱服刑之前被发现在家中死亡。

Operation Board Games: a federal fraud investigation initiated by United States Attorney Patrick Fitzgerald in December 2003, in order to investigate suspected fraud and extortion activity by Illinois Governor Rod Blagojevich. The investigation's name is a reference to two governing bodies in Illinois: one board controlling the Teacher's Pension System, and the second being the Health Facilities Planning Board.

经营局调查：此调查为联邦检察官帕特里克·菲兹杰拉德发起的旨在针对布拉戈耶维奇腐败案的调查。经营局指的是伊利诺斯州两个主要机构：教师津贴管理局和卫生设施规划委员会。

House Speaker: the presiding officer of the US House of Representatives.

众议院议长为美国众议院首席主持议会官员。这里的Illinois House Speaker指的是伊利诺斯州州议会议长。

Writing Tips 写作秘笈

本文是一篇关于美国政治人物、前伊利诺斯州州长布拉戈耶维奇的法庭判决与此案由来的特写。文中并没有详细列举布拉戈耶维奇的各条罪状及法庭的宣判，而是巧妙地从他手上的青筋悸动、观众席上其妻子的哭泣、书记员的声音节奏入手，惟妙惟肖地展现了这个貌似冷静、近乎麻木的政治家内心的波澜。作者在描述青筋时所用的拟人手法，如snake, slide, turn back, run to hide等，非常绝妙。

Unit 4

This is American Dream
梦想与现实

Part I. Get-go
给力起步

What are Americans like? What do Americans like? Is there really a national character in the United States? These are very different questions. To answer them, we need to know the American values, attitudes and beliefs.

> 虽说美国几乎容纳了世界上各个民族和肤色的人，谈不上外在统一性；但是美国人作为一个整体，又表现出极其鲜明的内在统一性。

The American Dream

The American Dream is a national ethos of the United States. It suggests an idea that all people can succeed through hard work, and that all people have the potential to live happy, successful lives.

The idea of an American Dream is older than the United States, dating back to the 1600s, when people began to come up with all sorts of hopes and aspirations for the new and largely unexplored continent. Many of these dreams focused on owning land and establishing prosperous businesses which would theoretically generate happiness, and some people also incorporated ideals of religious freedom into their American Dreams. As America fought for independence in the American Revolution, this idea of the American Dream is further expressed in the United States Declaration of Independence which proclaims that "all men are created equal" and that they are "endowed by their Creator with certain inalienable Rights" including "Life, Liberty and the pursuit of Happiness."

> 美国梦代表了美国的国民特质。"人生来平等"，只要你不懈地努力，你一定会成功。

The American character

America is a country of immigrants and there is great diversity in the ethnic makeup of America. Nevertheless, many writers have generalized about typical American character, as Mortimer B. Zuckerman, editor-in-chief of *U.S. News & World Report* sees his country as "a unique culture of self-reliance, independence, resourcefulness, pragmatism and novelty. " He goes on in detail: "we are comfortable with change and with people who make things happen. In America, the new is better than the old; taking charge is valued over playing it safe; making money is superior to inheriting it; education and merit are favored over family ties. " Despite the nation's great diversity, this generalization can be made about what the typical American believes in, admires, values and wants.

> 美国人崇尚自强、独立、智慧、务实、创新。

Democracy in Action

American democracy is based on the principle of majority rule. In a democratic legislative body, decisions are made by voting. In the U.S., voting is not just a tool for selecting political leaders and passing laws. It is also a way of making decisions in the business world, in social groups, in schools and even within the family. Americans believe that people should take part in making the rules they must live by. American children are introduced to the ideas of majority rule and representative government at very early age.

The statement that "All men are created equal" does not mean that all human beings are equal in ability or ambition. It means that all people should be treated equally before the law and given equal privileges and opportunities. Equal opportunity means (among other things) an equal chance for a good education and a good job.

> 美国认为，无论在社会上还是在普通家庭里，每个人都很看重民主。

Try it — You'll like it

The great American novelist and humorist Mark Twain described the typical English man or woman as a "person who does things because they have been done before" and the typical American as "a person who does things because they haven't been done before." Americans love to try something new out of curiosity and a belief that newer may be better.

As a nation of immigrants, the U.S. has had a continual influx of people with pioneering spirit, with the courage to make major changes in their lives. Americans love science and technology because these fields involve new discoveries.

Love of change is closely tied to faith in improvement. Americans have always been optimistic, believing in the perfectibility of people, the basic goodness of their country and the ability of American ingenuity to improve the quality of life.

> 美国人天生具有创新开拓精神。"喜新厌旧"被视为通向更美好生活的起跑线。

(Revised from Ethel Tiersky & Martin Tiersky《美国制度与文化》)

NOTES

American Revolution (1775–1783): also referred to as American War of Independence. It is a political upheaval during the last half of the 18th century in which thirteen colonies in North America joined together to break free from the British Empire, combining to become the United States of America.

美国革命：也叫美国独立战争，是指在18世纪后叶北美洲十三个州的殖民地脱离大英帝国并且创建了美利坚合众国的一连串事件与思想。

Declaration of Independence: a statement adopted by the Continental Congress(大陆会议) on July 4, 1776, which announced that the thirteen American colonies then at war with Great Britain were now independent states, and thus no longer a part of the British Empire. Written primarily by Thomas Jefferson, the Declaration is a formal explanation of why Congress had voted on July 2 to declare independence from Great Britain, more than a year after the outbreak of the American Revolutionary War. The birthday of the United States of America—Independence Day—is celebrated on July 4, the day the wording of the Declaration was approved by Congress.

《独立宣言》：北美洲十三个英属殖民地宣告脱离大不列颠王国，并宣告独立的纲领性文件。1776年7月4日，此宣言在费城由第二次大陆会议批准。7月4日从此成为美国独立纪念日。《独立宣言》的原件由大陆会议出席代表共同签署，并永久展示于美国华盛顿特区美国国家档案馆。该宣言为美国最重要的立国文书之一。

"*All men are created equal*" and that they are "*endowed by their Creator with certain inalienable Rights*" including "*Life, Liberty and the pursuit of Happiness.*": These are the beginning lines from the *Declaration of Independence* and the original is "We hold these truths to be self-evident, that all men are created equal, that they are endowed by their Creator with certain unalienable rights, that among these are life, liberty and the pursuit of happiness."

人人生而平等：这是美国《独立宣言》中的著名句子。其原文是这样的："我们认为下述真理是不言而喻的：人人生而平等，造物主赋予他们若干不可让与的权利，其中包括生存权、自由权和追求幸福的权利。"

Mortimer B. Zuckerman (1937–): Canadian-born self-made American billionaire magazine editor, publisher and real estate magnate. In 2008, Zuckerman was the 147th wealthiest American and, in 2007, the 188th per Forbes. He has been the publisher and owner of the *New York Daily News* since 1993 and, as of 2007, is the current editor-in-chief of *U.S. News & World Report*. He co-founded Boston Properties, Inc., in 1970 and serves as the chairman of the board and director.

莫特梅·朱克曼：生于加拿大，是一个白手起家的亿万富翁，杂志编辑、出版商、房地产大亨。时下为《美国新闻与世界报道》的主编和波士顿地产公司的董事会主席。

U.S. News & World Report: one of the big-three U.S. weekly newsmagazines published in Washington D.C. by U.S. News & World Report, L.P. founded in 1933 as *United States News*, it merged with *World Report* in 1948. Zuckerman purchased it in 1984.

《美国新闻与世界报道》：美国三大新闻杂志，在世界范围内影响力巨大。

take charge: to assume control or command, here can be understood as "take risk". 冒险

play it safe: to exercise caution and take few risks. 谨慎行事

majority rule: a rule or law that requires more than half of the members of a political organization who cast a vote to agree in order for the entire polity to make a decision on the measure beings voted on

多数决定原则、多数裁决：在投票表决时的一项原则或法律，指的是表决某一决议时只有多数投赞同票时此决议才能通过。

legislative body: an official body , usually chosen by election, with the power to make, change and repeal laws.

立法机构：制定、修改和废除法律的国家机关。资本主义国家的立法机关是议会。

representative government: a form of government or democracy founded on the exercise of popular sovereignty by the people's elected representatives.

代议制政府：政府划分为两类：一类是实行选举的代议制政府，称为"共和国"；另一类是世袭继承制政府，通称为"君主政体"或"贵族政体"。代议制和民主制结合起来，就能获得一种能够容纳和联合一切不同利益和不同大小领土与不同数量人口的、富有效力的政府体制。代议制政府论是近代西方政治民主化理论的主流。

Mark Twain (1835–1910)：an American writer and humorist, has been regarded as Father of American Literature . Twain is best known for his novels about *Tom Sawyer* and *Huckleberry Finn*.

马克·吐温：原名萨缪尔·兰亨·克莱门（Samuel Langhorne Clemens），是美国的幽默大师、小说家、作家，为19世纪后期美国现实主义文学的杰出代表，被誉为美国文学之父。威廉·福克纳称赞马克·吐温为"第一位真正的美国作家，我们都是继承他而来"。海明威曾经说过"一切当代美国文学都起源于马克·吐温一本叫《哈克贝里·费恩历险记》的书"。

Part II. cineWatch
光影星荟萃

Forrest Gump 《阿甘正传》

有种弱智叫大智；有种简单叫深刻；有种普通叫超越，有种奔跑叫人生；有个电影叫阿甘。

Storyline 好片抢先知

Forrest Gump is the story of an incredibly kind and gentle person who is also what some people might call "mildly retarded." But despite his lack of sophistication, and the fact that he was raised far from any major cities, Forrest manages to become personally involved in most of the critical events that take place in American History from the late 1950s until the early 1980s. This includes the Vietnam War, the Watergate Scandal, the Civil Rights and Anti-Vietnam War protest movements, and the Computer Revolution. Forrest even meets three American Presidents as well as Elvis Presley and John Lennon. In a way, this movie is a look at a period of American history through the eyes of a gentle soul who lacks cynicism, but simply accepts things for what they are.

阿甘（汤姆·汉克斯Tom Hanks饰）于第二次世界大战结束后不久出生在美国南方阿拉巴马州一个闭塞的小镇。他先天弱智，智商只有75；然而他的妈妈是一个性格坚强的女性，她常常鼓励阿甘"傻人有傻福"，要他自强不息。

阿甘像普通孩子一样上学，并且认识了一生的朋友和至爱珍妮（罗宾·莱特·潘Robin Wright饰）。在珍妮和妈妈的爱护下，阿甘凭着上帝赐予的"飞毛腿"开始了一生不停的奔跑。

阿甘成为橄榄球巨星、越战英雄、乒乓球外交使者、亿万富翁，但是，他始终忘不了珍妮，几次匆匆的相聚和离别，更是加深了阿甘的思念。

有一天，阿甘收到珍妮的信，他们终于又要见面……阿甘的一生是对美国梦的最好的诠释。

Cast 星光闪烁

Robert Zemeckis ⋯ Director 奥斯卡最佳导演奖

Tom Hanks ⋯ Forrest Gump 两届奥斯卡影帝

Gary Sinise ⋯ Lt. Dan 奥斯卡最佳男配角提名、金球奖

Robin Wright ⋯ Jenny 金球奖提名

Memorable quotes 余音绕梁

Mrs. Gump: You have to do the best with what God gave you.

Forrest Gump: Mama always said, dying was a part of life.

Forrest Gump: Mama says they were magic shoes. They could take me anywhere.

Forrest Gump: Mama always said life was like a box of a chocolates, you never know what you're gonna get.

Forrest Gump: Stupid is as stupid does.

Forrest Gump: My Mama always said you've got to put the past behind you before you can move on.

Forrest Gump: Lieutenant Dan got me invested in some kind of fruit company. So then I got a call from him, saying we don't have to worry about money no more. And I said, that's good! One less thing.

Forrest Gump: What's my destiny, Mama?

Mrs. Gump: You're gonna have to figure that out for yourself.

Forrest Gump: I don't know if we each have a destiny, or if we're all just floatin' around accidental-like on a breeze. But I, I think maybe it's both.

Mrs. Gump: Vacation's when you go somewhere... and you don't ever come back.

Jenny Curran: Do you ever dream, Forrest, about who you're gonna be?

Forrest Gump: Who I'm gonna be?

Jenny Curran: Yeah.

Forrest Gump: Aren't-aren't I going to be me?

Jenny Curran: Run, Forrest! Run!

Culture inside 文化反光镜

General Nathan Bedford Forrest (1821 – 1877): a cavalry and military commander, who is one of the American Civil War's most unusual figures. He was a lieutenant general in the Confederate Army during the War and is remembered both as a self-educated, innovative cavalry leader and as a leading southern advocate in the postwar years. He served as the first Grand Wizard of the Ku Klux Klan, a secret vigilante organization which launched a reign of terrorism against blacks, carpetbaggers, scalawags and Republicans during Reconstruction in the South.

内森·福瑞斯特将军：美国田纳西州的牛仔，奴隶主。美国内战爆发后，这个没进过西点军校，没读过一本军事书的人拉起了一支骑兵队伍为南方而战，成为美国南北战争时期的南方联盟将领，战后出任"三K党"的创始人，美国电影《阿甘正传》的主角就是为纪念他而命名的。

Elvis Presley (1935–1977): one of the most popular American singers of the 20th century. A cultural icon, he is widely known by the single name Elvis. He is often referred to as the "King of Rock and Roll" or simply "the King".

埃尔维斯·普雷斯利：猫王，美国摇滚乐史上影响力最大的歌手，有摇滚乐之王的誉称。20世纪50年代，猫王的音乐开始风靡世界。他的音乐超越了种族以及文化的疆界，将乡村音乐、布鲁斯音乐以及山地摇滚乐融会贯通，形成了具有鲜明个性的独特曲风，强烈地震撼了当时的流行乐坛，并让摇滚乐开始如同旋风一般横扫了世界乐坛。

Dr. Pepper: a soft drink, marketed as having a unique flavor. The drink was created in the 1880s by Charles Alderton of Waco, Texas and first served around 1885. Dr Pepper was first nationally marketed in the United States in 1904 and is now also sold in Europe, Asia, Australia (as an imported drink) and South America.

胡椒博士：美国七喜公司生产的一种焦糖碳酸饮料，是一种特殊的果汁混合物。

Beatnik: a member or follower of the Beat Generation in the 1950's US, whose behavior, views, and often style of dress are pointedly unconventional.

"垮掉的一代"的成员：第二次世界大战之后出现于美国的一群松散结合在一起的年轻诗人和作家的集合体。这一名称最早是由作家杰克·克鲁亚克于1948年前后提出的。

Dick Cavett show: most often refers to the shows on ABC-TV that Dick Cavett hosted between 1968 and 1975 in New York. The first daytime show featured Gore Vidal, Muhammad Ali, and Angela Lansbury. ABC pressured Cavett to "get big names," even though the shows without them got higher ratings and more critical acclaim.

迪克·卡维特秀：1968–1975年间美国ABC电视台的一档脱口秀节目，主持人为迪克·卡维特。

Reagan assassination attempt: it occurred on Monday, March 30, 1981, just 69 days into the presidency of Ronald Reagan. While leaving a speaking engagement at the Washington Hilton Hotel in Washington, President Reagan and three others were shot and wounded by John Hinckley, Jr. Reagan suffered a punctured lung, but prompt medical attention allowed him to recover quickly. The motivation behind Hinckley's attack stemmed from an obsession with actress Jodie Foster due to erotomania.

暗杀里根：就在里根总统入主白宫第69天的1981年3月30日下午，科罗拉多州的一名叫约翰·欣克利的25岁失业青年混在记者队伍里，在华盛顿希尔顿饭店门口向里根开枪。经过手术后，里根脱离了危险。

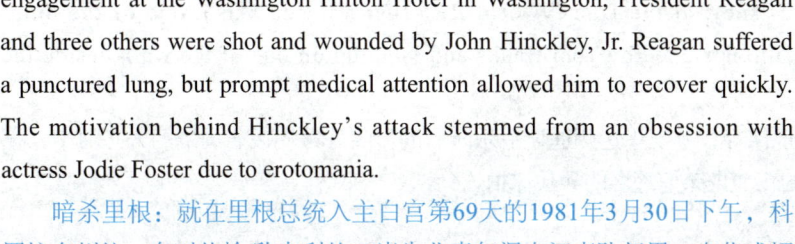

Trivia 八卦一下

The park bench that Tom Hanks sat on for much of the movie was located in historic Savannah, Georgia, at Chippewa Square. The fiberglass bench he sat on, since then, has been removed and placed into a museum to avoid being destroyed by bad weather, or possibly stolen.

剧中阿甘所坐的凳子原本位于佐治亚州萨凡纳市的卡皮瓦广场。电影《阿甘正传》拍完后，此玻璃纤维的凳子已被移至博物馆以防被破坏或被偷。

The necklace worn by Lt. Dan is a rosary with a Saint Christopher medal, inscribed "Protect Us In Combat". It was worn in Vietnam by Gary Sinise's brother-in-law, Jack Treese, in 1967-68.

丹中尉脖子上所带的念珠项链为"圣克里斯托弗"奖章，上面刻有"在战争中保护我们"。这枚奖章是丹中尉的扮演者加里·希尼斯的姐夫杰克·崔伊斯1967—1968年在越南战场上所佩戴的。

When Forrest gets up to talk at the Vietnam rally in Washington, the microphone plug is pulled and you cannot hear him. According to Tom Hanks, he says, "Sometimes when people go to Vietnam, they go home to their mommas without any legs. Sometimes they don't go home at all. That's a bad thing. That's all I have to say about that."

众所周知，阿甘在华盛顿对着游行抗议的群众讲话时有人蓄意拔掉了麦克风；而众所不知的是阿甘实际上说的是"有时候人们去越南参战，而回到母亲身边的时候他们没有了双腿，甚至是他们压根就回不来了。这太糟糕了。这就是我要说的全部。"

The movie's line "Mama always said life was like a box of chocolates. You never know what you're gonna get." was voted as the #40 movie quote by the American Film Institute (out of 100). In 2007, the American Film Institute ranked this as the #76 Greatest Movie of All Time.

影片中的"妈妈总是告诉我生活就像一盒巧克力,你永远都不知道你能吃到什么样的口味"在美国电影协会"百个著名台词"排行榜中荣登第40位。2007年美国电影协会又将此电影评为有史以来第76位最伟大的影片。

Almost all of John Lennon's dialogue is from his song "Imagine" ("No possessions", "No religion too", "It's easy if you try...").

约翰·列侬在影片中的台词几乎都来自他的著名歌曲《想象》(没有财产;也没有宗教信仰;如果你试着想象就会很容易……)

The shrimp boat used in the film now resides in the moat surrounding the Planet Hollywood restaurant in Downtown Disney, at the Disneyworld Resort in Florida. Also, one of the ping-pong paddles used in the film is signed by Tom Hanks and hung up on one of the walls inside the restaurant.

电影中阿甘的捕虾船现保存在佛罗里达州迪斯尼乐园里的星际好莱坞饭店周围的人工河中,在该饭店的墙上还挂着由汤姆汉克斯亲笔签名的乒乓球拍。

Part III. Extra Credit
美文品读

Wake up to American Dream
还做美国梦吗,该醒醒了!

Americans don't seem bothered enough by the country's growing wealth divide to do much about it, according to a recent Harvard Business School's survey.

In part, that's probably because they vastly underestimate the gap, believing the top 20 percent own 59 percent of the nation's wealth when they actually own 84 percent.

But there is another, less obvious reason for our passivity — the hope and glory pushed by an all-pervasive news, gossip and star-driven celebrity culture.

The core of the American dream teaches us that the formula for achieving wealth involves hard work, determination and luck.

Celebrities, and the coverage of them, seem to provide visible proof of this message every day: If it can happen to Justin Bieber, it can happen to me. So why change the system?

The connection between stardom and social mobility is as old as the first fan magazines of a century ago.

Silent-film star Ruth Clifford was an orphan who peered through a knothole at the Edison Studios lot in New Jersey before getting her big break, according to a 1919 issue of Photoplay.

Virginia Valli was a stenographer traveling through a dangerous part of Chicago while struggling to support her mother and sister before leading "the limousine life", a 1918 story in the same magazine details.

Just last week, in an obituary in the Los Angeles Times, the story was told again.

Mary Murphy, who played the sweet small-town girl opposite Marlon Brando in the *Wild Ones*, was a package wrapper at a department store when she was discovered by a talent scout.

The narrative persists like "once upon a time". Stories about contemporary celebrities — in fan magazines like *Us Weekly* and on star-driven websites such as E Online — typically highlight how much stars were like us before making it big.

We see their embarrassing high school pictures and read about their small hometowns, relationships, babies, body fat, marriages and divorces.

Oprah Winfrey is at least as famous for her rise from rural Mississippi to billionaire media mogul as she is for her "Live your best life" message.

Teen sensation Bieber personifies overnight success — from YouTube video to a recording deal and platinum album.

The very title of his album and biopic, *Never Say Never*, echoes the American dream of limitless opportunities for anyone who refuses to give up.

The rise of the Internet and reality TV, which has made fame and fortune seem ever more accessible, has further strengthened the illusion that our class system is wide open.

It also reaffirms the possibility of social mobility for those with few skills.

Celebrity culture sustains faith in our economic system in another way. It tells us whom to blame for failure — the individual.

Stories portray a star's addiction, weight gain or personality problems as the rationale behind their downfall.

Tabloid darling — Lindsay Lohan embodies this ethos. She is regularly portrayed as the architect of her career and life's collapse.

That's not without truth, but seldom does coverage of her antic go beyond individual responsibility to explore the vagaries of stardom and the challenges young people face navigating the pressures of the industry.

The "has beens" who unwittingly star in these morality tales shore up a convenient notion of the American dream: that downward mobility — even during economic hard times — is about individual character traits rather than the social system or catastrophic societal and industrial changes.

During the Depression, silent-film direct D.W. Griffith's career slide was portrayed in a 1934 issue of Photoplay as the result of his own poor business decisions.

Never mind the seismic shift that the rise of talkies brought to the industry.

More recently, when several of actor Nicolas Cage's homes went into foreclosure and it was revealed that he owed millions in back taxes, People magazine pointed its finger at the actor's out-of-control penchant for "lavish properties and prized toys."

Celebrity culture's focus on individual determination and, to some degree, blind luck as ingredients for success distracts us from the roles power and privilege actually play in upward mobility, even in Hollywood.

It makes it easy to forget that a percentage of today's A-list stars had A-list parents whose connections likely opened doors that remain closed for most.

Hollywood is perceived as a bastion of liberalism with a wide variety of progressive causes.

The great irony is that the celebrity on which it turns is among the most conservative social forces at play in shaping public attitudes about class and social mobility.

There's nothing wrong with the dream, except that it so rarely results in such spectacular reality.

（By Karen Sternheimer, *Los Angeles Times*, from *21st Century*, June 8, 2011）

 Making Sense 解文说词

① But there is another, less obvious reason for our passivity — the hope and glory pushed by an all-pervasive news, gossip and star-driven celebrity culture. (para. 3)

但是，对于贫富差距的消极态度有另一个那么不明显的原因：无孔不入的新闻、小道消息以及明星文化使我们对名望产生了渴求。

② Celebrities, and the coverage of them, seem to provide visible proof of this message every day.(para. 5)

名人和关于他们的报道似乎是对于"美国梦"的最好诠释。

③ social mobility (para. 6) refers to the change of people from one social class or social status to another.

社会流动。

④ The narrative persists like "once upon a time". Stories about contemporary celebrities — in fan magazines like *US Weekly* and on star-driven websites such as *E Online* — typically highlight how much stars were like us before making it big. (para. 11)

这些故事就像以"从前"为开头的童话故事那样有固定的套路。在诸如Us Weekly和E Online这样的关于名人的杂志和网站上，明星们的故事总是强调他们在成名之前是和我们大家一样的普通人。

Here "once upon a time" is used to refer to the beginning of a fairy tale when an old story is told. "making it big" means "to become famous".

⑤ The rise of the Internet and reality TV, which has made fame and fortune seem ever more accessible, has further strengthened the illusion that our class system is wide open.（para. 16）

互联网和真人秀的兴起使名气和财富看起来唾手可得，这更加使人们觉得要进入美国上层阶层并非难事。

⑥ Tabloid darling（para. 20）refers to somebody who is very much favored by the tabloid because he/she can cause sensation.

小报红人。

⑦ That's not without truth, but seldom does coverage of her antic go beyond individual responsibility to explore the vagaries of stardom and the challenges young people face navigating the pressures of the industry. The "has beens" who unwittingly star in these morality tales shore up a convenient notion of the American dream.（para. 21, 22）

有一部分（指对于林赛·罗韩的报道）是真实的。但是，这些关于罗韩的古怪行径的报道只限于指责她个人没有责任感，而没有探究娱乐圈的变幻莫测和年轻人在这个行业打拼所要面对的挑战。在这些道德教诲故事中，无意间做了主角的过气明星们验证了"美国梦"简单的另一面。

⑧ Never mind the seismic shift that the rise of talkies brought to the industry.（para. 24）

……从不提有声电影对娱乐业带来的震撼性冲击。

⑨ back taxes (para. 25)

refer to tames that an individual or corporation did not pay in a given year. Back taxes incur interest and penalties that add up quickly. The IRS allows for plans to pay back taxes over time, though they continue to accumulate interest in the interim.

欠缴税款。

⑩ The great irony is that the celebrity on which it turns is among the most conservative social forces at play in shaping public attitudes about class and social mobility.（para. 29）

最大的讽刺是：好莱坞的演艺名人圈在影响公众对阶级和社会流动性的态度问题上又是一股非常保守的社会力量。

（Some of the translations are also from *21st Century*, June 8, 2011）

Background 文化大本营

Harvard Business School: the graduate business school of Harvard University in Boston, Massachusetts. The school offers a full-time MBA program, doctoral programs, and many executive education programs. It owns *Harvard Business School Publishing*, which publishes business books, online management tools for corporate learning, case studies, and the monthly *Harvard Business Review*(《哈佛商业评论》). It is ranked 1st among American business schools by the *U.S. News & World Report*.

哈佛商学院：全球最著名的商学院之一，《美国新闻与世界报道》将其列为全美第一商学院。此商学院所拥有的"哈佛商学院出版社"以及期刊"哈佛商业评论"享誉全球。

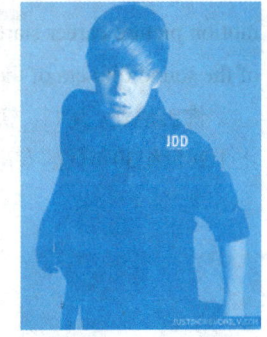

Justin Bieber (1994 –): a Canadian pop/R&B singer-songwriter and actor. Bieber was discovered in 2008 by Scooter Braun, who happened to come across Bieber's videos on YouTube and later became his manager. Bieber has won many awards, including Grammy Awards and is considered a teen idol.

贾斯汀·比伯：加拿大籍的流行乐坛音乐王子。音乐创作、打鼓、跳舞、弹吉他、弹琴等样样精通，而且长相帅气。他先在YouTube唱红了自己，随后被经纪人挖掘并被美国歌手音乐人Usher培养进入美国音乐歌坛。Baby的视频点击量超过七亿，全球第一。他是首位YouTube观看量达20亿的歌手，18岁就拥有四张冠军专辑，在首张专辑发行前就有4首单曲进入Top40。他还是2011《人物》杂志公布的年度好莱坞最富有的年轻人。在"福布斯全球百位巨星排行榜"上贾斯汀连续两年名列第三，微博粉丝全球第二。

Ruth Clifford (1900 –1998): an American actress of leading roles in silent films, whose career lasted from silent days into the television era.

露丝·克里福特：美国无声电影时代著名女演员。

Edison Studios: an American motion picture production company owned by the Edison Company of inventor Thomas Edison. The studio made close to 1,200 films as the Edison Manufacturing Company (1894–1911) and Thomas A. Edison, Inc. (1911–1918) until the studio's closing in 1918.

爱迪生电影公司：伟大的发明家托马斯·爱迪生所拥有的公司，成立于1894年，1918年关闭，期间拍过1200部电影，其中包括著名的《科学怪人》（*Frankenstein* 1910）、《火车大盗》（*Great Train Robbery* 1903）、《爱丽丝漫游仙境》（*Alice's Adventures in Wonderland* 1910）等。

Photoplay: one of the first American film fan magazines. It was founded in 1911 in Chicago. The magazine ceased publication in 1980 and its staff were moved to Us，a celebrity gossip magazine.

《电影剧》：美国最早的电影杂志之一，1911年在芝加哥创刊，1980年停刊。其员工转到名人八卦杂志Us。

Virginia Valli (1898 –1968): an American stage and film actress whose motion picture career started in the silent film era and lasted until the beginning of the sound film era of the 1930s.

佛吉尼亚·瓦利：美国话剧及电影演员，其演艺生涯始于默片时代，止于20世纪30年代的有声电影。

The Wild Ones: a 1953 outlaw biker film directed by László Benedek and produced by Stanley Kramer. It is famed for Marlon Brando's（马龙白·兰度）iconic portrayal of the gang leader Johnny Strabler.

《飞车党》：1953年László Benedek导演的摩托公路片，被誉为摩托车公路片的始祖，第一部反映美国非法机车团伙的电影。片中马龙·白兰度大放光彩。

E Online: a website providing source for entertainment news, celebrity gossip and pictures.

E在线：一个专注于娱乐新闻、名人八卦和照片的网站。

Oprah Winfrey （1954 –) an American television host, actress, producer, and philanthropist, best known for her self-titled, multi-award winning talk show, which has become the highest-rated program of its kind in history. She has been ranked the richest African American of the 20th century, the greatest black philanthropist in American history, and was once the world's only black billionaire .She is also, according to some assessments, the most influential woman in the world.

奥普拉·温弗里：当今世界上最具影响力的妇女之一，最成功的媒体人之一。她的成就是多方面的：通过控股哈普娱乐集团的股份，掌握了超过10亿美元的个人财富，一度为世界上唯一的黑人亿万富翁；其主持的电视谈话节目《奥普拉脱口秀》，平均每周吸引3300万名观众，并连续16年排在同类节目的首位。奥普拉也是世界上最伟大的慈善家之一。

YouTube: a video-sharing website on which users can upload, share, and view videos, created by three former PayPal employees in February 2005. It now operates as a subsidiary of Google.

YouTube：世界上最大的视频分享网站，早期的公司总部位于加利福尼亚州的圣布里诺，让用户下载、观看及分享影片或短片，2005年2月，由三名PayPal的前任员工所创站，网站的名称和标志都来自早期电视所使用的阴极射线管。2006年11月，Google公司以16.5亿美元收购了YouTube，并把其当做一家子公司来经营。

Lindsay Lohan (1986 –): an American actress, pop singer and model. She began her career as a child fashion model before making her motion picture debut in Disney's 1998 remake of *The Parent Trap* at the age of 11. Her career was interrupted in 2007 as two driving under the influence (DUI) incidents and three visits to drug rehabilitation facilities led to several lost movie deals.

林赛·罗韩：出生于美国纽约市的好莱坞话题女王、影视明星及女流行乐歌手。

The Depression: from about 1929 and lasted until the late 1930s or early 1940s. It was a severe worldwide economic depression in the decade preceding World War II, which was the longest, most widespread, and deepest depression of the 20th century. The depression originated in the U.S., starting with the fall in stock prices that began around September 4, 1929 and became worldwide news with the stock market crash of October 29, 1929 (known as Black Tuesday). From there, it quickly spread to almost every country in the world and caused devastating damage to the world economy.

经济大萧条：指1929年到20世纪30年代末之间全球性的经济大衰退，这是20世纪持续时间最长、影响面最广、最具灾难性的经济大萧条。

D. W. Griffith (1875 – 1948): a premier pioneering American film director. He is best known as the director of the controversial and groundbreaking 1915 film *The Birth of a Nation* and the subsequent film *Intolerance* (1916).

格里菲思：美国导演，被认为是对早期电影发展做出极大贡献的开创性人物。他著名的作品包括《一个国家的诞生》（*The Birth of a Nation*）和《党同伐异》（*Intolerance*）。

Nicolas Cage (1964 –): an American actor, producer and director, having appeared in over 60 films including *Face/Off* (1997). Cage, at age 32, became the fifth youngest actor ever to win the Academy Award for Best Actor for his performance in *Leaving Las Vegas*.

尼古拉斯·凯奇：好莱坞著名影星。1992年因在大卫·林奇的公路影片《我心狂野》中扮演男主角而获第43届戛纳电影节金棕榈大奖。1996年，他凭借《离开拉斯维加斯》中扮演的酒鬼一角夺得该年度奥斯卡最佳男主角奖，而后转型于动作类影片。

People magazine: a weekly American magazine of celebrity and human-interest stories, published by Time Inc. It was named "Magazine of the Year" by *Advertising* Age in October 2005, for excellence in editorial, circulation and advertising. *People* ranked *No*.6 on Advertising Age's annual. A-list "and *No*.3 on Adweek's" Brand "Blazers" list in October 2006.

《人物》杂志：1974年创刊，视角专注于美国的名人和流行文化，是时代华纳媒体集团旗下的杂志。此杂志被认为是美国文化的一部分。

Writing Tips 写作秘笈

本文是美国南加州大学著名的社会学家Karen Sternheimer发表在《洛杉矶时报》上的关于"美国梦"与明星文化的一篇文章。需特别注意的是作者运用了大量过去和现在的名人及他们的实例，有力地阐明了自己的观点："美国梦"只强调个人奋斗，而忽视了社会和经济背景对个人的影响。这种运用实例的方法比起空泛的说明观点更有效，也更能打动读者。

Unit 5

Come Together for Holidays

假日佳日：节日欢歌

Part I. Get-go
给力起步

New Year's Day

It's the first day of the year on the modern Gregorian calendar as well as the Julian calendar used in ancient Rome. The Romans dedicated this day to Janus, the god of gates, doors, and beginnings. The month of January was named after Janus, who had two faces, one looking forward and the other looking backward. With most countries using the Gregorian calendar as their main calendar, New Year's Day is the closest thing to being the world's only truly global public holiday, often celebrated with fireworks at the stroke of midnight as the New Year starts.

Some churches celebrate the Feast of the Circumcision of Christ on January 1, based on the belief that if Jesus was born on December 25, then according to Jewish tradition, his circumcision would have taken place on the eighth day of his life (January 1).

> 公元前46年，古罗马恺撒把这一天定为新年的开始，来祝福双面神"Janus"这位罗马神话中的门神。"Janus"后来也演化为英文一月"January"这个词。

Valentine's Day

Valentine's Day is an annual commemoration held on February 14 celebrating love and affection between intimate companions. The day is named after one or more early Christian martyrs named Saint Valentine. It is traditionally a day on which lovers express their love for each other by presenting flowers, offering confectionery, and sending greeting cards (known as "*valentines*"). The day first became associated with romantic love in the circle of Geoffrey Chaucer in the High Middle Ages, when the tradition of courtly love flourished.

Modern Valentine's Day symbols include the heart-shaped outline, doves, and the figure of the winged Cupid. Since the 19th century, handwritten valentines have given way to mass-produced greeting cards.

> 情人节，又名"圣瓦伦丁"节，为每年的2月14日。它是西方的传统节日之一。情侣们在这一天互相馈赠礼物，如巧克力、贺卡和花等，用以表达爱意或友好。

Easter

Easter marks the end of Lent, a forty-day period of fasting, prayer, and penance. The last week of the Lent is called Holy Week, and it contains Good Friday, commemorating the crucifixion and death of Jesus. Easter is followed by a fifty-day period called Eastertide or the Easter Season, ending with Pentecost Sunday.

Easter is a moveable feast, meaning it is not fixed in relation to the civil calendar. The First

Council of Nicaea (325) established the date of Easter as the first Sunday after the full moon following the northern hemisphere's vernal equinox. Ecclesiastically, the equinox is reckoned to be on March 21, and the "Full Moon" is not necessarily the astronomically correct date. The date of Easter therefore varies between March 22 and April 25. Eastern Christianity bases its calculations on the Julian Calendar whose March 21 corresponds, during the 21st century, to the 3rd of April in the Gregorian Calendar, in which calendar their celebration of Easter therefore varies between April 4 and May 8.

Easter customs vary across the Christian world, but decorating Easter eggs is a common motif. In the Western world, customs such as egg hunting and the Easter Bunny extend from the domain of church, and often have a secular character.

> 复活节是西方一个重要节日，为每年春分月圆之后第一个星期日。基督徒认为，复活节象征着重生与希望，是纪念耶稣被钉死在十字架之后第三天复活的日子。与复活节相关的物品有复活节兔和复活节彩蛋。有些人喜欢在蛋上画各种各样的鬼脸或花纹。

Halloween

It is an annual holiday observed on October 31, which commonly includes activities such as trick-or-treating, attending costume parties, carving jack-o'-lanterns, bonfires, apple bobbing, visiting haunted attractions, playing pranks, telling scary stories, and watching horror films.

Historian Nicholas Rogers, exploring the origins of Halloween, notes that while "some folklorists have detected its origins in the Roman feast of Pomona, the goddess of fruits and seeds, or in the festival of the dead called Parentalia", it is more typically linked to the Celtic festival of Samhain. The name of the festival historically kept by the Gaels in the British Isles is derived from Old Irish and means roughly "summer's end".

> 万圣节，源自古代凯尔特民族的新年节庆。此日也是祭祀亡魂的日子，人们在避免恶灵干扰的同时，也以食物祭拜祖灵及善灵以祈平安渡过严冬。它是西方传统节日。万圣节当晚小孩会穿上化妆服，戴上面具，挨家挨户索要糖果。

Thanksgiving Day

It is a holiday celebrated primarily in the United States and Canada. Traditionally, it has been a time to give thanks to God.

Thanksgiving in North America had originated from a mix of European and Native traditions. Typically in Europe, festivals were held before and after the harvest cycles to give thanks to God for a good harvest, to rejoice together after much hard work with the rest of the community. At the time, Native Americans had also celebrated the end of a harvest season. When Europeans first arrived to the Americas, they brought with them their own harvest festival traditions from Europe, celebrating their safe voyage, peace and good harvest. Though the origins of the holiday in both Canada and the United States are similar, Americans do not typically celebrate the contributions made in Newfoundland, while Canadians do not celebrate the contributions made in Plymouth, Massachusetts.

> 感恩节是美国和加拿大共有的节日，原意是为了感谢上天赐予的好收成。在美国，自1941年起，感恩节定为每年11月的第四个星期四。在这一天，成千上万的人们不管工作多忙，都要和自己的家人团聚。

Christmas

It is a holiday generally observed on December 25 to commemorate the birth of Jesus, the central figure of Christianity. Although nominally a Christian holiday, Christmas is celebrated by an increasing number of non-Christians worldwide and many of its popular celebratory customs have pre-Christian or secular themes and origins. Popular modern customs of the holiday include gift-giving, music, an exchange of Christmas cards, church celebrations, a special meal, and the display of various decorations; including Christmas trees, lights, garlands, mistletoe, nativity scenes, and holly. In addition, several figures, known as Saint Nicholas, Father Christmas, and Santa Claus, among other names, are associated with bringing gifts to children during the Christmas season.

Because gift-giving and many other aspects of the Christmas festival involve heightened economic activity among both Christians and non-Christians, the holiday has become a significant event and a key sales period for retailers and businesses. The economic impact of Christmas is a factor that has grown steadily over the past few centuries in many regions of the world.

> 圣诞节，是"基督弥撒"的缩写，是一个宗教节。因为人们把它当做耶稣的诞辰来庆祝，因而又名"耶诞节"。这一天，世界所有的基督教会都举行特别的礼拜仪式，是基督徒庆祝耶稣诞生的庆祝日。大部分的天主教教堂都会先在12月24日的耶诞夜，亦即12月25日凌晨举行子夜弥撒，而一些基督教会则会举行报佳音，然后在12月25日庆祝圣诞节。

(Revised from *A Guide to English-Speaking Countries*)

 NOTES

Gregorian calendar: also known as the Western calendar, or Christian calendar, is the internationally accepted civil calendar. It was introduced by Pope Gregory XIII, after whom the calendar was named, by a decree signed on 24 February 1582.

公历：现在国际通用的历法，又称"里历"，通称"阳历"。"阳历"是以地球绕行太阳一周为一年，为西方各国所通用，故又名"西历"。公历前身是儒略历。1582年罗马天主教教宗里十三世把全面儒略历1582年10月4日的下一天定为格列历10月15日，中间销去10天，同时修改了儒略历置闰法则。

Julian calendar: began in 45 BC as a reform of the Roman calendar by Julius Caesar. It was chosen after consultation with the astronomer Sosigenes of Alexandria and was probably designed to approximate the tropical year (known at least since Hipparchus).

罗马儒略历格里历的前身，由罗马共和国独裁官儒略·恺撒采纳埃及亚历山大的希腊数学家兼天文学家索西琴尼计算的历法，在公元前46年1月1日起执行，取代旧罗马历法的一种历法。儒略历将一年设12个月，大小月交替；四年一闰，平年365日，闰年于二月底增加一闰日；年平均长度为365.25日。由于累积误差随着时间越来越大，1582年后该历被教皇格里高利十三世改善，变为格里历，即沿用至今的公历。

Feast of the Circumcision of Christ: a Christian celebration of the circumcision of Jesus in accordance with Jewish tradition, eight days after his birth, the occasion on which the child was formally given his name.

基督洗礼日：这是基督教徒的一个节日。洗礼一般在小孩生下来后第八天进行，意味着此人正式接受基督教。

Geoffrey Chaucer (1342 – 1400): known as the Father of English literature, is widely considered the greatest English poet of the Middle Ages and was the first poet to have been buried in Poet's Corner of Westminster Abbey. Chaucer is a crucial figure in developing the legitimacy of the vernacular, Middle English, at a time when the dominant literary languages in England were French and Latin.

杰弗里·乔叟：英国中世纪最伟大的诗人，常被誉为"英国文学之父"，其代表作为《坎特伯雷故事集》。

High Middle Ages: refers to the period of European history around the 11th, 12th, and 13th centuries. The High Middle Ages were preceded by the Early Middle Ages and followed by the Late Middle Ages, which by convention end around 1500.

中世纪鼎盛时代：一般认为11世纪为欧洲中世纪的鼎盛时期。

Cupid in Roman mythology: the god of desire, affection and erotic love. He is the son of goddess Venus and god Mars. In popular culture, Cupid is frequently shown shooting his bow to inspire romantic love, often as an icon of Valentine's Day. He is now in the current culture the personification of love and courtship in general.

丘比特：一直被人们喻为爱情的象征。相传他是一个顽皮的、身上长

着翅膀的小神。他的箭一旦插入青年男女的心上，便会使他们深深相爱。在古希腊神话中，他是爱与美的女神阿芙罗狄忒与战神阿瑞斯的小儿子厄洛斯。在罗马神话中，他叫丘比特，他的母亲是维纳斯（即古希腊神话中的阿芙罗狄忒）。

Lent in the Christian tradition: the period of the liturgical year from Ash Wednesday to Easter. The traditional purpose of Lent is the preparation of the believer — through prayer, repentance, almsgiving and self-denial — for the annual commemoration during Holy Week of the Death and Resurrection of Jesus, which recalls the events linked to the Passion of Christ and culminates in Easter, the celebration of the Resurrection of Jesus Christ.

大斋节：亦称"封斋节"是基督教的斋戒节期。教会通常在圣灰礼拜三也就是大斋节的首日，开始换上象征"忏悔"、"警醒"及"禁戒"等意义的紫色来布置。大斋期由大斋首日（圣灰星期三/涂灰日）开始至复活节前日止，一共四十天。

Good Friday: a religious holiday observed primarily by Christians commemorating the crucifixion of Jesus Christ and his death at Calvary. The holiday is observed during Holy Week as part of the Paschal Triduum on the Friday preceding Easter Sunday. It is also known as Holy Friday, Great Friday, or Easter Friday, though the latter normally refers to the Friday in Easter week.

耶稣受难日：一个基督教节日，为复活节的前一个星期五。耶稣受难日是纪念耶稣生命中最高潮的一周（即"圣周"，又称"受难周"）中最重大的日子。这一周是从复活节前的一个星期日（棕榈主日——耶稣光荣地进入耶路撒冷城，民众手持棕榈枝欢迎他）开始，经复活节前的星期四（立圣餐日——纪念耶稣与门徒进"最后的晚餐"时设立圣餐礼）和星期五（受难日——纪念耶稣为世人的罪被钉十字架而死）到复活节（星期日）结束。

Easter eggs: The oldest tradition is to use dyed or painted chicken eggs, but a modern custom is to substitute chocolate eggs, or plastic eggs filled with confectionery such as jelly beans. These eggs are often hidden, allegedly by the Easter Bunny, for children to find on Easter morning. Otherwise, they are generally put in a basket filled with real or artificial s traw to resemble a bird's nest.

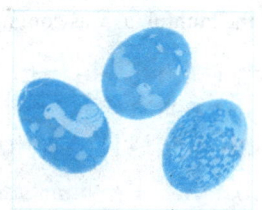

复活节彩蛋：包括各种真实的蛋，以及所有制作出来、形状像蛋的物品，可以作为复活节的礼物及纪念品。因为蛋蕴藏有生机，可以孵化出生命，是"复活"、"再生"、"重生"的最佳代表物品。因而，每到复活节时，整个西方世界最风行的东西就是蛋。

Trick-or-treating: a customary practice for children on Halloween seen in many countries. Children in costumes, either in large groups or accompanied by an adult, travel from house to house in order to ask for treats such as candy with the question " Trick or treat? ". The "trick" is a threat to perform mischief on the homeowners or their property if no treat is given.

不给糖就捣乱：万圣夜时孩子们玩的一种游戏。万圣节前夜孩子们成群结队到邻居家去讨要糖果，如果得不到糖果，孩子们就会在主人家恶作剧。

Costume parties: mainly in contemporary Western culture, is a type of party where guests dress up in a costume. As for the costume parties in Halloween teenagers and adults who may be considered too old for trick-or-treating attend a costume party instead.

化妆舞会：这也是万圣节的一种习俗。

Jack-o'-lantern: typically is a carved pumpkin. It is associated chiefly with the holiday of Halloween and was named after the phenomenon of strange light flickering over peat bogs, called ignis fatuus or jack-o'-lantern. In a jack-o'-lantern, typically the top is cut off, and the inside flesh then scooped out; an image, usually a monstrous face, is carved onto the outside surface, and the lid replaced. At night, a light is placed inside to illuminate the effect.

南瓜灯：庆祝万圣节的标志物。传说有一个名叫杰克的人非常吝啬，因而死后不能进入天堂，而且因为他取笑魔鬼也不能进入地狱。所以，他只能提着灯笼四处游荡，直到审判日那天。人们为了在万圣节前夜吓走这些游魂，便用芜菁、甜菜或马铃薯雕刻成可怕的面孔来代表提着灯笼的杰克，这就是南瓜灯的由来。

Saint Nicholas: a historic 4th-century saint and Greek Bishop of Myra. He had a reputation for secret gift-giving, such as putting coins in the shoes of those who left them out for him, and thus became the model for Santa Claus, whose modern name comes from the Dutch Sinterklaas. His reputation evolved among the faithful, as was common for early Christian saints.

圣诞老人：圣·尼古拉斯是圣诞老人原型，生前为当地的主教，并且还是一位慈善家，因慷慨而被人们爱戴。圣·尼古拉斯喜欢以匿名的方式赠送给当地穷人各种礼物。在公元346年去世后，他被当地人尊称为"圣人"，其生前事迹被逐渐演绎成今天的圣诞老人传说。他的遗体在800年前被埋葬在爱尔兰东南部城市基尔肯尼的哲伯恩特修道院内。

Part II. cineWatch
光影星荟萃

The Holiday 《恋爱假期》

爱是盲目的，有时给爱情放个假，也许会获得惊喜。

Storyline 好片抢先知

The Story stars as two lovelorn women from opposite sides of the Atlantic Ocean, who temporarily exchange homes to escape heartbreak during the holiday season, only to find that a change of address can change their lives. With new found romance, both their lives change forever.

爱丽斯（凯特·温斯莱特 Kate Winslet饰）住在英国伦敦的乡村，而阿曼达（卡梅隆·迪亚兹 Cameron Diaz饰）则是洛杉矶的美国丽人。她们在天南地北的两端，却遇上了同样的问题：感情上遭受的挫败令生活灰暗无光。二人在网上聊天，商议在圣诞节到来之前，到对方的环境去生活，交互双方的住所作为度假场地。于是，一场令人兴奋的旅行开始了。爱丽斯来到美国大都市，阿曼达则乘班机前往极具英伦情调的英国乡村。除了新鲜的生活环境，当地男生的魅力更让她们猝不及防。

 Cast 星光闪烁

Nancy Meyers ⋯Director 金球奖最佳编剧提名

Kate Winslet ⋯Iris 奥斯卡、金球奖影后、四次奥斯卡提名、四次金球奖提名、艾美奖提名

Cameron Diaz ⋯Amanda 四次金球奖最佳女主角、女配角提名

Jude Law ⋯Graham 恺撒奖荣誉奖、两次奥斯卡提名、三次金球奖提名

Jack Black ⋯Miles 金球奖最佳男主角提名

 Memorable quotes 余音绕梁

Iris: I have found almost everything ever written about love to be true. Shakespeare said journeys end in lovers meeting. Oh, what an extraordinary thought! Personally, I have not experienced anything remotely close to that, but I'm more than willing to believe Shakespeare had.

Iris: I suppose I think about love more than anyone really should. I'm constantly amazed by its sheer power to alter and define our lives. It was Shakespeare who also said, Love is blind.

Iris: For some, quite inexplicably, love fades. For others, love is simply lost. But then, of course, love can also be found, even if just for the night. And then there's another kind of love, the cruelest kind, the one that almost kills its victims. It's called unrequited love.

Iris: Most love stories are about people who fall in love with each other, but what about the rest of us? What about our stories, those of us who fall in love alone? We are the victims of the one-sided affair. We are the cursed of the loved ones. We are the unloved ones, the walking wounded, the handicapped without the advantage of a great parking space.

Iris: Oh, God, just the sight of him. Heart pounding, throat thickening, absolutely can't swallow. All the usual symptoms.

Amanda: A fairy tale English cottage set in a tranquil country garden. Snuggle up by an old stone fireplace and enjoy a cup of cocoa.

Miles: The wind. It's what makes it so warm this time of year. Legend has it when the Santa Anas blow, all bets are off. Anything can happen.

Arthur: Iris, in the movies we have leading ladies and we have the best friend. You, I can tell, are a leading lady, but for some reason you're behaving like the best friend.

Iris: And after all that, however long all that may be, you'll go somewhere new and you'll meet people who make you feel worthwhile again, and little pieces of your soul will finally come back. And all that fuzzy stuff, those years of your life that you wasted, that will eventually begin to fade.

Miles: It is Christmas Eve, and we are going to sit out on that patio, gonna make ourselves a little fire, gonna pop some bubbly, and we are gonna celebrate being young and being alive.

Miles: I'm making him a CS of this tune. Every time he hears it, it should give him the confidence to walk right out there.

Graham: I apologize for the blunt delivery, but as problematical as this fact may be, I am in love with you.

Miles: That's what you said to me once, that we weren't really right for each other. We were a square peg and a round hole.

 ## Culture inside 文化反光镜

Bordeaux: the world's major wine industry capital. It is home to the world's main wine fair, Vinexpo, while the wine economy in the metro area moves 14.5 billion Euros each year. Bordeaux wine has been produced in the region since the 8th century.

波尔多：法国一地区，以生产久负盛名的波尔多红酒而名扬世界。

Louis B. Mayer (1884–1957): an American film producer. He is generally cited as the creator of the "star system" within Metro-Goldwyn-Mayer (MGM) in its golden years. Known always as Louis B. Mayer and often simply as "L.B.", he believed in wholesome entertainment and went to great lengths so that MGM had "more stars than there are in the heavens".

路易斯·梅尔：好莱坞著名制片人，米高梅公司创建人，美国电影学院终身成就奖获得者。人们不仅因为《宾虚》记住了他，而且还因为他在好莱坞的黄金时代在米高梅创立了明星体制，从而使米高梅出现了"明星比天上的星星还要多"的盛世。

MGM: an American media company, involved primarily in the production and distribution of films and television programs. MGM was founded in 1924 when the entertainment entrepreneur Marcus Loew gained control of Metro Pictures, Goldwyn Pictures Corporation and Louis B. Mayer Pictures. Its headquarters are in the MGM Tower in Century City, Los Angeles.

米高梅电影制片公司：好莱坞五大电影公司之一。它拍摄了电影史上最出色的影片之一——《乱世佳人》，创造出经久不衰的银幕经典——007，塑造了不朽的卡通形象——猫和老鼠，发起成立了美国电影艺术与科学学院，并推出了学院奖（奥斯卡奖）。米高梅电影公司的雄狮利奥标志一度被当成了美国的象征，它旗下巨星云集，曾创造每周推出一部电影的神话。2005年索尼公司买下米高梅，2010年米高梅正式宣布破产。

Random House: the largest general-interest trade book publisher in the world. It has been owned since 1998 by the German private media corporation Bertelsmann and has become the umbrella brand for Bertelsmann book publishing. Random House also has a movie production arm, Random House Films, of which the most recent release was One Day. The company is also currently developing a division responsible for creating story content for media including video games, social networks on the web, mobile platforms, in print and on film.

兰登书屋：号称世界最大的英语商业国际性出版社，是世界超级媒体集团贝塔斯曼的子公司。它在整个20世纪的世界图书界中扮演着举足轻重的角色。这并不仅仅因为它是全世界最大的出版集团，更是因为它在现代西方文化发展中起到了潜移默化的引领作用。该出版社所出图书多次获诺贝尔和普利策奖。

FedEx: originally known as FDX Corporation, is a logistics services company, based in the United States with headquarters in Memphis, Tennessee. The name "FedEx" is a syllabic abbreviation of the name of the company's original air division, Federal Express, which was used from 1973 until 2000.

联邦快递：一家国际性速递集团，提供隔夜快递、地面快递、重型货物运送、文件复印及物流服务，总部设于美国田纳西州。其品牌商标FedEx由公司原来的英文名称Federal Express合并而成。

Hanukkah: also known as the Festival of Lights, is an eight-day Jewish holiday commemorating the rededication of the Holy Temple (the Second Temple) in Jerusalem at the time of the Maccabean Revolt of the 2nd century BCE. Hanukkah is observed for eight nights and days, starting on the 25th day of Kislev according to the Hebrew calendar, which may occur at any time from late November to late December in the Gregorian calendar.

光明节又称"哈努卡节"、"灯节"，意在纪念公元前2世纪犹太人针对希腊——叙利亚王国发动的反对在耶路撒冷的犹太教神殿中供奉希腊神像的起义。整个节日共持续8天，人们每天都要在烛台上点燃一支蜡烛以示纪念。

Casablanca: an 1942 American romantic drama film directed in 1942 by Michael Curtiz, Set during World War II, it focuses on a man torn between, in the words of one character, love and virtue. He must choose between his love for a woman and helping her and her Czech Resistance leader husband escape from the Vichy-controlled Moroccan city of Casablanca to continue his fight against the Nazis.

《卡萨布兰卡》：好莱坞经典电影，拍摄于1942年。该片被认为不只是一部令人心碎的爱情电影，实际上更是一部宣扬民族主义和爱国主义的电影。本片荣获1944年奥斯卡最佳影片、最佳导演和最佳改编剧本奖。2007年美国编剧协会公布影史"最伟大的101部电影剧本"名单，《卡萨布兰卡》位居首位。

Chariots of Fire: a 1981 British film. It tells the fact-based story of two athletes in the 1924 Olympics: Eric Liddell, a devout Scottish Christian who runs for the glory of God, and Harold Abrahams, an English Jew who runs to overcome prejudice.

《烈火战车》：一部英国电影，拍摄于1981年。影片讲述了1924年英国两名奥运健将的故事。他们一个是虔诚的基督徒，为上帝而跑；一个是犹太人，为克服偏见而战。

Driving Miss Daisy: an American comedy-drama film adapted from the Alfred Uhry play of the same name. The film was directed by Bruce Beresford in 1989, with Morgan Freeman reprising his role as Hoke Colburn and Jessica Tandy playing Miss Daisy. The story defines Daisy and her point of view through a network of relationships and emotions by focusing on her home life, synagogue, friends, family, fears, and concerns. Hoke is rarely seen out of Miss Daisy's presence, although the title implies that the story

is told from his perspective. Driving Miss Daisy won the Academy Award for Best Picture, and three more, including Academy Award for Best Actress and Academy Award for Best Adapted Screenplay.

《为戴茜小姐开车》：布鲁斯·贝尔斯福德1989年执导的一部电影。影片通过一个老年寡妇与忠实黑人之间的主仆关系，再现了美国南部25年来种族关系转变的时代特点。在1990年第62届奥斯卡奖角逐中，《为戴茜小姐开车》一举夺得了最佳影片、最佳女主角、最佳改编剧本、最佳化妆4个奖项。

The Lady Eve: an American screwball comedy film written and directed by Preston Sturges in 1941, and starring Barbara Stanwyck and Henry Fonda. The film is based on a story by Monckton Hoffe about a mismatched couple who meet on board a luxury liner. In 1994, The Lady Eve was selected for preservation in the United States National Film Registry by the Library of Congress as being "culturally, historically, or aesthetically significant."

《淑女伊芙》：一部拍于1941年的美国喜剧片。影片讲述了一个百万富翁在一次乘坐豪华油轮旅行中差点成为一对骗子的牺牲品的故事。亨利·方达完美地把握了这个浪漫的百万富翁的心理特征，精彩的演绎让影片形象活灵活现。此外，芭芭拉·斯坦威克的精彩对手戏，也让影片锦上添花。

 Trivia 八卦一下

If you're willing to embrace a bit of corniness for the sake of some incisive humor, a few poignant moments and enjoyable scenarios, make time for *The Holiday*.

如果有兴趣体验英伦乡下之味，那么《恋爱假期》正是为你量身定做的。

Dustin Hoffman appears in the video rental store in an uncredited cameo as Jack Black talks about the score from *The Graduate*. According to Hoffman, this was unscripted and unexpected. He was going to Blockbuster for a movie, saw all the light and came over to see what was going on. He knew director Nancy Meyers, who scripted a short scene with him in it.

在英国的音像店里，杰克在品评《毕业生》的音乐，这时达斯汀·霍夫曼走进镜头。此桥段完全没有剧本，而是霍夫曼去伦敦出席一个电影的首映时无意中在街上看见熟人、导演南希·迈耶斯，于是导演即兴加了这个小片段。

Lindsay Lohan, who had made her motion picture debut in Meyers' remake of *The Parent Trap* (1998), and James Franco, a friend of Meyers, make uncredited appearances in the fictional *Deception* trailer, on which Amanda and her team are working on.

电影中的阿曼达和她的团队所制作的电影中的人物一个是林赛·罗韩（因导演迈耶斯的电影《天生一对》而出名）；另一个是詹姆斯·弗兰卡，导演的朋友。

The official soundtrack contains music by various artists, Heitor Pereira and Hans Zimmer, and is released on the Varèse Sarabande label.

著名作曲家汉斯·季默携手黑特·佩雷拉为电影配乐，并由声名显赫的瓦雷泽·萨拉班德（Varèse Sarabande）发行大碟。

Released to mixed or average reviews by critics, the film became a global box office success, grossing $205 million worldwide, mostly from its international run.

本片获得了全球票房的成功，创票房20多亿美元的好成绩。

Diaz garnered an ALMA Award nomination for her performance, while Winslet was nominated for an Irish Film and Television Award the following year. The film itself won the 2007 Teen Choice Award in the Chick Flick category.

卡梅伦·迪亚兹因此片获得ALMA（美国拉丁裔媒体艺术奖）大奖提名；而凯特·温丝莱特获得爱尔兰电影电视奖提名。2007年此片获"青少年选择奖"。

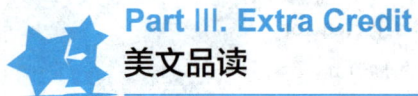

Part III. Extra Credit
美文品读

Christmas Morning, 1949
1949年的圣诞节早晨

A light drizzle was falling as my sister Jill and I ran out of the Methodist Church, eager to get home and play with the presents Santa had left for us and our baby sister, Sharon. Across the street from the church was a Pan American gas station where the Greyhound bus stopped. It was closed for Christmas, but I noticed a family standing outside the locked door, huddled under the narrow overhang in an attempt to keep dry. I wondered briefly why they were there but then forgot about them as I raced to keep up with Jill.

Once we got home, there was barely time to enjoy our presents. We had to go off to our grandparents' house for our annual Christmas dinner. As we drove down the highway through town, I noticed that the family was still there, standing outside the closed gas station.

My father was driving very slowly down the highway. The closer we got to the turn off for my grandparents' house, the slower the car went. Suddenly, my father U-turned in the middle of the road and said, "I can't stand it!"

"What?" asked my mother.

"It's those people back there at the Pan Am, standing in the rain. They've got children. It's Christmas. I can't stand it."

When my father pulled into the service station, I saw that there were five of them, the parents and three children—two girls and a small boy.

My father rolled down his window. "Merry Christmas," he said.

"Howdy," the man replied. He was very tall and had to stoop slightly to peer into the car.

Jill, Sharon, and I stared at the children, and they stared back at us.

"You waiting on the bus?" my father asked.

The man said that they were. They were going to Birmingham, where he had a brother and prospects of a job.

"Well, that bus isn't going to come along for several hours, and you're getting wet standing here. Winborn's just a couple miles up the road. They've got a shed with a cover there, and some benches," my father said. "Why don't y'all get in the car, and I'll run you up there."

The man thought about it for a moment, and then he beckoned to his family. They climbed into the car. They had no luggage, only the clothes they were wearing.

Once they were settled in, my father looked back over his shoulder and asked the children if Santa had found them yet. Three glum faces mutely gave him his answer.

"Well, I didn't think so," my father said, winking at my mother, "because when I saw Santa this morning, he told me that he was having trouble finding y'all, and he asked me if he could leave your toys at my house. We'll just go get them before I take you to the bus stop."

All at once, the three children' faces lit up, and they began to bounce around in the back seat, laughing and chattering.

When we got out of the car at our house, the three children ran through the front door and straight to the toys that were spread put under our Christmas tree. One of the little boy grabbed Sharon's ball. And the other girl picked up something of mine. All this happened a long time ago, but the memory of it remains clear. That was the Christmas when my sisters and I learned the joy of making others happy.

My mother noticed that the middle child was wearing a short-sleeved dress, so she gave the girl Jill's only sweater to wear.

My father invited them to join us at our grandparents' for Christmas dinner, but the parents refused. Even when we all tried to talk them into coming, they were firm in their decision.

Back in the car, on the way to Winborn, my father asked the man if he had money for bus fare.

His brother had sent tickets, the man said.

My father reached into his pocket and pulled out two dollars, which was all he had left until his next payday. He pressed the money into the man's hand. The man tried to give it back, but my father insisted. "It'll be late when you get to Birmingham, and these children will be hungry before then. Take it. I've been broke before, and I know what it's like when you can't feed your family."

We left them there at the bus stop in Winborn. As we drove away, I watched out the window as long as I could, looking back at the little girl hugging her new doll.

SYLVIA SEYMOUR AKIN

Memphis, Tennessee

(From *True Tales from NPR's National Story Project*)

 Making Sense 解文说词

① A light drizzle was falling as my sister Jill and I ran out of the Methodist Church, eager to get home and play with the presents Santa had left for us and our baby sister, Sharon. (para. 1)

天上下着毛毛细雨，我和姐姐吉尔跑出卫理公会教堂，满心只想着快点回到家玩圣诞老人给我们和小妹妹莎伦准备的礼物玩具。

② The closer we got to the turnoff for my grandparents' house, the slower the car went. (Para. 3)

越接近去爷爷奶奶家的分岔路口，车子就越慢。

③ Why don't y'all get in the car, and I'll run you up there. (Para. 12)

不如上车我送你们到那里吧。

y'all: a contraction of the words "you" and "all". It is used as a plural second-person pronoun.

④ Three glum faces mutely gave him his answer. (Para. 14)

三张忧郁的脸无声地回答了他。

⑤ All at once, the three children' faces lit up, and they began to bounce around in the back seat, laughing and chattering. (Para. 16)

三个孩子的脸顿时阴霾尽散，还在后排座位蹦蹦跳跳，笑笑嚷嚷起来。

⑥ That was the Christmas when my sisters and I learned the joy of making others happy. (Para. 17)

因为在那个圣诞节我和我的姐妹领会到了让别人快乐而获得的愉悦。

Background 文化大本营

Methodist Church: the largest of the Protestant Free Churches in Britain and the U.S. It was established in 1739 by John Wesley as part of the Church of England but it became separate from it in 1795. It was introduced into the U.S in the 18th century and today has over 50 million members around the world. It emphasized the importance of moral issues, both personal and social.

卫理公会：英国约翰·卫斯理创立了基督新教卫斯理宗。教会主张圣洁生活和改善社会，注重在群众中进行传教活动。在美国独立后，美国卫斯理宗脱离圣公会而组成独立的教会。其后教会分裂为美以美会、坚理会、美普会、循理会和圣教会等。1939年，美以美会、坚理会和美普会合并成现今的卫理公会。

Greyhound: an intercity common carrier of passengers by bus serving over 3,700 destinations in the United States, Canada and Mexico, operating under the well-known logo of a leaping greyhound. It was founded in Hibbing, Minnesota, USA, in 1914 and incorporated as "Greyhound Corporation" in 1929. Today, it is headquartered at 350 North St. Paul Street in Downtown Dallas, Texas, and under the ownership of British transport firm FirstGroup, which operates Greyhound as an independent subsidiary, and a division of FirstGroup America.

灰狗巴士：美国最著名的全国性长途汽车公司，客运于美国与加拿大之间，开业于1914年美国明尼苏达州希宾市，在1929年成为有限公司，现在的公司总部在达拉斯。

Santa: a figure in North American culture who reflects an amalgamation of the Dutch Sinterklaas, the English Father Christmas, and Christmas gift-bringers in other traditions. Santa Claus is said to bring gifts to the homes of good children during the late evening and overnight hours of Christmas Eve, December 24.

圣诞老人：一位专门为好孩子在圣诞节前夜送上礼物的神秘人物。传说每到12月24日晚上，有个神秘人会驾乘由12只驯鹿拉的雪橇，挨家挨户地从烟囱进入屋里，然后偷偷把礼物放在好孩子床头的袜子里，或者堆在壁炉旁的圣诞树下。虽然没有人真的见过神秘人的样子，但是人们通常将其装扮成头戴红色圣诞帽子，留着大大的白色胡子，身穿一身红色棉衣，脚穿红色靴子的样子，因为总在圣诞节前夜出现派发礼物，所以习惯地称他为"圣诞老人"。

Pan Am: the principal United States international air carrier from the late 1920s until its collapse on December 4, 1991. Founded in 1927 as a scheduled air mail and passenger service operating between Key West, Florida and Havana, Cuba, the airline became a major company credited with many innovations that shaped the international airline industry, including the widespread use of jet aircraft, jumbo jets, and computerized reservation systems. Identified by its blue globe logo and the use of the word "Clipper" in aircraft names and call signs, the airline was a cultural icon of the 20th century and the unofficial flag carrier of the United States

Pan Am：泛美航空公司的简称。泛美航空公司自20世纪30年代成立至1991年倒闭前，一直是美国的主要航空公司之一，其母公司为Pan Am Corp。在达美航空停止注资后，泛美航空公司于1991年12月4日停业。

Howdy: an informal greeting, commonly thought to have originated as a shortened form of the greeting "How do ye?" It was first recorded as part of the Southern U.S. dialect in 1840. Literature from that period includes the use of "How-do, how-do" as a greeting used by Indians when addressing Anglo settlers in greeting.

Howdy：美国南方方言，"How do ye？"，"你好"的意思。

Birmingham: the largest city in Alabama
伯明翰市：美国南方阿拉巴马州的最大城市。

 Writing Tips 写作秘笈

本文开门见山，在首句交代了时间、地点、人物和事件，典型的记叙文写作手法。文中大量的对话，向读者展现了生活中口语表达的不完整性和简洁性。文中并不富裕的一家人，慷慨地把自己的圣诞礼物和生活费送给了更需要它的人。然而，他们并没有因此而感到失落，而是为了能够帮到别人而感到更加幸福。通往快乐的道路有很多条，我们偶尔也要改变一下方向，选择另一条通往快乐的路。

Unit 6

To love is not only to accept but to give
爱字从心：这是心的接受和给予

Part Ⅰ. Get-go
给力起步

The legend of white snake

  The legend of white snake is a love story between two snakes and a man .The white snake had been lived on earth for thousands of years, and she had practiced herself during the years to master a lot of magic. One day she was going to be an immortal, but she still remembered a man who saved her five hundred years ago, and she wanted to repay an obligation. Finally she found the man whose previous life saved her and that man is Xu Xian at the broken bridge of West Lake. They together overcame a lot of difficulties and had a boy, but after the boy was born, the white snake Bai Suzhen, was controlled in the Fall of pagoda by a monk named Fahai on behalf of subdued demons. When the boy grew up , he saved her mother Bai Suzhen . At last Bai Suzhen and her husband Xu Xian became the immortal together.

>   这个传说发生在宋朝时的杭州。白素贞是千年修炼的蛇妖，为了报答书生许仙前世的救命之恩，化为人形欲报恩。白素贞施展法力，巧施妙计与许仙相识，并嫁给了他。婚后，金山寺和尚法海告诉许仙，说白素贞是蛇妖。许仙最初将信将疑。后来，他按法海的办法在端午节让白素贞喝下带有雄黄的酒，白素贞不得不显出原形，却将许仙吓死。白素贞上天庭盗取仙草灵芝将许仙救活后，法海将许仙骗至金山寺并将其软禁。白素贞同小青一起与法海斗法，水漫金山寺，因此伤害了其他生灵。白素贞因为触犯天条，在生下孩子后被法海收入钵内，镇压于雷峰塔下。后来，白素贞的儿子长大得中状元，他到塔前祭母并将母亲救出，全家最终团聚。

The cowherd and the girl weaver

  The cowherd was a poor guy. The weaver, the granddaughter of the God of heaven, often came down with other fairies from heaven and took a bath in a lake. One day the cowherd got across. Encouraged by the old cow, he stolen a red clothes. The fairy sisters pull out as soon as quickly when they saw the cowherd. But the girl weaver unable to return to the heaven without clothes. She married the cowherd and had a son and a daughter. They led a happy life. When the God of heaven learned it, he brought the weaver back. The cowherd and their children came back home to find her gone. With the help of the old cow, he would go to heaven to find his wife. However the Queen Mother separated them by the Milky Way. At the same time, many magpies were touched by their true love, and they turned into a bridge to help the two lovers. Finally they were allowed to meet only on the magpies' bridge on every 7th July in lunar calendar.

传说在很久以前，有一个名叫牛郎的孤儿。在老牛的指点下，牛郎找到了下凡仙女们洗澡游玩的地方，拿起了其中一个仙女的衣服，那个仙女名字叫织女。两人由此相识，坠入爱河，后生育一对龙凤胎。但被王母娘娘发现了，织女因此被带回天界。老牛告诉牛郎，它死之后把它的皮做成鞋就可以穿着它腾云驾雾。后来，牛郎终于上了天界，眼看就要和织女团聚，但被王母娘娘头上银簪所变的银河拦住去路。天上的喜鹊被他们的爱情感动了，化作"鹊桥"，牛郎织女终于团聚。王母娘娘有些动容，每年农历七月初七才允许两人在鹊桥相会。后来，每年七夕牛郎就把两个小孩放在扁担中，上天与织女团聚，他们的爱情成为佳话。

The butterfly lovers

Zhu Yingtai, a beautiful and intelligent young woman, attended classes in disguise as a young man. She met Liang Shanbo in school. They chatted and felt a strong affinity for each other at their first meeting. They studied together for the next three years in school and Zhu gradually fell in love with Liang, but Liang was a bookworm and failed to notice the feminine characteristics exhibited by his classmate. One day, Zhu's father asked her to return home as soon as possible. Liang accompanied Zhu for 18 miles to see her off. Months later, when Liang visited Zhu, he discovered that Zhu was actually a woman. They loved each other, but Zhu's parents have already arranged for her to marry a rich man. Liang was heartbroken when he heard the news, then he died. On the day of Zhu's marriage, mysterious whirlwinds prevented the wedding procession from escorting the bride beyond Liang's grave, which lied along the journey. Zhu left the procession to pay her respects for Liang. Liang's tomb split apart, and Zhu dived into it to join him. A pair of butterflies emerged from the tomb and flew away.

富家女祝英台女扮男装，赴杭州求学，途遇梁山伯，结拜为兄弟。两人同窗共读，三载相伴。分别之时祝英台自许终身。但英台之父已将英台许配别人，梁山伯悲愤成疾而亡。迎亲之日，花轿途经梁山伯坟墓，英台哭祭。墓裂，英跃入墓中。二人双双化为彩蝶。

Romeo and Juliet

The story takes place in Verona, Italy. Two noble families, the Montagues and Capulets, hate each other and are feuding. A nobleman, Paris, wants to marry Juliet Capulet, the beautiful daughter of the family. Her father tells him to come to a party he is planning that night so he can meet her. Romeo, the son of the Montague family, also goes to the party. He is in disguise so none of his enemies will recognize him. At the party, he meets Juliet. It is love at first sight, and they spend the night dancing and talking. The two young lovers decide to marry in secret, which they do the very next day. However, there is a fight between two families. Romeo kills a person to get revenge, so he has to leave the city, and Juliet's father tells her she must marry Paris. Juliet asks a friend to help her. He gives her a potion that will make everyone think she is dead. In fact, she will just be sleeping. Then, when she wakes up, she can escape and be with Romeo. Unfortunately, Romeo returns to the city in secret. He sees Juliet lying there and thinks she is dead. He is so heartbroken, he takes poison and kills himself. When Juliet wakes up she sees Romeo is dead, and takes his dagger and kills herself too. Although both lovers are dead, something good comes out of the tragedy. The two families agree to stop fighting and live in peace. But it is too late for Romeo and his young love, Juliet.

在意大利维洛那城，两大家族蒙太古和凯普莱特结下了宿怨。在一次宴会上，蒙太古家的罗密欧和凯普莱特家的朱丽叶一见钟情。他们偷偷地来到了修道院，在神父的主持下结成了夫妻。冤家路窄，在一次械斗中，朱丽叶的表兄杀死了罗密欧的朋友，而罗密欧一怒之下复仇成功，从而被流放，并与朱丽叶进行了最后一次约会。而后，朱丽叶被迫答应帕里斯伯爵的求婚。朱丽叶在神父的帮助下，在婚礼的前夜服药假死，等待罗密欧来带她远走高飞。不明真相的罗密欧，闻讯来到朱丽叶的墓穴旁，杀死了阻拦他的帕里斯，在吻了朱丽叶后，饮药自尽。醒来的朱丽叶见到此景，悲痛欲绝，毫不犹豫地吻着罗密欧嘴唇残留的毒液，并用匕首直刺自己的胸膛倒在罗密欧身上死去。迟到的劳伦斯神父向大家讲述了罗密欧和朱丽叶的故事，老凯普莱特惭愧地握住老蒙太古的手，就这样罗密欧和朱丽叶以死的代价换取了两家的彻底言和。

Titanic

Titanic, the ship of dreams is also known as Unsinkable, and it was unsinkable on its departure on April 10th, 1912. And on its epic journey a poor artist named Jack Dawson and a rich girl Rose DeWitt fall in love, until one night, their fairytale love for one another turns into a struggle for survival on a ship. Rose leaves her fiancée Caledon Hockley for this poor artist. When the Titanic collides with the Iceberg and sinks, to make Rose alive, Jack chooses to die and Rose survives. 84 years later Rose tells the story about her life on Titanic to her granddaughter and friends and explains the first sight of Jack that falls into love, then into a fight for survival. When Rose gets saved, The Officer asks Rose what her name is. She loved Jack so much she says her name is Rose Dawson. And now 84 years later, Rose Calvert is 100 years old. She tells her granddaughter the whole story from departure until the death of Titanic on its first and last voyage. To Rose all Titanic and the real love of her life Jack Dawson is all an existence inside of her memory.

萝丝在泰坦尼克号上，因不想嫁给未婚夫卡尔，于是准备跳海自杀，被刚好得到船票，登上这座豪华巨轮的杰克所救。杰克带她参加下等舱的舞会，给她画像……他们很快坠入情网，但是这份甜美的爱情还没过多久，历史上最重大的灾难之一，泰坦尼克号的沉没便发生了。他们刚刚萌生的爱情幼苗也历经生死的考验。最后，杰克为了救萝丝，为她取暖并鼓励她活下来，而自己却冻死在寒冷的海水里。萝丝得救了，她从没有忘记杰克，不仅仅是因为他们有一段凄美的爱情，还因为杰克给了她很多快乐，也给了她新的希望和未来……

NOTES

West Lake: a freshwater lake located in the historic area of Hangzhou, the capital of Zhejiang province in eastern China. The lake is divided by the causeways of Su Di, Bai Di, and Yanggong Di. There are numerous temples, pagodas, gardens, and artificial islands within the lake. West Lake has influenced poets and painters throughout the ages for its natural beauty and historical relics, and it has been among the most important sources of inspiration for Chinese  garden designers, as evidenced by the impact it had on various Chinese classical gardens.It was made a UNESCO World Heritage Site in 2011, and was described as having "influenced garden design in the rest of China as well as Japan and Korea over the centuries" and as reflecting "an idealized fusion between humans and nature."

西湖：位于浙江省杭州市的西南方，它以秀丽的湖光山色和众多的名胜古迹而成为闻名中外的旅游胜地并被世人赋予"人间天堂"的美誉。西湖凭借千年的历史积淀所孕育出的特有江南风韵和大量杰出的文化景观而入选世界文化遗产，同时也是现今《世界遗产名录》中为数不多的湖泊类文化遗产之一，是中国唯一一处入选的湖泊类文化遗产。

The Lei feng Pagoda: a five-story tall tower with eight sides, located on Sunset Hill, south of West Lake in Hangzhou. Originally it was constructed in the year AD 975, during Five Dynasties and Ten Kingdoms period, at the order of King Qian Chu of Wuyue. It was built to celebrate the birth of Qian Chu's son, born to Huang Fei. The Leifeng Pagoda was an octagonal, five-story structure built of brick and wood and with a base built out of bricks. It collapsed in 1924 but was rebuilt in 2002, since then it has been a popular tourist attraction.

雷峰塔：一名"黄妃塔"，又称"西关砖塔"。在西湖南岸夕照山上，南屏山日慧峰下净慈寺前。雷峰塔为吴越国王钱俶因黄妃得子而建，初名"黄妃塔"。因建于雷峰，后人改称"雷峰塔"。旧塔已于1924年倒塌，现已重建。"雷峰夕照"为西湖十景之一。

Milky Way: refers to the galaxy that contains our Solar System. This name derives from its appearance as a dim "milky" glowing band arching across the night sky, in which the naked eye cannot distinguish individual stars. The term "Milky Way" is a translation of the Classical Latin from the Hellenistic Greek.The Milky Way appears like a band because it is a disk-shaped structure being viewed from inside. The fact that this faint  band of light is made up of stars was proven in 1610 when Galileo Galilei used his telescope to resolve it into individual stars. In the 1920s, observations by astronomer Edwin Hubble showed that the Milky Way is just one of many galaxies.

银河：横跨星空的一条乳白色亮带，由一千亿颗以上的恒星组成。银河在天鹰座与天赤道相交，处在北半天球。银河在天球上勾画出一条宽窄不一的带，称为"银道带"。它的最宽处达30°，最窄处只有4°～5°，平均约20°，它只是银河系中的一部分。

Romeo: the son of old Montague, secretly loves and marries Juliet, a member of the rival House of Capulet. Romeo is one of the most important characters of the play, and has a consistent presence throughout it. His role as an idealistic lover has led the word "Romeo" to become a synonym for a passionate male lover in various languages. Although often treated as such, it is not clear that "Montague" is a surname in the modern sense.

罗密欧：威廉·莎士比亚著名戏剧作品《罗密欧与朱丽叶》中的男主角。该故事讲述二人于舞会一见钟情后方知对方身份，最后二人为了在一起，朱丽叶先服假毒，醒来发现罗密欧自尽，也相继自尽。该剧因其知名度高而常被误称为莎翁"四大悲剧"之一。

Juliet: one of the title characters in William Shakespeare's tragedy Romeo and Juliet. She is the daughter of old Capulet, head of the House of Capulet. The story has a long history that precedes Shakespeare himself. Shakespeare's Juliet is a headstrong and intelligent character in spite of her young age, though she often seems timid to the audience because of her young age. She is considered by many to be the true hero of the play, acting as a sounding board and a balance against the impulsive Romeo.

朱丽叶：《罗密欧与朱丽叶》中的女主角，凯普莱特的女儿，拥有他人无法媲美的美貌与坚强的意志力。虽然因为年轻，朱丽叶总给人留下羞涩的印象，但许多人认为她才是剧中真正的英雄。

Verona: a city in the Veneto, northern Italy. It is the second largest city municipality in the region and the third of northeast Italy. It is one of the main tourist destinations in northern Italy, owing to its artistic heritage, several annual fairs, shows and operas, such as the lyrical season in the Arena, the ancient amphitheatre built by the Romans. The city has been awarded World Heritage Site status by UNESCO because of its urban structure and architecture.

维罗纳：位于意大利北部的一座历史悠久的城市。该城市有古代罗马的圆形露天剧场和许多造型精美的教堂。维罗纳风靡全世界的另一个原因是罗密欧和朱丽叶的故乡，朱丽叶家的阳台，成为"爱的圣地"。2000年，维罗纳入选为联合国教科文组织评选的世界遗产。

Montagues: the patriarch of the House of Montague, and the father of Romeo. As with Capulet, it would be incorrect to refer to him as "Lord Montague". He worries over Romeo's relationship with Rosaline (with whom Romeo was in love at the beginning of the story), but cannot get through to his son. He later pleads with the Prince to prevent his son from being executed, and gets his wish when the Prince lowers Romeo's punishment to banishment.

蒙太古：莎士比亚的著名戏剧《罗密欧与朱丽叶》中罗密欧的父亲，蒙太古家族的族长。蒙太古和凯普莱特是一座城市的两大家族，这两大家族有宿仇，经常械斗。

Capulets: the patriarch of the Capulet family, the father of Juliet. He is very wealthy. He is sometimes commanding but also convivial, as at the ball: when Tybalt tries to incite a duel with Romeo, Capulet tries to calm him and then threatens to throw him out of the family if he does not control his temper; he does the same to his daughter later in the play.

凯普莱特：《罗密欧与朱丽叶》中朱丽叶的父亲，是凯普莱特家族的族长。

Paris: a kinsman of Prince Escalus and seeks to marry Juliet. He is described as handsome, somewhat self-absorbed, and very wealthy. Although Paris is not as developed as other characters in the play, he stands as a complication in the development of Romeo and Juliet's relationship. His love of Juliet stands as a counterpoint to Romeo's impetuous love.

帕里斯：剧中朱丽叶的追求者，一个古代"高富帅"的典范。

Titanic: a British passenger liner that sank in the North Atlantic Ocean on 15 April 1912 after colliding with an iceberg during her maiden voyage from Southampton, UK to New York City, US. The sinking of Titanic caused the deaths of 1,502 people in one of the deadliest peacetime maritime disasters in modern history. The Titanic

was the largest ship afloat at the time of her maiden voyage. She was the second of three Olympic class ocean liners operated by the White Star Line, and she was built by the Harland and Wolff shipyard in Belfast. On her maiden voyage, she carried 2,224 passengers and crew.

泰坦尼克号：一艘奥林匹克级邮轮，于1912年4月处女航时撞上冰山后沉没。泰坦尼克号由位于爱尔兰岛贝尔法斯特的哈兰德与沃尔夫造船厂兴建，是当时最大的客运轮船。在她的处女航中，泰坦尼克号从英国南安普敦出发，途经法国瑟堡-奥克特维尔以及爱尔兰昆士敦，计划中的目的地为美国纽约。1912年4月14日，船上时间夜里11时40分，泰坦尼克号撞上冰山；4月15日凌晨2时20分，船裂成两半后沉入大西洋。泰坦尼克号海难为和平时期死伤人数最惨重的海难，船上1500多人丧生。

Part II. cineWatch
光影星荟萃

Stepmom 《继母》

母爱是伟大的。一份无私的爱，最难的是放手。

Storyline 好片抢先知

Anna and Ben, the two children of Jackie and Luke, have to cope with the fact that their parents divorced and that there is a new woman in their father's life: Isabel, a successful photographer. She does her best to treat the kids in a way that makes them still feel at home when being with their dad, but also loves her work and does not plan to give it up. But Jackie, a full-time mother, regards Isabel's efforts as offensively insufficient. She can't understand that work can be important to her as well as the kids. The conflict between them is deepened by the sudden diagnose of cancer, which may be deadly for Jackie. They all have to learn a little in order to grow together.

贾姬（苏珊·萨兰登 Susan Sarandon 饰）是路克（艾德·哈里斯 Ed Harris 饰）的前任妻子。她为他生下一对儿女，精心操持家务，却终因性格不合而宣告婚姻失败。离婚三年来，儿女一直由贾姬和路克轮番照料，生活倒也波澜不惊，直到女摄影师伊莎贝尔（朱莉娅·罗伯茨 Julia Roberts 饰）和路克堕入情网，矛盾开始繁衍激化。伊莎贝尔搬到路克家来，一心一意要做一个合格的继母。即使她没有多少持家经验，但还是设法和孩子们快乐相处，让他们接受自己。事与愿违，在孩子的心中，谁也无法替代生母贾姬的地位。贾姬的心情更是复杂。她已经身患癌症，当然盼望有个好继母照顾孩子。可是，妒嫉心却让她不愿看到伊莎贝尔和孩子们情如骨肉。病症一天天恶化，心理挣扎的贾姬，终于有了令人释怀的决定。

Cast 星光闪烁

Chris Columbus … Director 土星奖最佳导演提名

Julia Roberts … Isabel Kelly 奥斯卡最佳女主角，金球奖最佳女主角

Susan Sarandon … Jackie Harrison 奥斯卡最佳女主角，金球奖最佳女主角提名

Ed Harris … Luke Harrison 奥斯卡最佳男主角提名、奥斯卡最佳男配角、金球奖最佳男配角

Memorable quotes 余音绕梁

Ben Harrison: Do you think Isabel's pretty?

Jackie Harrison: Sure... if you like big teeth.

Ben Harrison: Can you fall out of love with your kids?

Luke: No. That is impossible!

Ben Harrison: Like Mission: Impossible!

Isabel: Why don't we name the puppy?

Anna Harrison: I know: Isabel.

Isabel: I beg your pardon?

Anna Harrison: Well, it kind of smells like you, and I'm allergic to you too, so it fits perfectly.

Jackie Harrison: I'm never, never going to forget this.

Anna Harrison: Never say "never."

Jackie Harrison: Well there's a loophole, you know. You can say "never, never" if you mean it enough to say it twice.

Isabel: You look tired.

Jackie Harrison: I hate when people say that. It's like a polite way of telling you that you look like shit.

Jackie Harrison: Just because you can't see something, doesn't mean it isn't there.

Jackie Harrison: Yep. Life's a tradeoff. It's finally legal to smoke dope, but you got to have cancer.

Isabel: Are you dying?

Jackie Harrison: Not today.

Ben Harrison: Mommy...

Jackie Harrison: What, sweetie?

Ben Harrison: If you want me to hate her I will.

Jackie Harrison: The thing is, they [the children]

Jackie Harrison: Don't have to choose. They can have us both. I have their past, you can have their future.

Culture inside 文化反光镜

Betty Ford: First Lady of the United States from 1974 to 1977 during the presidency of her husband Gerald Ford. As First Lady, she was active in social policy and created precedents as a politically active presidential wife.

贝蒂·福特：美国前总统杰拉德·福特的妻子、前美国第一夫人。她在其有生之年致力于全美的健康事业。美国历史学家安东尼称赞贝蒂在过去20年中是影响全美进行康复运动的"圣母"。

Girl Scouts: a youth organization for girls. It aims to empower girls and to help teach values such as honesty, fairness, courage, compassion, character, sisterhood, confidence, and citizenship through activities including camping, community service, learning first aid, and earning badges by acquiring other practical skills. Girl Scouts' achievements are recognized through rank advancement and by various special awards such as the bronze award. Girl Scouts welcomed girls with disabilities early in their history, at a time when they were not included in most other activities.

美国女童子军：创立于1912年3月12日，是世界最大的女童组织，其创始人是洛夫人。该组织强调女性领导、培养女孩品德、树立女孩信心。女童子军还提供其他学习生活或工作技能的机会。据它的网站介绍，美国女童子军还学习传统的烹饪、手工艺品制作和户外野营，还可以学习财务知识、产品设计、商业开发、数码电影制作和网站设计，并获得这些方面的徽章。

Central Park: a public park at the center of Manhattan in New York City. The park initially opened in 1857, on 843 acres (3.41km^2) of city-owned land. In 1858, Frederick Law Olmsted and Calvert Vaux won a design competition to improve and expand the park with a plan they entitled the Greensward Plan. Construction began the same year, continued during the American Civil War, and was completed in 1873. Central Park is one of the world's largest urban public parks comparable to other great parks in the world. Designated a National Historic Landmark in 1962, the park is currently managed by the Central Park Conservancy under contract with the city government.

中央公园：号称纽约"后花园"，由第59大街、第110大街、第五大街、中央公园西路围绕着。它坐落在纽约曼哈顿岛的中央，是一块完全人造的自然景观，里面有绿色的草地、树木郁郁的小森林、庭院、溜冰场、回转木马、露天剧场、两座小动物园，还有可以泛舟水面的湖、网球场、运动场、美术馆等。

Big Apple Circus: a circus that is based in New York City. Opened in 1977, it has become a tourist attraction as well. The Big Apple Circus began the 1980s decade with a lot of media attention, having established a special holiday celebration in honor of the circus and its staff, and then appearing in a Hollywood film.

大苹果马戏团：1977年成立于纽约的一个马戏团。

Pearl Jam: an American rock band that formed in Seattle, Washington, in 1990. To date, the band has sold over 31.5 million records in the U.S, and an estimated 60 million worldwide. Pearl Jam has outlasted many of its contemporaries from the alternative rock breakthrough of the early 1990s, and is considered one of the most influential bands of the decade. Stephen Thomas Erlewine of All music referred to Pearl Jam as "the most popular American rock & roll band of the '90s."

珍珠果酱乐队：一支美国摇滚乐队，1990年成立于华盛顿州西雅图。

Lady Godiva: an 11th-century Anglo-Saxon noblewoman who, according to a legend dating back at least to the 13th century, rode naked through the streets of Coventry in order to gain a remission of the oppressive taxation imposed by her husband on his tenants. The name "Peeping Tom" for a voyeur originates from later versions of this legend in which a man named Tom had watched her ride and was struck blind or dead.

葛黛瓦夫人：11世纪一名英格兰盎格鲁—萨克逊的贵族妇女。依据传说，她为了争取减免丈夫强加于市民们的重税，裸体骑马绕行了考文垂的大街。

New York University (*NYU*): a private, nonsectarian American research university based in New York City. NYU's main campus is situated in the Greenwich Village neighborhood of Lower Manhattan. Founded in 1831, NYU is one of the largest private nonprofit institutions of American higher education.

纽约大学：成立于1831年，是全美最大的私立大学之一；也是美国唯一一座坐落于纽约心脏地带的名校。学生称其"所设课程压力不大，但要求甚高"。作为一所一流的学术机构，纽约大学拥有33名诺贝尔奖得主，3名阿贝尔奖得主，21名奥斯卡奖、艾美奖、格莱美奖、东尼奖得主，9名美国国家科学勋章获奖者，16名普利策奖得主，以及19名美国科学院勋章获奖者。纽约大学较为偏重人文艺术及社会科学，在这些方面的校友们大都有杰出的表现。另外，如小约翰·菲茨杰拉德·肯尼迪、鲁迪·朱利安尼等名人也皆为纽约大学的毕业校友。

Disneyland: the first of two theme parks built at the Disneyland Resort in Anaheim, California, opened on July 17, 1955. Spanning 160 acres and the only theme park to be designed and built under the direct supervision of Walt Disney, it is dedicated to fairy tales and Disney characters. Disneyland has a larger cumulative attendance than any other theme park in the world, hosting approximately 600 million guests since its opening. In 2011, the park hosted approximately 16.14 million guests, making it the second most visited park in the world that calendar year.

迪士尼：全称为The Walt Disney Company，名字缘自其创始人沃尔特·迪士尼。它是一家总部设在美国伯班克的大型跨国公司，主要业务包括娱乐节目制作、主题公园、玩具、图书、电子游戏和传媒网络。皮克斯动画工作室（PIXAR Animation Studio）、惊奇漫画公司（Marvel Entertainment Inc）、试金石电影公司（Touchstone Pictures）、米拉麦克斯（Miramax）电影公司、博伟影视公司（Buena Vista Home Entertainment）、好莱坞电影公司（Hollywood Pictures）、ESPN体育、美国广播公司（ABC）都是其旗下的公司（品牌）。

Parent-teacher Association (PTA) or Parent-Teacher-Student Association (PTSA): a formal organization composed of parents, teachers and staff that is intended to facilitate parental participation in a school. They occur in the United States, the United Kingdom, and Japan and may occur in other countries.

家庭及教师协会：一个由家长、学校、教师组成的组织，旨在致力于家长对学生教育和学校工作的参与。

Trivia 八卦一下

Each of the leads (Julia Roberts, Susan Sarandon, Ed Harris) was nominated for an Oscar for playing real people - Sarandon as Sister Helen Prejean in *Dead Man Walking*, Roberts as Erin Brockovich-Ellis in *Erin Brockovich*, and Harris as Jackson Pollock in *Pollock*. Roberts and Sarandon both won, but Harris lost.

电影中每个主要演员都因曾经扮演真人而被奥斯卡奖提名：苏珊·萨兰登扮演《死囚漫步》中的修女海伦·普雷金；茱莉亚·罗伯茨扮演《艾琳·布罗克维奇》中的布罗克维奇；艾德·哈里斯扮演《杰

克逊·波拉克》中的波拉克。萨兰登和罗伯茨都最终获奖。

The restaurant called "The '76 House", featured in two dinner scenes, one with Jackie and Luke and one with Jackie and Isabel, is a National Historical Site in Tappan, Rockland County, New York. Major John Andre, a British officer who assisted turncoat Benedict Arnold, was held there while awaiting trial by then General George Washington. At the time, it was a tavern and inn, but located across from the town meeting hall and church where the trial was held; another National Historic Site.

电影中两次出现的晚饭场景（卢克与前妻，贾姬和伊萨贝尔）都是在一个叫做"76人家"的饭店拍摄的，此处也是一处美国历史遗址，位于纽约。当年美国独立战争时曾帮助叛变者阿诺德的英国上尉正是在此等候华盛顿将军的审判，当年这是一个位于市政厅对面的小酒馆。

Stepmom received mixed reviews from critics. It earned a 43% rating on Rotten Tomatoes.
评论界对此电影的评价好坏参半。它在"烂番茄"评选上获得43%的评率。

The deidi catio of the film, "In loving memory of Irene Columbus" is dedicated to, director Chris Columbus's mother, who in the year before the movie was released had died of cancer, a similar circumstance to one of the main characters in the movie.

本片头中的"谨以此片献给艾琳，哥伦布"是导演克里斯·哥伦布献给自己已逝母亲的。她与剧中主人公一样罹患癌症，在影片公映前去逝。

The song that Isabel (Julia Roberts) sings to Ben (Liam Aiken) in the hospital is "If I Needed You". It was recorded by Roberts' ex-husband Lyle Lovett on his 1998 album *Step Inside This House*.
片中伊莎贝尔在医院里唱给本的歌《我需要你》是来自茱莉亚·罗伯茨前夫的一首歌。

The film is known internationally by numerous alternate titles. For example: *Stay to My Side* (Spanish), *My Best Enemy* (French), and *Side by Side* (Portuguese, German).
片名在国外被译成多个版本：西班牙语译成《与我在一起》；法语为《我最好的敌人》；德语和葡萄牙语为《肩并肩》。

Part III. Extra Credit
美文品读

College girl stops home for a spray tan
我的小潮女，爸爸就爱你！

Spray tans are everywhere these days. It's like the entire nation has been lightly toasted.

Soon, there will be an app for that. Hold your smartphone directly to your face. Click.

The other day, my wife, Posh, got her car spray-tanned, a discretionary expense that a lot of people might frown upon. Not me.

"For all I care, you can spray tan the house," I told her.

"Really?"

"Spray tan whatever you like," I said.

"The dog?"

"The kids."

"The luggage?"

"The income taxes."

The college girl, back for spring break, went out and got herself spray-tanned the other day.

She came back looking guilty about something, and I noticed that her mid-March Midwestern complexion had been minked ever so slightly.

"What'd you do?" I asked her.

"Nothing."

"What'd you do?"

"Nothing."

"What'd you do?"

"Nothing."

This is a line of questioning every parent will recognize. Eventually, you annoy your child to the point of surrender. Because, within the past few hours, a teenager will have always done something morally or financially foolish.

And if you've raised them right, they eventually start to feel guilty about lying to their parents, the only people in the world who would ever pick up their wedding tab.

Though sometimes an interrogation can take hours.

"What'd you do?"

"Spray tan."

"Huh?"

She claimed to have paid for it with "that 20 (dollars) I found at the Pacific Design Center".

For two years now, our daughter has been paying for questionable purchases- shoes, scarves, trips to Catalina- with "that 20 (dollars) I found at the Pacific Design Center".

So, if you happened to lose 20 bucks at the Pacific Design Center in 2009, you now owe me a little over 4,000 (dollars).

I told my daughter about the best bargain in town, the Irish spray tan, which is two beers and a Slim Jim. It works best when you're Irish, of course, but anyone with a pale-pink northern European skin tint can use it. After two beers, I always look like I've wintered on a burro in Mazatlan. After three beers, the capillaries begin to rise in my face till I look like a sewer map of Manhattan. No worries. I'm proud to be a person of color.

"So, you're drunk all the time," my daughter said.

"Yes."

"What kind of example is that?" she asked.

Depends on what you're after. But it does occur to me, as the father of four, that I've got to start being a better role model.

This is difficult, for I'm easily as flawed as my children, maybe more so. I rely on a certain amount of wisdom to maintain the upper hand. When that doesn't work, I just explode.

That's the other Irish spray tan, anger. We Celts are a wonderful people, but we're always a little miffed about something someone said, and we reserve our greatest miffs for the people we care about the most.

As I've confessed before, farewells still do me in as well, and when the little girl returned to college the other morning, with a suitcase thick with fashion choices you just can't find in Indiana, my heart went with her too. Not the whole heart, just a chamber or two, a ventricle, a couple of valve covers.

Really, I'd prefer to be shot.

You know, parenthood is really an amazing thing, a 60-year symphony of wars and happy hours. Or maybe a 60-year polka.

But tell me, do you ever get used to them going away?

(By CHRIS E RSKINE, Los Angeles Times from "*21st Century*, June 8, 2011")

Making Sense 解文说词

① "For all I care, you can spray tan the house," I told her.（para. 4）

你把整栋房子都喷上防晒喷雾吧，我无所谓。For all I care的意思是"我不在乎，与我无关，我管不着"。

② This is a line of questioning every parent will recognize. Eventually, you annoy your child to the point of surrender.（para. 19）

这番问话做父母的都懂的。你会不停地这么烦扰你的孩子，直到他们老实交代。

③ I told my daughter about the best bargain in town, the Irish spray tan, which is two beers and a Slim Jim. It works best when you're Irish, of course, but anyone with a pale-pink northern European skin tint can use it. After two beers, I always look like I've wintered on a burro in Mazatlan. After three beers, the capillaries begin to rise in my face till I look like a sewer map of Manhattan. No worries. I'm proud to be a person of color.（para. 28）

我告诉女儿要想把皮肤弄成小麦色有个最划算的办法：爱尔兰式的"防晒喷雾"，也就是两杯啤酒外加一根Slim Jim牌香肠。如果你是爱尔兰人，效果最好。只要你有北欧人的苍白中带粉色的皮肤，就都能用这个办法。两杯啤酒下肚，我看起来就像是骑在毛驴背上在墨西哥马萨特兰过的冬。三杯啤酒，能让我脸上的毛细血管膨胀，整张脸看起来好像是曼哈顿的下水管道图。别担心，看起来像有色人种让我很自豪。

④ That's the other Irish spray tan, anger. We Celts are a wonderful people, but we're always a little miffed about something someone said, and we reserve our greatest miffs for the people we care about the most.（para. 34）

愤怒，是另一种爱尔兰式的防晒喷雾。我们凯尔特人是一个伟大的民族，但我们很容易因为某人说的某句话而闷闷不乐。而且，越是面对我们在乎的人，我们发的脾气就越大。

⑤ As I've confessed before, farewells still do me in as well, and when the little girl returned to college the other morning, with a suitcase thick with fashion choices you just can't find in Indiana, my heart went with her too. Not the whole heart, just a chamber or two, a ventricle, a couple of valve covers.（para. 35）

我以前就承认过，我无法忍受分别。当这个小女孩（他的女儿）拎着一大箱子你在印第安纳州买不到的时尚玩意儿返校的时候，我的心都随她而去了。也不是整颗心，也就是一两个心房，一个心室，几个心脏瓣膜吧。Do me in的意思是"对我情绪的影响很大"，甚至是"让我很生气"。

Background 文化大本营

Pacific Design Center: or PDC is a 1,200,000 square feet multi-use facility for the design community located in West Hollywood, California. One of the buildings is often described as the Blue Whale because of its outsize nature relative to surrounding buildings and its brilliant blue glass cladding.

太平洋设计中心：位于美国加州洛杉矶市。自1975年建成以来，它一直是人们议论的焦点，成为南加州现代建筑一个令人尊敬的标志。这一由美国著名建筑师希撒·佩利设计的、抽象刻画海洋特征的建筑物，被人们戏称为"蓝鲸"，它使洛杉矶的非传统性和五颜六色的城市结构显得极具现代化。

Slim Jim: a brand of jerky snacks or dried sausage manufactured by ConAgra Foods, Inc., the food conglomerate based in Omaha. They are popular in the United States. More than 500 million are produced annually in at least 20 varieties.

"瘦吉姆"：世界500强的美国康尼格拉食品公司的产品，是种牛肉干。

Irish: an ethnic group who originate in Ireland, an island in northwestern Europe. Ireland has been populated for around 9,000 years. The Irish people's earliest ancestors are recorded in legends – they are claimed to be descended from groups such as the Nemedians, Fomorians, Fir Bolg, Tuatha Dé Danann and the Milesians. Lebor Gabála Érenn, a book of Irish mythology tells that Milesians were Scythian descendants.

爱尔兰人：狭义上指爱尔兰共和国的公民，广义上来讲是自古居住在爱尔兰岛上的人们。广义的爱尔兰人属于凯尔特人种。

Mazatlan: a city in the Mexican state of Sinaloa. The city was founded in 1531 by an army of Spaniards and Indian settlers. By the mid-19th century a large group of immigrants had arrived from Germany. These new citizens developed Mazatlan into a thriving commercial seaport, importing equipment for the nearby gold and silver mines. Mazatlan is the second-largest city in the state. It is also a popular tourist destination, with its beaches lined with resort hotels.

马萨特兰：墨西哥西部太平洋沿岸最大的港口和游览胜地。

Manhattan: the most densely populated and smallest in area of the five boroughs of New York City. Manhattan is a major commercial, economic, and cultural center of the United States. Anchored by Wall Street in Lower Manhattan, New York City functions as one of the financial centers of the world, and is home of both the New York Stock Exchange and NASDAQ. Many major radio, television, and telecommunications companies in the United States are based here, as well as many news, magazine, book, and other media publishers.Manhattan has many famous landmarks, tourist attractions, museums, and universities. It is also the location of the United Nations Headquarters. It is the center of New York City and the New York metropolitan area.

曼哈顿：纽约的市中心，纽约最重要的商业、金融、保险机构均分布在这里。世界金融中心——华尔街分布在曼哈顿下城，而纽约的大企业、商业中心分布于曼哈顿中城。整个曼哈顿耸立着5500多栋高楼，其中35栋超过了200米，是世界上最大的摩天大楼集中区。该地区拥有纽约标志性的帝国大厦、洛克菲勒中心、克莱斯勒大厦、大都会人寿保险大厦等建筑。

Celts or Kelts: an ethno-linguistic group of tribal societies in Iron Age and Medieval Europe who spoke Celtic languages and had a similar culture.

凯尔特人：公元前2000年活动在中欧的一些有着共同文化和语言特质的、有亲缘关系的民族的统称。他们主要分布在当时的高卢、北意大利（山南高卢）、西班牙、不列颠与爱尔兰。现代意义上的凯尔特人，或凯尔特人后裔仍坚持使用他们自己的语言（爱尔兰语、威尔士语、苏格兰盖尔语和布列塔尼语），并以自己的凯尔特人血统而自豪。

Indiana: a U.S. state located in the midwestern and Great Lakes regions of North America. Indiana is the 38th largest by area and the 15th most populous of the 50 United States. Its capital and largest city is Indianapolis. Indiana was admitted to the United States as the 19th U.S. state on December 11, 1816. Before it became a territory, varying cultures of indigenous peoples and historic Native Americans inhabited Indiana for thousands of years. Since its founding as a territory, settlement patterns in Indiana have reflected regional cultural segmentation present in the Eastern United States.

印第安纳州：美国中北部偏东的一个州。由于该州是美国中西部各州往来必经之地，所以也叫"美国十字路口"（The Crossroads of America）。

 Writing Tips 写作秘笈

作者用诙谐的语气从spray tan（防晒喷雾）着手，讲述了他对女儿深厚的感情。为了达到幽默的效果，作者运用了多种手法，如：夸张（Soon, there will be an app for that. Hold your smart-phone directly to your face. Click.）；反讽（they eventually start to feel guilty about lying to their parents, the only people in the world who would ever pick up their wedding tab.）；双关（if you happened to lose 20 bucks at the Pacific Design Center in 2009, you now owe me a little over four grand）。

Unit 7

The salad bowl: Cultural diversity
什锦色拉：多元文化交相辉映

Part Ⅰ. Get-go
给力起步

The great melting-pot of America, the place where we are all made Americans of, is the public school, where men of every race, and of every origin, and of every station of life send their children, or ought to send their children, and where, being mixed together, they are all infused with the American spirit and developed into the American man and the American woman.

——Woodrow Wilson

在美国，公立学校是把我们全都培养成美国人的大熔炉。不同种族，不同国籍，处于不同生命阶段的人把子女送去（也理应送去），他们在那里融为一体，都被赋予了美国精神，并成为美国人。

——伍德罗·威尔逊

Cultural diversity

Cultural diversity is tricky to quantify, but a good indication is thought to be a count of the number of languages spoken in a region or in the world as a whole. By this measure, there are 4 signs that we may be going through a period of precipitous decline in the world's cultural diversity. America has drawn to its shores individuals from all over the world. This has produced a blending of different ways of life that many Americans find disturbing. Ishmael Reed, however, sees this mixing of customs as neither new nor a thread. On the contrary, it is typically American.

美国，一个多元化的国家，来自不同种族背景、宗教背景的世界各地的人生活在这里。他们一方面会为美国的多元文化注入强大的动力，另一方面也会带来人和人之间文化上的矛盾问题。不同生活方式的交融或许让美国人感到些许不安。可是无法否认，这种不同习俗的融合既非新鲜事物，又非什么威胁；相反，这正是典型的美国风格。

American history

The US has established a highly developed national economy within a matter of about two hundred years, counting from the time of its independence. Perhaps no other country has left as great an impression on the contemporary world as the US—a big achievement for such a relatively young nation. Lauded as a beacon of freedom, where over the centuries millions of immigrants have come to better their lives, and reviled as an international bully, perhaps never more so than in recent years, it's a place you have to explore in order to understand and appreciate.

美国的历史虽说只有短短两百年，可它的成长与壮大，融入了来自不同国家，不同地区的移民特色。这也是美国多元化文化产生的原因。

Immigration & American diversity

In fact, the US history is one of immigration. In 1620, about 100 English colonists, so-called "Mayflower Pilgrims" left for America seeking religious freedom. They landed near Plymouth, Massachusetts, making an early successful European migration to North America, which had been inhabited by American people for more than 16,000 years. Throughout the 19th and 20th centuries, American ports teemed with German, Chinese, Irish, Italian, Polish immigrants from all over the world.

> 自1620年首批清教徒登陆马萨诸塞州之后，美国陆续又接纳了许多来自世界各个国家的移民。

American culture

The US is called the melting pot because there are people from everywhere around the world. They have different cultures, different customs, but when they come to the US, they are one, one nation. Americans take pride in their "melting pot" society that encourages new comers to assimilate into the American culture. But the melting pot imagery has been contested by the idea of multiculturalism, the "salad bowl theory", or as it is known in Canada, the "cultural mosaic", whereby the immigrants retain their own national characteristics while integrating into a new society.

> 美国到底应该被称之为"大熔炉"，还是"沙拉碗"？

American religion

The US is a religious country, and the influence of the God on the American people can be seen everywhere. Because of the complexity of the nationality of the American people and their right to choose their own church to worship, there are as many as over 333,000 local church groups, and more than 250 religious sects throughout the country. That is because the country is largely composed of immigrants, and those overseas workers came to the US with different religions. In general, Christianity and Judaism have the greatest influence on nation. According to the principle of "separation of church and state", the government of the US gives no direct subsidies to any faiths, but exempts them from paying taxes on income and property.

> 美国是个多民族、多宗教的国家。居民主要信奉基督教和天主教，犹太教、东正教、佛教、伊斯兰教、道教等宗教亦有一定信众。

(Revised from *American Society & Culture*)

NOTES

Woodrow Wilson (1856 –1924): the 28th President of the United States, from 1913 to 1921. A leader of the Progressive Movement, he served as President of Princeton University from 1902 to 1910, and then as the Governor of New Jersey from 1911 to 1913. Running against Republican incumbent William Howard Taft, Socialist Party of America candidate Eugene V. Debs, and former President Progressive ("Bull Moose") Party candidate Theodore Roosevelt, Wilson was elected President as a Democrat in 1912.

托马斯·伍德罗·威尔逊：美国第28任总统。作为进步主义时代的一个领袖级知识分子，他曾先后任普林斯顿大学校长、新泽西州州长等职。1912年总统大选中，由于西奥多·罗斯福和威廉·塔夫托的竞争分散了共和党选票，威尔逊以民主党人身份当选总统。迄今为止，他是唯一拥有哲学博士（Ph.D.）头衔的美国总统（法律博士衔除外），也是唯一一名任总统以前曾在新泽西州担任公职的美国总统。

Ishmael Reed (1938 –): a bearded, paunchy but powerful-looking journalist, editor, author, poet, essayist whose activism extends beyond his writings. He is a tireless yet realistic promoter of Oakland, California as an integrated city, where blacks hold positions of power. In the New York Times and elsewhere he has criticized the networks' unfair reportage on black crime. Few writers have provoked more controversy than Ishmael Reed. His books have been attacked by other black writers, feminists, and Establishment critics, who have accused him of being overly cynical and of harboring a hatred of women.

伊什梅尔·里德：美国最有才华、最有争议的后现代派作家，也是继拉尔夫·埃利森以来最受评论界关注的非裔美国男作家。他是继马克·吐温之后美国文坛出现的最优秀的讽刺大师，是多元文化主义的积极倡导者。当然，也有人称之为"保守派、激进分子、黑人民族主义者、性别歧视者……自命不凡的狂人"。

Mayflower: a merchant ship that set sail from Plymouth, a port on the southern coast of England. Typically, the Mayflower's cargo was wine and dry goods, but on this trip the ship carried passengers: 102 of them, all hoping to start a new life on the other side of the Atlantic. Nearly 40 of these passengers were Protestant Separatists–they called themselves "Saints"–who hoped to establish a new church in the New World. Today, we often refer to the colonists who crossed the Atlantic on the Mayflower as "Pilgrims."

《五月花号》：1620年9月，102名英国清教徒因不满受残酷迫害从英国的普利茅斯港出发驶向大西洋的另一边，决定移居到北美的新大陆，在那里完全按照自己的方式来信仰上帝，过着一种自由，不受迫害的生活。

Plymouth: the first permanent colony in New England (1620) which is a destination best known for the Pilgrim. It is nestled between Boston & Cape Cod in the States.

普利茅斯：美国新英格兰地区的一个地名，是英殖民者于1620年在美洲创建的第一个永久殖民地。

Massachusetts: a state that has played a significant role in American history since the Pilgrims, seeking religious freedom, founded Plymouth Colony in 1620. As one of the most important of the 13 colonies, Massachusetts became a leader in resisting British oppression. During the 19th century, Massachusetts was famous for the intellectual activity of its writers and educators and for its expanding commercial fishing, shipping, and manufacturing interests. Massachusetts pioneered the manufacture of textiles and shoes. Today, these industries have been replaced in importance by the electronics and communications equipment fields.

马萨诸塞州：美国的一个州，正式名称为"马萨诸塞联邦"（Commonwealth of Massachusetts），位于美国东北，是新英格兰地区的一部分。在中文中，通常简称"麻州"或"麻省"。马萨诸塞州东濒大西洋，海岸线曲折，属温带大陆性气候，1788年加入联邦，为美国独立时最初13个州之一。

Melting Pot: a metaphor for a heterogeneous society becoming more homogeneous, the different elements "melting together" into a harmonious whole with a common culture. It is particularly used to describe the assimilation of immigrants to the USA. This metaphor was in use by the 1780s.

"大熔炉"：一种贴切的形容，指美国可以融合世界各种不同的文化为美国文化，有欧洲的、南美的、非洲的、亚洲的等。

Salad Bowl: a concept that suggests the integration of the many different cultures of United States residents combine like a salad, as opposed to the more traditional notion of a cultural Melting Pot. In Canada, this concept is more commonly known as the cultural Mosaic.

"沙拉碗"：意指美国多元文化背景的移民群体联合在一起，像一个大的沙拉碗，不同文化各自保持特色，根本没有合并融合为某种单一的文化。这一说法是相对于早期学者提出的"大熔炉"观点的，该观点认为，美国文化可以将不同种族的文化很好地融合起来，可事实证明并非如此。美国的大部分移民都保持着自己的文化传统几十年不变。在加拿大，这种观点被普遍称作是"文化马赛克"。

Part II. cineWatch
光影星荟萃

My Big Fat Greek Wedding
《我盛大的希腊婚礼》

面对自己庞大的家族，在多种文化冲突碰撞中，他和她把爱情进行到底了……

Storyline 好片抢先知

Toula Portokalos is 30, Greek, and works in her family's restaurant, Dancing Zorba's, in Chicago. All her father Gus wants for her is to get married to a nice Greek boy. But Toula is looking for more in life. Her mother convinces Gus to let her take some computer classes at college (making him think it's his idea). With those classes under her belt, she then takes over her aunt's travel agency (again making her father think it's his idea). She meets Ian Miller, a high school English teacher, they date secretly for a while before her family finds out. Her father is livid over her dating a non-Greek. He has to learn to accept Ian; Ian has to learn to accept Toula's huge family, and Toula has to learn to accept herself.

Toula（妮娅·瓦达拉斯 Nia Vardalos 饰）虽然在美国出生长大，却是生活在一个巨型的希腊世界中，整个庞大的家族以父亲权威般的意志为代表坚持着希腊是世界之源的精神动力。从小就眼观着家人古怪行为的Toula听得最多的就是母亲与神经质祖母的言论：嫁给一个希腊人，生一大堆希腊小孩，喂饱自己的肚子直到世界的最后一天。长到30岁的Toula邋遢肥胖，在一次夜雨中她继续听着父亲的唠叨，然而当她走进日复一日工作的家庭餐馆时，她决定要改变自己的命运！她去学习，去美容院整理自己的仪容，当她浑身散发出自信时，白马王子Ian（约翰·考伯特 John Corbett 饰）出现了。二人一见钟情，迫不及待要组织自己的新家庭。对这个庞大的希腊家族来说，Ian不折不扣是一个外人，婚礼的繁琐和斗争才刚刚开始，不同的价值观引发了一连串笑料。

Cast 星光闪烁

Nia Vardalos … Toula Portokalos MTV 电影奖最具突破女演员提名，全球奖最佳女主角提名

Michael Constantine … Gus Portokalos ——最佳希裔美国演员奖

Memorable quotes 余音绕梁

Gus Portokalos: You'd better get married soon. You're starting to look... old!

Gus Portokalos: There are two kinds of people - Greeks, and everyone else who wish they were Greek.

Toula Portokalos: My dad believed in two things: That Greek would educate non Greeks about being Greek and every ailment from psoriasis to poison ivy can be cured with Windex.

Gus Portokalos: Give me a word, any word, and I show you that the root of that word is Greek.

Maria Portokalos: Toula, on my wedding night, my mother, she said to me, "Greek women, we may be lambs in the kitchen, but we are tigers in the bedroom."

Toula Portokalos: There are three things that every Greek woman must do in life: marry Greek boys, make Greek babies, and feed everyone.

Ian Miller: May I please date your daughter?

Gus Portokalos: No!

Toula Portokalos: Ma, Dad is so stubborn. What he says goes："Ah, the man is the head of the house!"

Maria Portokalos: Let me tell you something, Toula. The man is the head, but the woman is the neck. And she can turn the head any way she wants.

Toula Portokalos: My family is big and loud but they're my family. We fight and we laugh and yes, we roast lamb on a spit in the front yard. And where ever I go, whatever I do they will always be there.

Nick Portokalos: I've never seen my sister this happy, Ian. If you hurt her, I'll kill you and make it look like an accident.

Toula Portokalos: If nagging were an Olympic sport, my Aunt Voula would win a gold medal!

Culture inside 文化反光镜

Chicago: the third lagest US city. It is in the state of Illinois on Lake Michigan and sometimes called the "Windy City". Chicago is the center of the American Mid-west and has the busiest airport in the world.

芝加哥：位于美国中西部，属伊利诺伊州，东临密歇根湖，是美国仅次于纽约市和洛杉矶的第三大城市。芝加哥地处北美大陆的中心地带，为美国最重要的铁路、航空枢纽。芝加哥同时也是美国重要的金融、文化、制造业、期货和商品交易中心之一。

Parthenon: the Parthenon in Athens, Greece was under construction from 449 BC to 421 BC. The Parthenon was created to honor the Greek goddess Athena, whom was called the protector of the city. Though the Parthenon is considered a temple, it was never meant to be used as a religious spot; there was no cult activity there. Instead, it is believed that the Parthenon was used as a sort of treasury.

（希腊）雅典娜神殿：建于公元前449—前421年，也称为"雅典娜胜利女神庙"、"尼基神庙"、"无翼胜利女神庙"，位于卫城山上，采用爱奥尼亚柱式，台基长8.15米，宽5.38米，前后柱廊雕饰精美，是居住在雅典的多利亚人与爱奥尼亚人共同创造的建筑艺术结晶。在希腊人心目中，雅典娜是代表着智慧、技艺与胜利的女神。

Corinthian column: the most highly decorated of the five classical types. The ancient and classical Greeks made some of their most astonishing contributions to successive societies and cultures in the field of architecture. Divided into three orders, Doric, Ionic and Corinthian, each architectural order has a specific column associated with it, which makes it easy to differentiate among the three. The Corinthian order is the newest and most elaborate of the three, and this is typified by the Corinthian column.

古希腊有三种基本柱式：陶立克柱式（或译作多立克）、爱奥尼柱式和科林斯柱式。陶立克柱式形态简洁，其柱高是直径的6倍，雄健威武，象征男性美；爱奥尼柱式纤巧修长，柱高是直径的8~9倍，柱头用卷涡装饰，富有曲线美，象征女性美；科林斯柱式形态更复杂、更修长，上部是藤蔓似的卷涡，下面是曼妙的花纹，更具女性美。

Windex: a famous brand of glass cleaner which can do more than just cleaning the glass.

稳洁：一款有名的玻璃清洗剂，用途广泛。在该影片中就有消炎、止痒、止痛之功效。

Hamlet: one of the four great tragedies of William Shakespeare's and was once adapted for the screen and directed by Kenneth Branagh, who also stars in the titular role as Prince Hamlet. It was highly acclaimed by the majority of critics and has been regarded as one of the best Shakespeare film adaptations ever made.

《哈姆雷特》：著名悲剧，是莎士比亚最负盛名的剧本，同《麦克白》、《李尔王》和《奥赛罗》一起组成莎士比亚"四大悲剧"。在《哈姆雷特》中，复仇的故事中交织着爱恨情愁。同时，哈姆雷特也是该剧主人公丹麦王子的名字。后有据此改编的同名电影和越剧、京剧等艺术作品。

Sunday School: a kind of class organized by a church that some children and youth go to on Sundays in order to learn about Christianity and the Holy World.

主教日学校：在西方，基督教会在礼拜天开办课程，开设"基督教教义"和"查经班"等课程。这种就叫做"主教日学校"。

PNR: refers to Passenger Name Record. There are five parts of a PNR required before the booking can be completed. They are: The name of the passenger(s); Contact details for the travel agent or airline office; Ticketing details, either a ticket number or a ticketing time limit; Itinerary of at least one segment, which must be the same for all passengers listed; Name of the person making the booking.

旅客订座纪录：PNR即Passager Name Record的缩写，它反映了旅客的航程、航班座位占用的数量及旅客信息，适用民航订座系统。一个PNR记录了旅客订座的完整信息，计算机赋于每个PNR一个编号，也称"订座记录编号"。电脑号一般为五位数字与字母的组合。

Vegas: a short form for Las Vegas and is in the southern part of the state of Nevada, about 50 miles east of the California border and 30 miles west of the Arizona border. The city is famous for its casinos and hotels.

拉斯维加斯：地处美国内华达州沙漠边陲，是世界三大赌城之一。

Niagara Falls is situated on the Niagara river, it is one of the world's greatest natural wonders, can only be described as breath taking. The falls are on the international line between the cities of Niagara Falls, N.Y., and Niagara Falls, Ont. Goat Island splits the cataract into the American Falls and the Horseshoe, or Canadian, Falls. The governments of the United States and Canada control the appearance of the surrounding area. No matter what time of

year, whether its the beautiful rainbow glistening in the mist, or the magnificent ice bridge created by the cold of winter, Niagara Falls always seem to amaze its viewers.

尼亚加拉瀑布：北美东北部尼亚加拉河上的大瀑布，堪称世界著名的奇景之一。瀑布位于加拿大安大略省和美国纽约州的交界处，一直由加拿大和美国共同管理周边地区。无论冬夏，过去数十年，美丽独特的尼亚加拉瀑布一直吸引人们到此度蜜月、走钢索横越瀑布或者坐木桶漂游瀑布。

Fiji: an island country of the southwest Pacific Ocean comprising 322 islands. The island were discovered by the Dutch Navigator Abel Tasman in 43, and it was annexed by Great Britain in 874 and became independent in 970. Suva, on the island of Viti Levu is the capital which owns about population of 8000.

斐济：南太平洋上著名的群岛国家。它是个多种族的国家，包含322个岛屿，其中1/3岛屿上有人居住。最大的岛屿为维提岛与瓦努阿岛。位于维提岛上的首都苏瓦是全国政治中心和服装业基地，也是南太平洋著名的天然良港，有8000人口。

Trivia 八卦一下

The opening scene where Nia Vardalos and Michael Constantine travel in the early morning to open the restaurant was one of the very last scenes filled. Vardalos said that all of the other cast members had finished their scenes and had left, and so the sadness she and Constantine had in that car scene reflected the tearful goodbyes.

电影开篇时妮娅·瓦达拉斯和迈克尔·康斯坦丁早起开店的那一幕实际是最后拍摄的。据说当时剧组人员都离开了，因此，瓦达拉斯和康斯坦丁表现出的悲伤情绪也含有挥泪告别的意味。

Nia Vardalos is a Ryerson University graduate. The university was used for several scenes in the film. Kerr Hall is the school where Ian Miller teaches. The Rogers Communications building plays Harry S. Truman College.

妮娅·瓦达拉斯是瑞尔森大学的毕业生，而瑞尔森大学在电影里多次出现。

In the movie poster, the two E's in the word "Greek" are made to look like the Greek letter Sigma, which is S, not E. To a Greek, it reads "My Big Fat Grssk Wedding".

电影宣传海报上的Greek中的两个E印刷得像是希腊字母S。

Nia Vardalos's real-life husband, Ian Gomez, plays Ian's best friend, Mike.

妮娅·瓦达拉斯本人的老公在剧中扮演伊恩的好朋友迈克。

The song playing at the wedding reception, "All My Only Dreams", first appeared in *That Thing You Do!* which was written, directed, and produced by Tom Hanks, who also produced this film.

婚礼现场播放的那首"我唯一的梦想"首次出现在电影《挡不住的奇迹》中，这两部电影都是由汤姆·汉克斯自编自导的。

When Toula walks to the front porch of her house in the blue shirt, in the background we see the Greek god of love.

当图拉身着蓝色衬衫走向她家门廊时，画面背景显示希腊爱神形象。

At the wedding reception, no one was doing the dance correctly. The cast was too tired.

婚礼现场没有一个人的舞步是对的，只因大家都太累了。

According to Nia Vardalos, paying for catering during the film proved not to be a problem. Wherever the film was being shot, whenever local Greek restaurants learned about it, they sent over lots of free food.

据妮娅·瓦达拉斯称，电影中的宴席菜肴基本没有花钱，因为电影无论在哪里一开拍，只要当地的希腊餐厅耳闻，就立刻送去大量免费的食物。

It was the fifth highest-grossing film of 2002 in the United States, with USD$241,438,208, and the highest-grossing romantic comedy in history.

该片在美国2002年票房排行中位列第五，入账241438208美元，创下喜剧电影票房历史之最。

Part III. Extra Credit
美文品读

Audacity of Hope
无畏的希望
——2004年7月24日奥巴马在美国民主党代表大会上的演说

On behalf of the great state of Illinois, crossroads of a nation, land of Lincoln, let me express my deep gratitude for the privilege of addressing this convention. Tonight is a particular honor for me because, let's face it, my presence on this stage is pretty unlikely. My father was a foreign student, born and raised in a small village in Kenya. He grew up herding goats, went to school in a tin-roof shack. His father, my grandfather, was a cook, a domestic servant.

But my grandfather had larger dreams for his son. Through hard work and perseverance my father got a scholarship to study in a magical place: America, which stood as a beacon of freedom and opportunity to so many who had come before. While studying here, my father met my mother. She was born in a town on the other side of the world, in Kansas. Her father worked on oil rigs and farms through most of the Depression. The day after Pearl Harbor he signed up for duty, joined Patton's army and marched across Europe. Back home, my grandmother raised their baby and went to work on a bomber assembly line. After the war, they studied on the GI Bill, bought a house through FHA, and moved west in search of opportunity.

And they, too, had big dreams for their daughter, a common dream, born of two continents. My parents shared not only an improbable love; they shared an abiding faith in the possibilities of this nation. They would give me an African name, Barack, or "blessed," believing that in a tolerant America your name is no barrier to success. They imagined me going to the best schools in the land, even though they weren't rich, because in a generous America you don't have to be rich to achieve your potential. They both passed away now. Yet, I know that, on this night, they look down on me with pride.

I stand here today, grateful for the diversity of my heritage, aware that my parents' dreams live on in my precious daughters. I stand here knowing that my story is part of the larger American story, that I owe a debt to all of those who came before me, and that, in no other country on earth, is my story even possible. Tonight, we gather to affirm the greatness of our nation, not because of the height of our skyscrapers, or the power of our military, or the size of our economy. Our pride is based on a very simple premise, summed up in a declaration made over two hundred years ago, "We hold these truths to be self-evident, that all men are created equal. That they are endowed by their Creator with certain inalienable rights. That among these are life, liberty and the pursuit of happiness."

That is the true genius of America, a faith in the simple dreams of its people, the insistence on small miracles. That we can tuck in our children at night and know they are fed and clothed and safe from harm. That we can say what we think, write what we think, without hearing a sudden knock on the door. That we can have an idea and start our own business without paying a bribe or hiring somebody's son. That we can participate in the political process without fear of retribution, and that our votes will be counted —or at least, most of the time.

This year, in this election, we are called to reaffirm our values and commitments, to hold them against a hard reality and see how we are measuring up, to the legacy of our forbearers, and the promise of future generations. And fellow Americans — Democrats, Republicans, Independents —I say to you tonight: we have more work to do. More to do for the workers I met in Galeurg, Illinois, who are losing their union jobs at the Maytag plant that's moving to Mexico, and now are having to compete with their own children for jobs that pay seven bucks an hour. More to do for the father I met who was losing his job and choking back tears, wondering how he would pay $4,500 a month for the drugs his son needs without the health benefits he counted on. More to do for the young woman in East St. Louis, and thousands more like her, who has the grades, has the drive, has the will, but doesn't have the money to go to college.

Don't get me wrong. The people I meet in small towns and big cities, in diners and office parks, they don't expect government to solve all their problems. They know they have to work hard to get ahead and they want to. Go into the collar counties around Chicago, and people will tell you they don't want their tax money wasted by a welfare agency or the Pentagon. Go into any inner city neighborhood, and folks will tell you that government alone can't teach kids to learn. They know that parents have to parent, that children can't achieve unless we raise their expectations and turn off the television sets and eradicate the slander that says a black youth with a book is acting white. No, people don't expect government to solve all their problems. But they sense, deep in their bones, that with just a change in priorities, we can make sure that every child in America has a decent shot at life, and that the doors of opportunity remain open to all. They know we can do better. And they want that choice.

In this election, we offer that choice. Our party has chosen a man to lead us who embodies the best this country has to offer. That man is John Kerry. John Kerry understands the ideals of community, faith, and sacrifice, because they've defined his life. From his heroic service in Vietnam to his years as prosecutor and lieutenant governor, through two decades in the United States Senate, he has devoted himself to this country. Again and again, we've seen him make tough choices when easier ones were available. His values and his record affirm what is best in us.

John Kerry believes in an America where hard work is rewarded. So instead of offering tax breaks to companies shipping jobs overseas, he'll offer them to companies creating jobs here at home. John Kerry believes in an America where all Americans can afford the same health coverage our politicians in Washington have for themselves. John Kerry believes in energy independence, so we aren't held hostage to the profits of oil companies or the sabotage of foreign oil fields. John Kerry believes in the constitutional freedoms that have made our country the envy of the world, and he will never sacrifice our basic liberties nor use faith as a wedge to divide us. And John Kerry believes that in a dangerous world, war must be an option, but it should never be the first option.

A while back, I met a young man named Shamus at the VFW Hall in East Moline, Illinois. He was a good-looking kid, six-two or six-three, clear-eyed, with an easy smile. He told me he'd joined the Marines and was heading to Iraq the following week. As I listened to him explain why he'd enlisted, his absolute faith in our country and its leaders, his devotion to duty and service, I thought this young man was all any of us might hope for in a child. But then I asked myself: Are we serving Shamus as well as he was serving us? I thought of more than 900 service men and women, sons and daughters, husbands and wives, friends and neighbors, who will not be returning to their hometowns. I thought of families I had met who were struggling to get by without a loved one's full income, or whose loved ones had returned with a limb missing or with nerves shattered, but who still lacked long-term health benefits because they were reservists. When we send our young men and women into harm's way, we have a solemn obligation not to fudge the numbers or shade the truth about why they're going, to care for their families while they're gone, to tend to the soldiers upon their return, and to never ever go to war without enough troops to win the war, secure the peace, and earn the respect of the world.

Now let me be clear. We have real enemies in the world. These enemies must be found. They must be pursued, and they must be defeated. John Kerry knows this. And just as Lieutenant Kerry did not hesitate to risk his life to protect the men who served with him in Vietnam, President Kerry will not hesitate one moment to use our military might to keep America safe and secure. John Kerry believes in America. And he knows it's not enough for just some of us to prosper. For alongside our famous individualism, there's another ingredient in the American saga.

A belief that we are connected as one people. If there's a child on the south side of Chicago who can't read, that matters to me, even if it's not my child. If there's a senior citizen somewhere who can't pay for her prescription and has to choose between medicine and the rent, that makes my life poorer, even if it's not my grandmother. If there's an Arab American family being rounded up without benefit of an attorney or due process, that threatens my civil liberties. It's that fundamental belief —I am my brother's keeper, I am my sister's keeper — that makes this country work. It's what allows us to pursue our individual dreams, yet still come together as a single American family. "E pluribus unum." Out of many, one.

Yet even as we speak, there are those who are preparing to divide us, the spin masters and negative ad peddlers who embrace the politics of anything goes. Well, I say to them tonight, there's not a liberal America and a conservative America - there's the United States of America. There's not a black America and white America and Latino America and Asian America; there's the United States of America. The pundits like to slice-and-dice our country into Red States and Blue States; Red States for Republicans, Blue States for Democrats. But I've got news for them, too. We worship an awesome God in the Blue States, and we don't like federal agents poking around our libraries in the Red States. We coach Little League in the Blue States and have gay friends in the Red States. There are patriots who opposed the war in Iraq and patriots who supported it. We are one people, all of us pledging allegiance to the stars and stripes, all of us defending the United States of America.

In the end, that's what this election is about. Do we participate in a politics of cynicism or a politics of hope? John Kerry calls on us to hope. John Edwards calls on us to hope. I'm not talking about blind optimism here — the almost willful ignorance that thinks unemployment will go away if we just don't talk about it, or the health care crisis will solve itself if we just ignore it. No, I'm talking about something more substantial. It's the hope of slaves sitting around a fire singing freedom songs; the hope of immigrants setting out for distant shores; the hope of a young naval lieutenant bravely patrolling the Mekong Delta; the hope of a mill worker's son who dares to defy the odds; the hope of a skinny kid with a funny name who believes that

America has a place for him, too. The audacity of hope!

In the end, that is God's greatest gift to us, the bedrock of this nation; the belief in things not seen; the belief that there are better days ahead. I believe we can give our middle class relief and provide working families with a road to opportunity. I believe we can provide jobs to the jobless, homes to the homeless, and reclaim young people in cities across America from violence and despair. I believe that as we stand on the crossroads of history, we can make the right choices, and meet the challenges that face us. America!

Tonight, if you feel the same energy I do, the same urgency I do, the same passion I do, the same hopefulness I do — if we do what we must do, then I have no doubt that all across the country, from Florida to Oregon, from Washington to Maine, the people will rise up in November, and John Kerry will be sworn in as president, and John Edwards will be sworn in as vice president, and this country will reclaim its promise, and out of this long political darkness a brighter day will come. Thank you and God bless you.

Making Sense 解文说词

① On behalf of the great state of Illinois, crossroads of a nation, land of Lincoln, let me express my deep gratitude for the privilege of addressing this convention. (para. 1)

伟大的伊利诺伊州，既是全国的交通枢纽，又是林肯的故乡。作为州代表，我将在大会上致词，并因受此殊荣而深感自豪。

② Through hard work and perseverance my father got a scholarship to study in a magical place: America, which stood as a beacon of freedom and opportunity to so many who had come before. (para. 2)

凭借着刻苦的努力和坚韧的毅力，父亲荣获赴美留学的机会，而且还拿到了奖学金。美国这片神奇的土地，对于很多踏上这片国土的人而言，意味着自由和机遇。

③ My parents shared not only an improbable love; they shared an abiding faith in the possibilities of this nation. They would give me an African name, Barack, or "blessed," believing that in a tolerant America your name is no barrier to success. (para. 3)

我的父母不仅不可思议地彼此相爱，而且对这个国家有了坚定不移的信念。他们赐予我一个非洲名字——巴拉克，意为"上天庇佑"。因为他们相信，在如此包容的国度里，这样的名字不会成为成功的羁绊。

④ that I owe a debt to all of those who came before me, and that, in no other country on earth, is my story even possible. (para. 4)

owe a debt 欠债 owe v. +to/for

我更深知自己无法忘却那些更早踏上这片土地的先人，因为如果不是在美国，我的故事无论如何都不会发生。

⑤ Don't get me wrong.（para.7）

请正面理解我的意思。这里相当于口语中的 "Don't misunderstand me." 当担心对方不同意自己的观点时，可以此为开场白，继而提出自己的观点。

⑥ From his heroic service in Vietnam to his years as prosecutor and lieutenant governor, through two decades in the United States Senate, he has devoted himself to this country.（para.8）

他曾在越南英勇战斗，回国后又出任检察官和副州长，在参议院度过了20个年头，把全部的精力都献给了国家。

⑦ "E pluribus unum." Out of many, one.（para.12）

合众为一。

⑧ Tonight, if you feel the same energy I do, the same urgency I do, the same passion I do, the same hopefulness I do. (para.16)

今晚，如果你我感同身受，有同样的力量、同样的紧迫感、同样的冲动和同样的希望。作者在这里用了三个以上结构相同、语气相同的词组并列，增加了节奏感和条理性。

 Background 文化大本营

Illinois(IL): a state in the US Midwest, also called the Prairie State. Its largest city is Chicago and its capital city is Springfield. It has industry and produces coal and agricultural products such as corn and wheat. Illinois became a state in 1818 and is associated with Abraham Lincoln, who was a lawyer in Springfield.

伊利诺伊州：美国中西部地区的一个州，又叫"草原州"，最大城市是芝加哥，首府为斯普林菲尔德。该州有制造业，出产煤炭和玉米、小麦等农产品。伊利诺伊在1818年建州，该州常和林肯联系在一起，因为林肯曾在斯普林菲尔德当过律师。

Lincoln (1809 – 1865): the sixteenth President of the United States, successfully led his country through its greatest internal crisis, the American Civil War, only to be assassinated less than a week after the war's end. Before his election as President, Lincoln was a lawyer, an Illinois state legislator, a member of the United States House of Representatives, and an unsuccessful candidate for election to the Senate.

亚伯拉罕·林肯：美国政治家，第16任总统（任期：1861年3月4日—1865年4月15日），也是首位共和党籍总统。在其总统任内，美国爆发内战，史称南北战争。林肯废除了奴隶制度，击败了南方分离势力，维护了国家的统一。内战结束后不久，林肯遇刺身亡。他是第一个遇刺身亡的美国总统。

Kenya: a country that *lies astride* the equator on the eastern coast of Africa. It is a medium-sized country by continental standards, covering an area of about 586,600sq km. Inland water bodies cover some 10,700km sq, the bulk of this in Lakes Victoria and Turkana. Kenya has tremendous topographical diversity, including glaciated mountains with snow-capped peaks, the Rift Valley with its scarps and volcanoes, ancient granitic hills, flat desert landscapes and coral reefs and islets.

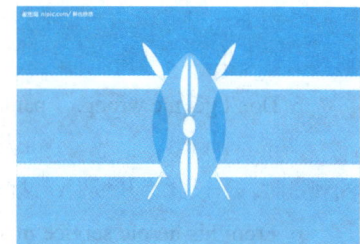

肯尼亚：位于非洲东部，与埃塞俄比亚、索马里、苏丹共和国、坦桑尼亚、乌干达接壤。肯尼亚国土面积58.6600万平方公里，分为8个省，第一次世界大战前被德国占领，后被让予英国。1963年12月12日独立。

Kansas: a US state in the Middle West, the most central of all the states. It forms part of the Great Plains and suffered badly during the Dust Bowl. Its popular name is the Sunflower State and its capital city is Topeka.

堪萨斯州：美国中西部的一个州，是所有各州里位置最靠中间的州。该州是大平原的一部分，曾是干旱沙暴地区，受灾非常严重。堪萨斯州别称向日葵州，首府为托皮卡。

Pearl Harbor: a lagoon harbor on the island of Oahu, Hawaii, west of Honolulu. Much of the harbor and surrounding lands is a United States Navy deep-water naval base. It is also the headquarters of the United States Pacific Fleet. The attack on Pearl Harbor by the Japan on Sunday, December 7, 1941 brought the United States into World War II.

珍珠港：地处瓦胡岛南岸的科劳山脉和怀阿奈山脉之间平原的最低处，与唯一的深水港火奴鲁鲁港相邻，是美国海军的基地和造船基地，也是北太平洋岛屿中最大最好的安全停泊港口之一，一般的民用船舶及外国舰船无美国海军部特殊许可是不得进入的。日本偷袭珍珠港事件发生在1941年12月7日清晨，该事件也使美国卷入了第二次世界大战。

Patton(1885 – 1945): a senior US Army officer during World War II and he was known as "Old Blood and Guts." He was one of the most colorful generals of World War II. After D-Day, General Patton led the US 3rd Army rapidly through France and into Germany. He was a tough man who demanded strict discipline and was either loved or hated by his soldiers.

乔治·巴顿：美国陆军四星上将，是第二次世界大战中著名的美国军事统帅，号称"铁胆将军"。在登陆日后，指挥美国快速穿过法国，进入德国。巴顿将军非常强硬，实行严格的纪律，因此，他要么受士兵爱戴，要么招来嫉恨。乔治·巴顿是一个具有政治、军事、哲学头脑的人。

GI Bill: full name "The GI Bill of Rights" is a US law passed in 1944 to give financial help to members of the armed forces when they returned from World War II. This included money given to help pay for homes and education. By 1947, about 4 million people had benefited from the law. It now helps anyone leaving the US armed forces.

退伍军人福利法案：1944年美国通过的一项法律，保证对第二次世界大战退伍军人给予财政援助，其中就包括提供资金帮助安家和接受教育。到1947年，大约有400万人受益于该法案。现在这一法律适用于任何退伍军人。

FHA: Federal Housing Administration is a government-run entity within the U.S. Department of Housing & Urban Development and provides mortgage insurance on loans made by FHA-approved leaders. Such insured loans include mortgage on single family, multifamily, manufactured homes and families.Created by Congress during the Great Depression, FHA was tasked to help American home owners struggling to make their monthly mortgage payment. In addition, the FHA is a self-funded by home mortgage insurance payment.

美国联邦住房管理局（FHA）：隶属美国住房与城市发展部，主要为购房抵押贷款提供保险。FHA是美国1934年大萧条时期罗斯福总统为经济复苏推行新政的产物之一，其初衷是为了在20世纪30年代的大萧条中稳定住房业，而长期策略是为美国中低收入的家庭建造更多的房屋。这个策略为美国房地产行业的发展起到了至关重要的历史作用。

Mexico: officially the United Mexican States is a federal constitutional republic in North America. It is bordered on the north by the United States of America; on the south and west by the Pacific Ocean; on the southeast by Guatemala, Belize, and the Caribbean Sea; and on the east by the Gulf of Mexico. Covering almost two million square kilometers (over 760,000 sq mi), Mexico is the fifth largest country in the Americas by total area and the thirteenth largest independent nation in the world. With an estimated population of over 113 million, it is the world's eleventh most populous country and the most populous Spanish-speaking country.

墨西哥合众国：位于北美洲，北部与美国接壤，东南与危地马拉与伯利兹相邻，西部是太平洋，东部有墨西哥湾与加勒比海的阻隔，占地逾200万平方公里，为美洲第五大国家，世界排名11，人口超过1.13亿，在拉美仅次于巴西，居第二位，位居世界第十一位。官方语言为西班牙语，有7.1%的人讲印第安语，居民中89%信奉天主教，6%信奉基督教新教，首都为墨西哥城。

The Pentagon: the headquarters of the United States Department of Defense, located at 48 N. Rotary Road, Arlington, Virginia. As a symbol of the US military, "the Pentagon" is often used metonymically to refer to the Department of Defense rather than the building itself. Those who work within its walls often simply call it the Building.

五角大楼：位于美国华盛顿特区西南方的弗吉尼亚州阿灵顿县，是美国国防部办公地，美国最高军事指挥机关所在地。由于其特殊的职能，有时"五角大楼"一词不仅仅代表这座建筑本身，也常常用作美国国防部的代名词。

John Kerry（1943 – ）: an American politician who is the 68th and current United States Secretary of State. He was a United States Senator from Massachusetts from 1985 to 2013, and was chairman of the Senate Foreign Relations Committee. He was the presidential nominee of the Democratic Party in the 2004 presidential election, but lost to President George W. Bush.

约翰·克里：美国政治家，现任国务卿。自1985—2013年任马萨诸塞州参议员。2004年7月29日获民主党提名为该党2004年美国总统选举的候选人，同当时的在任总统小布什竞选美国总统一职，落选。2008年12月，克里当选为美国参议院外交委员会主席。2013年，接替希拉里出任新一任美国国务卿，这是16年来美国第一位白人男性国务卿。

VFW: full name "the Veterans of Foreign Wars", is a large organization for former members of the US armed forces who fought wars abroad. It helps those in need, has campaigns to influence the government on military matters, and does community service. It was established in 1899 and has more than 2.8 million members.

海外战争退役军人协会（VFW）：成立于1898年，现有会员280多万人。VFW是由参加过海外战争的美国退伍军人组成的大型组织，旨在给困难者提供帮助，为影响政府的军事事务而进行活动，也提供社区服务。

Red States & Blue States：In American politics, the color red and the animal elephant are symbolic Republican Party while the color blue and the animal donkey are symbolic of Democratic Party.

红州和蓝州：在美国政治中，红色以及大象代表共和党，而蓝色以及驴子是民主党的表征。因此，红州和蓝州分别代表支持共和党和民主党的州。

John Edwards(1953 –)：a US politician, member of the Democratic Party, Senator from North Carolina from 1999 to 2005 , candidate for vice Presidency of the United States in 2004 and a candidate for the Democratic nomination for the US presidential election of 2008 .

约翰·爱德华兹：美国民主党前参议员（1999—2005），2004年民主党美国副总统选举候选人，曾角逐2008年美国总统选举民主党候选人提名。

Mekong Delta: the region in Southeast Vietnam where the Mekong River approaches and empties into the sea through a network of tributaries. The Mekong delta region encompasses a large portion of southeastern Vietnam of 39,000 km². The area covered by water depends on the season.

湄公河三角洲：或称下高棉，位于越南东南部的一个地区，湄公河在入海口形成的三角洲。湄公河三角洲地区面积39000km²，是越南南方最大的平原和鱼米之乡，也是越南最富庶的地方。

Florida: the most southern state in the US. It is internationally famous for its hot weather and white beaches. Florida's popular name is the Sunshine State.The largest city is Miami and the capital city is Tallahassee. Florida was discovered by Spanish explorer Juan Ponce Leon in AD1513, and he named it "La Pascua Florida" which means "flowered Easter".

佛罗里达：美国最南部的一个州。它的国际知名度源于其炎热的气候和白色的海滩。佛罗里达的别称是"阳光州"，首府是塔拉哈西，最大城市是迈阿密。佛罗里达是西班牙探险家德莱昂1513年发现的，并命名为"佛罗里达"，西班牙语意为"鲜花盛开的地方"。

Oregon: a state in the north-western US, also called the Beaver State. The largest city is Portland, and the capital is Salem. Captain James Cook sailed along its coast in 1778, and Lewis and Clark visited the area in 1805. Oregan became state in 1859. Its products include salmon and other fish, wood, paper and fruit.

俄勒冈：美国西北部的一个州，位于美国的太平洋沿岸。该州又称海狸州，最大城市是波特兰，首府为塞勒姆。库克船长1778年曾沿此海岸航行，刘易斯和克拉克1805年也到过这里。该州主要出产大马哈鱼以及其他鱼类、木材、纸张和水果。

Maine: the largest of the New England states in area, with the popular name of "The Pine Tree State," as 90 percent of its land is forest, and its economy is related to timber and the production of paper and paper products. The capital is Augusta. Maine is a popular area for outdoor holidays and sports. It was separated from Massachusetts in 1820 to become a free state.

缅因州：美国东北部新英格兰地区的一个州，俗称"松树州"，因为其90%的土地都是森林，大部分产业都与木材业、造纸业及纸制品相关。缅因州的首府是奥古斯塔，此州是受人喜爱的户外休假和运动的地方。缅因州于1820年脱离马萨诸塞州，成为自由州。

Writing Tips 写作秘笈

本文是奥巴马2004年在美国民主党代表大会上发表的一次重要演说，据英国《独立报》报道，此次演讲使他声名鹊起，并且在2006年出版同名著作。实际上，"无畏的希望"一词出自他的前牧师赖特对于一幅画的评论，奥巴马本人曾经也被那幅画感动得热泪盈眶。演讲一开篇，奥巴马就引用自己的亲身经历生动而真切地唤起民众的情绪，为后来的文章做好铺垫。整个文章观点鲜明，深刻，令人深受鼓舞。尤其是文中一个个排比句的使用更加增加了演讲的语势，魅力无穷，听众无不深受感动。

Unit 8

Something racial: I still have a dream
曾经时刻：密西西比在燃烧

Part Ⅰ. Get-go
给力起步

The development of slavery

The first slaves were taken to North America from Africa by the Dutch in 1619. By the time of the American Revolution there were 500 000 slaves, mostly in the South. After the Revolution the northern states made slavery illegal but the South needed cheap labor for the cotton plantations. As the South's economy became dependent on slaves, the slave markets continued.

The quality of life for slaves depended on the treatment they received from their master and on the kind of work they did. Those working on the cotton plantations of the Deep South suffered most. Families were regularly broken up. The worst situation was to be sold further down the Mississippi River.

> 第一批奴隶是由荷兰人在1916年从非洲运到美洲的。截至美国革命时期,美国已有50万奴隶,大多在南方。美国革命后蓄奴制在北方各州均为非法,但南方的种植园经济却高度依赖奴隶。奴隶的生活充满苦难,常常是妻离子散。

Opposition to slavery

It is hard to understand how slavery was allowed to continue in a country that thought of itself as the "land of the free." But not everyone believed it was right to treat slaves like that, and in 1830s opposition to slavery grew. Leaders of the abolition movement included William Lloyd Garrison, publisher of an anti-slavery newspaper, the Liberator , and Harriet Beecher Stowe who wrote Uncle Tom's Cabin, a novel about a slave who was badly treated.

Some abolitionists took direct action. In 1831 a former slave, Nat Turner organized an uprising of slaves in Virginia. In 1859 a white man , John Brown tried to free some slaves. The work of the Underground Railroad had more impact. One of its most famous workers was Harriet Tubman.

Laws were made to restrict the growth of slavery. But the South wanted slavery to expand westward, and politicians found it increasingly difficult to reach agreement.

Conflicts between the North and South increased, and it became clear that supporters and opponents of slavery could not continue to exist in the same country. In 1861, the slave states left the US and formed their government. This was the beginning of the Civil War.

> 令人费解的是在一个自诩"自由国度"的国家,怎么就会容忍奴隶制存在下去?许多人有各种解释的理由,但是也有更多的废奴者站了出来:加里森和他的《解放者》,斯陀夫人和她的《汤姆叔叔的小屋》,特纳和他的奴隶起义,还有创建地下铁道的塔布曼……

The end of the slavery

After the North won the Civil War and brought the southern states back into the US, slavery was ended. But little changes for former slaves. Some moved to the North but there were not enough jobs there and many suffered prejudice from the whites. Those that stayed in the South often worked on the plantations where they had been slaves. They were paid for their work, but had to buy food and clothes and wages were low and they got into debt.

On average, blacks got less education, earn less money, have less respect and die younger. Blacks and whites often find it difficult to trust each other and things get worse and worse until one day the nationwide Civil Rights movement came.

> 南北战争之后，虽说奴隶制被废除，可是曾经的奴隶的生活政治状况并未有多大改变。随着矛盾日积月累，民权运动最终全面爆发。

I have a dream

Therefore in the 1950s and 1960s, the national campaign for equal rights came all over the American land. The campaign included boycotts, the actions of freedom riders, and 1963 a march to Washington led by Martin Luther King. It succeeded in causing the introduction of bussing and affirmative action. The Civil Rights Act of 1964 and the Voting Rights Act of 1965 were also introduced as the result, which helped to change the attitudes of many white Americans.

Today, the world is happy to see the first black man to be the president of the United States and America made the history.

> 20世纪50和60年代经历了风起云涌的黑人争取平等权利的运动，感谢马丁·路德·金的那个梦想才使我们今天拥有了第一位黑人总统。

(Revised from *Oxford Guide to British and American Culture*)

 NOTES

The South: Commonly referred to as the American South, Dixie, or the Southern US — is an area in the southeastern and south-central United States. The region is known for its distinct culture and history, having developed its own customs, musical styles and varied cuisines that have helped distinguish it from the rest of the United States. The South owes its unique heritage to a variety of sources, including Native Americans; early European settlements of Spanish, English, German, French, Scotch-Irish, and Scottish; importation of hundreds of thousands of enslaved Africans; historic dependence on slave labor; the presence of a large proportion of African Americans in the population; and the aftermath of the Confederacy after the Civil War.

美国南方：指美国中南部和东南部诸州，共含14个州，分别是马里兰州、佛吉尼亚州、西佛吉尼亚州、肯塔基州、田纳西州、北卡罗来纳州、南北卡罗来纳州、佐治亚州、佛罗里达州、亚拉巴马州、密西西比州、阿肯色州、路易斯安那州和得克萨斯州。这些州除了马里兰州、西佛吉尼亚州和肯塔基州以外均为南北战争时期的南方邦联成员。美国南方在文化、历史、饮食等方面与其他各州不同，它的独特性来源于早期的印第安人和欧洲殖民者、奴隶制以及南北战争中南方的邦联等。

The Deep South: a descriptive category of the cultural and geographic subregions in the American South. Historically, it is differentiated from the "Upper South" as being the states which were most dependent on plantation type agriculture during the pre-Civil War period. The Deep South was also commonly referred to as the Lower South or the Cotton States. People of English ancestry traditionally predominate in every part of the Deep South except for southern Louisiana. Deep South includes South Carolina, Mississippi, Florida, Alabama, Georgia, Louisiana, and Texas.

美国最南部诸州：指美国东南地区最南部诸州，包括南卡罗来纳州、密西西比州、佛罗里达州、阿拉巴马州、佐治亚州、路易斯安那州以及得克萨斯州。这些州曾经蓄奴并在南北战争中脱离联邦，居民在政治和宗教观点上也多趋于保守。

Mississippi River: the chief river of the largest river system in North America. Flowing entirely in the United States (though its drainage basin reaches into Canada), it rises in northern Minnesota and meanders slowly southwards for 2,530 miles (4,070 km) to the Mississippi River Delta at the Gulf of Mexico. With its many tributaries, the Mississippi's watershed drains all or parts of 31 US states and 2 Canadian provinces between the Rocky and Appalachian Mountains. The Mississippi ranks as the fourth longest and tenth largest river in the world. The river either borders or cuts through the states of Minnesota, Wisconsin, Iowa, Illinois, Missouri, Kentucky, Tennessee, Arkansas, Mississippi, and Louisiana.

密西西比河是世界第四长河，也是北美洲流程最长、流域面积最广、水量最大的河流。它位于北美洲中南部，最终注入墨西哥湾。"密西西比"是英文"mississippi"的音译，来源于印第安人阿耳冈昆族语言，"密西"（misi）和"西比（sipi）分别是"大、老"和"水"的意思，"密西西比"即"大河"或"老人河"。

Land of the free: *this is the line* "the land of the free and home of the brave" from the American anthem "The Star-Spangled Banner", so Land of the free is used to refer to the USA.

自由的国度：缘自美国国歌"星条旗之歌"中的一句"这自由国家，勇士的家乡"，用来指美国。

Abolition Movement: a reform movement during the 18th and 19th centuries. Often called the antislavery movement, it sought to end the enslavement of Africans and people of African descent in Europe, the Americas, and Africa itself. It also aimed to end the Atlantic slave trade carried out in the Atlantic Ocean between Africa, Europe, and the Americas.

废奴运动：指18到19世纪的反奴隶制的运动，旨在废除欧洲、美洲和非洲的奴隶制以及大西洋的奴隶贩卖活动。

William Lloyd Garrison (1805 –1879): a prominent American abolitionist, journalist, and social reformer. He is best known as the editor of the abolitionist newspaper *The Liberator*, and was one of the founders of the American Anti-Slavery Society.

威廉·劳埃德·加里森：美国著名的废奴主义者、记者以及社会进步家，美国反对奴隶制协会的创始人之一。加里森所创的报纸《解放者》是当时著名的反奴隶制的报纸。

Harriet Beecher Stowe (1811 –1896): an American abolitionist and author. Her novel Uncle Tom's Cabin (1852) was a depiction of life for African-Americans under slavery; it reached millions as a novel and play, and became influential in the United States and United Kingdom. It energized anti-slavery forces in the American North, while provoking widespread anger in the South.

比彻·斯陀夫人：美国著名的女作家、废奴主义者。她的小说《汤姆叔叔的小屋》被认为是美国废奴运动的开端。

Uncle Tom's Cabin: a novel written by American author Harriet Beecher Stowe. Published in 1852, the novel "helped lay the groundwork for the Civil War". Lincoln declared. "So this is the little lady who started this great war."

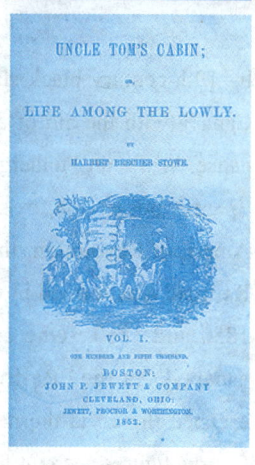

《汤姆叔叔的小屋》：美国著名作家斯托夫人的一部现实主义作品。小说着力刻画了信仰基督教、具有崇高牺牲精神的黑奴汤姆，在不平等的社会制度下遭受的悲惨命运，借此揭示了奴隶制度的罪恶本质。《汤姆叔叔的小屋》一经出版，立即引起了社会各界的强烈反响，在一定程度上推动了美国人民的反奴隶制情绪，从而成为导致美国内战爆发的因素之一。林肯总统曾说，"一个小女人引发一场伟大的战争。"

Nat Turner (1800 –1831): also called Nathaniel "Nat" Turner was an American slave who led a slave rebellion in Virginia on August 21, 1831 that resulted in 60 white deaths and at least 100 black deaths. He gathered supporters in Southampton County, Virginia. Turner was convicted, sentenced to death, and hanged. In the aftermath, the state executed 56 blacks accused of being part of Turner's slave rebellion. Two hundred blacks were also beaten and killed by white militias and mobs reacting with violence. Across Virginia and other southern states, state legislators passed new laws prohibiting education of slaves and free blacks, restricting rights of assembly and other civil rights for free blacks, and requiring white ministers to be present at black worship services.

纳特·特纳：美国黑人起义领袖。1831年夏，在弗吉尼亚的南汉普敦县，纳特·特纳通过传教布道，集结了大约70名奴隶，发动了一场暴动。他们攻打一个又一个种植园，至少杀死55个男人、妇女和儿童。他们拥有很多支持者，但弹药用尽后，他们被抓获。包括特纳在内，大约有19人最后被绞死。

John Brown (1800 –1859): an American abolitionist who believed armed insurrection was the only way to overthrow the violent system of slavery in the United States. In 1856 in Kansas, Brown commanded forces at the Battle of Black Jack and the Battle of Osawatomie. Brown's followers also killed five pro-slavery supporters at Pottawatomie. In 1859, Brown led an unsuccessful raid on the federal armory at Harpers Ferry that ended with his capture. Brown's trial resulted in his conviction and a sentence of death by hanging.

约翰·布朗：美国白人，约翰·布朗起义的发动者。1859年发生的约翰·布朗起义，是美国人民群众试图用武装斗争消灭黑人奴隶制的一次英勇尝试。1800年，布朗出生于康涅狄格州一个白人农民家庭，其父为废奴主义者。布朗从小受反奴隶制思想的熏陶。他1856年曾参加堪萨斯内战并赢得胜利。1859年他领导美国人民在哈伯斯费里举行武装起义，要求废除奴隶制，并逮捕一些种植园主，解放了许多奴隶。他的起义最后被镇压，他最终被逮捕并杀害。大部分历史学家对他持肯定态度，包括作家爱默生及梭罗均称赞约翰·布朗。

Underground Railroad: a network of secret routes and safe houses used by 19th-century black slaves in the United States to escape to free states and Canada with the aid of abolitionists and allies who were sympathetic to their cause. While an "underground railroad" running south toward Florida, then a Spanish possession, existed from the late 17th century until shortly after the American Revolution, the network now generally known as the Underground Railroad was formed in the early 19th century, and reached its height between 1850 and 1860. One estimate suggests that by 1850, 100,000 slaves had escaped via the "Railroad". More than 30,000 people were said to have escaped there via the network during its 20-year peak period, although U.S. Census figures account for only 6,000.

地下铁道：指人们通过隐蔽的方式，经由秘密的路线和食宿站，指引和协助大批黑人奴隶逃离南方。到美国内战爆发之前，估计至少有6万人因此获得自由。

Harriet Tubman（1820 –1913): an African-American abolitionist, humanitarian, and Union spy during the American Civil War. Born into slavery, Tubman escaped and subsequently made more than thirteen missions to rescue more than 70 slaves using the network of antislavery activists and safe houses known as the Underground Railroad. She later helped John Brown recruit men for his raid on Harpers Ferry, and in the post-war era struggled for women's suffrage.

哈瑞特·塔布曼：美国废奴主义者，杰出的黑人废奴主义运动家。她本人就是一个逃跑的奴隶，曾帮助许多黑奴逃亡，被称为"黑摩西"或"摩西祖母"。美国废奴主义运动的领袖约翰·布朗称她为"塔布曼将军"。

Civil Rights Movement: refers to the social movements in the United States aimed at outlawing racial discrimination against black Americans and restoring voting rights to them. Nearly 100 years after the Emancipation Proclamation, African Americans in Southern states still inhabited a starkly unequal world of disenfranchisement, segregation and various forms of oppression, including race-inspired violence. "Jim Crow" laws at the local and state levels barred them from classrooms and bathrooms, from theaters and train cars, from juries and legislatures. In 1954, the U.S Supreme Court struck down the "separate but equal" doctrine that formed the basis for state-sanctioned discrimination, drawing national and international attention to African Americans' plight. In the turbulent decade and a half that followed, civil rights activists used nonviolent protest and civil disobedience to bring about change, and the federal government made legislative headway with initiatives such as the Voting Rights Act of 1965 and the Civil Rights Act of 1968.

民权运动：指第二次世界大战后美国黑人反对种族隔离与歧视，争取民主权利的群众运动。

Martin Luther King, Jr. (1929 – 1968): an American clergyman, activist, and leader in the African-American Civil Rights Movement. He is best known for his role in the advancement of civil rights using nonviolent civil disobedience. King has become a national icon in the history of American progressivism.

马丁·路德·金：著名的美国民权运动领袖。1963年，马丁·路德·金晋见了肯尼迪总统，要求通过新的民权法，给黑人以平等的权利。1963年8月28日，他在林肯纪念堂前发表了题为《我有一个梦想》的演说。他是1964年度诺贝尔和平奖获得者。1968年4月，马丁·路德·金前往孟菲斯市领导工人罢工时被人刺杀，年仅39岁。1986年起美国政府将每年1月的第三个星期一定为"马丁·路德·金全国纪念日"。

Freedom Riders: refer to groups of black and white people from the northern US who in 1961 rode together in buses in the Deep South as a protest against segregation on public transport there. The first Freedom Riders were organized by the Congress of Racial Equality. The Freedom Riders were often attacked by angry crowds, but in November that year the Interstate Commerce Commission legally ended segregation on buses.

自由乘车者：1961年美国很多黑人和白人在最南部诸州一起乘坐公共汽车以抗议公共交通中实

行的种族隔离制度。第一批自由乘车活动是由种族平等大会组织起来的。当时,自由乘车者经常受到愤怒人群的攻击,但同年11月州际商务委员会就从法律上废除了公共汽车上的种族隔离制度。

Bussing: the system of transporting children in buses from their homes to schools in a different area, in order to achieve a greater mixture of races in schools. Usually African-American children travel to better white schools. This began in 1954 and was approved by the US Supreme Court in 1971.

校车接送:在美国是指为实现学校中的种族混合而采取的一种用校车接送孩子们到另一地区的学校上学的措施。通常非洲裔美国儿童坐车到较好的白人学校去读书。这一措施自1954年开始实施,1971年得到联邦最高法院的许可。

Affirmative action: a US government policy requiring that minorities (including women) should be favoured when people are chosen for jobs and entry to college. Americans are divided about this practice and often say it is "reverse discrimination". It has existed since the 1960s, but the Supreme Court has since decided against strict quotas and forcing affirmative action on private businesses.

反歧视行动:美国政府采取的一项政策,鼓励人们优先雇用、录取少数民族(包括女性)。美国人对此常有分歧。这一政策自20世纪60年代起就存在,但是最高法院已经裁决取消严格的配额。

Civil Rights Act of 1964: a landmark piece of legislation in the United States that outlawed major forms of discrimination against racial, ethnic, national and religious minorities, and women. It ended unequal application of voter registration requirements and racial segregation in schools, at the workplace and by facilities that served the general public ("public accommodations").

民权法案:美国国会于1964年通过的法案,内容规范了美国境内不得采取种族隔离,也规定对黑人、少数民族与妇女的歧视性作为为非法。它结束了美国自立国以来长期的黑白种族隔离政策,被认为是人权进步的里程碑。

Voting Rights Act of 1965: a landmark piece of national legislation in the United States that outlawed discriminatory voting practices that had been responsible for the widespread disenfranchisement of African Americans in the US. It was signed by President Johnson.

选举权法:美国民权运动时期通过的一个法案,由约翰逊总统签署,废除了许多限制非洲裔美国人投票的条款。这也是美国司法史上的一个里程碑式的法案。

Part II. cineWatch
光影星荟萃

The Help 《女仆》

惊天动地的轰塌，从来就积累自静默的细小裂纹——无论生活，无论电影。

Storyline 好片抢先知

Set in Mississippi during the 1960s, Skeeter (Stone) is a southern society girl who returns from college determined to become a writer, but turns her friends' lives – and a Mississippi town – upside down when she decides to interview the black women who have spent their lives taking care of prominent southern families. Aibileen (Davis), Skeeter's best friend's housekeeper, is the first to open up – to the dismay of her friends in the tight-knit black community. Despite Skeeter's life-long friendships hanging in the balance, she and Aibileen continue their collaboration and soon more women come forward to tell their stories – and as it turns out, they have a lot to say. Along the way, unlikely friendships are forged and a new sisterhood emerges, but not before everyone in town has a thing or two to say themselves when they become unwittingly – and unwillingly – caught up in the changing times.

1962年美国南方密西西比州，23岁的白人女孩史基特（艾玛·斯通 Emma Stone 饰）刚从大学毕业返乡，她梦想成为作家，但在保守家乡的母亲认为一桩好婚事才是女人的归宿。史基特从小由女佣带大，但她发现为白人一手带大孩子的黑佣，不论在生活或态度上，时常得到不平等的待遇。年轻的白人太太平日和好姐妹交际打牌，主持非洲慈善义卖，把家事还有小孩丢给帮佣，但是却仇视这些长时间相处，深入她们家庭的人。而如果这些黑人女帮佣稍微不服从或是回嘴，白人女性会以"偷窃"为由解雇她们，其他白人家庭也都抵制，让不听话的帮佣找不到活路，对此感到不平的史基特，决意着手一个大胆的写作计划：采访黑佣在白人家庭工作的甘苦，并从她们的角度写成一本书……

Cast 星光闪烁

 Tate Taylor … Director 棕榈泉国际电影节大奖得主

Emma Stone … Skeeter Phelan 美国青少年观众票选大奖提名

Viola Davis … Aibileen Clark 奥斯卡最佳女主角提名

Bryce Dallas Howard … Hilly Holbrook 棕榈泉国际电影节新星奖、美国青少年观众票选大奖提名

Octavia Spencer … Minny Jackson 奥斯卡和金球奖最佳女配角

Memorable quotes 余音绕梁

Aibileen Clark: You is kind. You is smart. You is important.

Charlotte Phelan: Your eggs are dying. Would it kill you to go on a date?

Aibileen Clark: 18 people were killed in Jackson that night. 10 white and 8 black. I don't think God has color in mind when he sets a tornado loose.

Preacher Green: If you can love your enemy, you already have victory.

Aibileen Clark: I ain't never had no white person in my house before.

Charlotte Phelan: Courage sometimes skips a generation. Thank you for bringing it back to our family.

Mae Mobley: You are my real mama, Aibi.

Charlotte Phelan: Love and hate are two horns on the same goat, Eugenia. And you need a goat.

Elizabeth Leefolt: You will get a disease from those toilets!

Minny Jackson: Eat my shit.

Hilly Holbrook: Excuse me!

Minny Jackson: I said eat… my… shit.

Hilly Holbrook: Have you lost your mind?

Minny Jackson: No, ma'am but you is about to. 'Cause you just did.

Aibileen Clark: I was born 1911, Chicksaw County, Piedmont Plantation.

Woman: And did you know as a girl growing up that one day you'd be a maid?

Aibileen Clark: Yes ma'am, I did.

Woman: And you knew that because…

Aibileen Clark: My mama was a maid. My grandmama was a house slave.

Woman: "house slave…" Did you ever dream of being something else?

Aibileen Clark: [nods yes]

Woman: What does it feel like to raise a white child when your own child's at home being looked after by somebody else?

Aibileen Clark: It feel…

Mr. Blackly: I guarantee you, one day they're going to figure out cigarettes will kill you.

Aibileen Clark: Miss Leefolt got so much hairspray on her head, she gonna blow us all up if she light a cigarette.

Constantine Jefferson: [to Eugenia] Every day you're not dead in the ground, when you wake up in the morning, you're gonna have to make some decisions. Got to ask yourself this question: "Am I gonna believe all them bad things them fools say about me today?" You hear me today? "Am I gonna believe all them bad things them fools say about me today? You hear me today?" All right? As for your mama, she didn't pick her life. It picked her. But you, you're gonna do something big with yours. You wait and see.

Stuart Whitworth: I've never met a woman that says exactly what she's thinking.

Eugenia 'Skeeter' Phelan: Well, I got plenty to say.

Missus Walters: I may ave trouble remembering my own name, or what country I live in, but there are two things I can't seem to forget: that my own daughter threw me into a nursing home, and that she ate Minny's shit.

Hilly Holbrook: Maybe I can't send you to jail for what you wrote, but I can send you for being a thief.

Aibileen Clark: I know something about you. Don't you forget that. From what Yule Mae says, there's a lot of time to write letters in jail. Plenty of time to write the truth about you. And the paper is free.

Aibileen Clark: In just ten minutes, the only life I knew was done.

Mae Mobley: [calling after her through the window] A-a-a-aibee!

Aibileen Clark: God says we need to love our enemies. It hard to do. But it can start by telling the truth. No one had ever asked me what it feel like to be me. Once I told the truth about that, I felt free. And I got to thinking about all the people I know. And the things I seen and done. My boy Trelaw always said we gonna have a writer in the family one day. I guess it's gonna be me.

Hilly Holbrook: They carry different diseases than we do. That's why I've drafted the Home Health Sanitation Initiative.

Eugenia 'Skeeter' Phelan: The what?

Hilly Holbrook: A disease-preventative bill that requires every white home to have a separate bathroom for the colored help. It's been endorsed by the White Citizen's Council.

Eugenia 'Skeeter' Phelan: Maybe we should just build you a bathroom outside, Hilly.

Culture inside 文化反光镜

Jackson: the capital of the US state of Mississippi. Jackson is the most populous city in Mississippi. The current slogan for the city is "Jackson, Mississippi: City with Soul." The city is named after Andrew Jackson, who was a general at the time of the naming but later became president of the United States.

杰克逊市：密西西比州首府，得名于美国第七任总统安德鲁·杰克逊，它是南北战争的主战场之一，其非洲裔美国人占城市总人口的65%以上，曾是美国种族歧视最严重的城市。

Ole Miss Rebels: refer to University of Mississippi sports teams, originally known as the "Mississippi Flood", were renamed the Rebels in 1936 and compete in the fourteen-member Southeastern Conference of the NCAA's Division I. The school's colors are cardinal red and navy blue, purposely chosen to mirror the school colors of Harvard and Yale, respectively. With a long history in intercollegiate athletics (Ole Miss began football in 1890), the university competes in 18 men's and women's sports. Student-athletes, 630 in all, received all-conference academic honors from 1995–2004.

密西西比大学体育队：成立于1936年，为美国体育总会的成员。

The Association of Junior Leagues International, Inc. (AJLI): a non-profit organization of 293 Junior Leagues in Canada, Mexico, United Kingdom and the United States. Junior Leagues are educational and charitable women's organizations aimed at improving their communities through voluntarism and building their members' civic leadership skills through training.

青少年联盟：它的前身是一个女性青年互助组织，成立于1927年。这是一个非营利性的组织，旨在发展和培养社区志愿者。

Harper & Row Publishing: an American publishing house, currently the flagship imprint of global publisher Harper Collins，from 1962 – 1990 ,it is called Harper & Row.

哈珀罗伊出版集团：哈珀柯林斯出版集团(Harper Collins)的前身公司（1962-1990）。哈珀柯林斯出版集团系新闻集团(News Corp.)的全资子公司，是全球最大的英文书籍出版商之一，总部位于纽约。

Kentucky Derby: the most famous US horse-racing event. It is one of the triple crown races and is run every year on the first Saturday in May at Churchill Downs in Louisville, Kentucky. The horses are all 3 years old, and the race is 1.25 miles in length. The Kentucky Derby was begun in 1875 by Colonel M Lewis Clark and has become part of a social event that lasts several days.

肯塔基马赛：美国最著名的赛马比赛，为三王冠跑马赛之一，每年5月的第一个星期六在肯塔基州路易斯维尔的丘吉尔草地上举行。参赛马匹的年龄都是三岁，赛程为1.25英里。该项赛事1875年由克拉克上校创办，现已成为一个历时几天的社会活动的一部分。

The Guiding Light: an American television soap opera that is credited by the Guinness Book of World Records as the longest-running television drama history, broadcast from 1952 until 2009, preceded by a 19-year broadcast on radio.

《指路明灯》：美国最早的电视肥皂剧。它最初是1936年的一部系列广播剧，于1952年搬上银幕，2009年停播，是吉尼斯纪录最长的电视剧。

Life: a US magazine which is known especially for its photographs. It was first published in 1936 by Henry Luce who owned Time magazine. His aim was to enable reader "to see life; to see the world; to witness great events." After television became popular, *Life* went out of business in 1972, but it was brought back in 1978, appearing once a month. It is now published by Time Warner.

《生活》：美国杂志，尤以其刊登的照片闻名。它1936年发刊，出版人是拥有《时代》杂志的亨利·卢斯。他的目标是让读者能够"看到生活；看到世界；见证重大事件"。电视普及后，《生活》杂志在1972年停刊，但1978年又复刊，每月一期，由时代华纳出版。

Jackie Kennedy (1929 – 1994): the wife of the 35th President of the United States, John F. Kennedy and First Lady of the United States during his presidency from 1961 until his assassination in 1963. Five years later she married Greek shipping magnate Aristotle Onassis; they remained married until his death in 1975. For the final two decades of her life, Jacqueline Kennedy Onassis had a career as a book editor. She is remembered for her contributions to the arts and preservation of historic architecture, her style, elegance, and grace. A fashion icon, her famous pink Chanel suit has become a symbol of her husband's assassination and one of the lasting images of the 1960s.

杰奎琳·肯尼迪：约翰·肯尼迪总统的夫人，美国前第一夫人。她的穿戴极富个性，其独到的审美情趣，成功地引导了美国的流行时尚。

Robert Kennedy (1925 – 1968): an American politician, a Democratic senator from New York, and a noted civil-rights activist. An icon of modern American liberalism and a member of the Kennedy family, he was a younger brother of President John F. Kennedy, and he served as the president's chief advisor during his presidency. From 1961 to 1964 he served as the US Attorney General. In March 1968 Kennedy began a campaign for the presidency and was a front-running candidate of the Democratic Party. In the California presidential primary, on June 4, Kennedy defeated Eugene McCarthy, the hero of the New Left and student elements in the Democratic Party. That night Kennedy was shot by Sirhan Sirhan, a Palestinian Arab. Mortally wounded, he survived nearly 26 hours, then died early in the morning of June 6.

罗伯特·肯尼迪：第35任美国总统约翰·肯尼迪的弟弟，在约翰·肯尼迪总统任内担任美国司法部长，在和平解决古巴导弹危机和促进民权方面发挥了极大的作用。1965年，他当选美国纽约州参议员，是著名的反对越战和林登·约翰逊的民主党人，1968年，他成为民主党无可争议总统候选人，享有极高的威望，但突然被暗杀而死，导致共和党的理查德·尼克松最终赢得总统选举。

Edward "Ted" Kennedy (1932 –2009): a United States Senator from Massachusetts and a member of the Democratic Party. He was the second most senior member of the Senate when he died and was the fourth-longest-serving senator in United States history, having served there for almost 47 years. As the most prominent living member of the Kennedy family for many years, he was also the last surviving son of Joseph P. Kennedy, Sr.; the youngest brother of President John F. Kennedy and Senator Robert F. Kennedy, both victims of assassination; and the father of Congressman Patrick J. Kennedy.

爱德华·肯尼迪：在参议院供职近半个世纪，被誉为美国近代最伟大的议员；见证了十位美国总统的任期；被奥巴马称为"导师"；在传奇的肯尼迪九兄妹中是排行最小男丁。

White Citizens' Council: an American white supremacist organization formed on July 11, 1954. After 1956, it was known as the Citizens' Councils of America. With about 60,000 members, mostly in the South, the group was well known for its opposition to racial integration during the 1950s and 1960s, when it retaliated with economic boycotts and other strong intimidation against black activists, including depriving them of jobs. By the 1970s, following passage of federal civil rights legislation in the mid-1960s and stronger enforcement of rights by the federal government, the influence of the WCC had waned considerably.

白人市民议会：成立于1954年的"白人至上主义"组织。1956年，其会员超过6万人，其中大部分来自南方。该组织反对种族融合，通过经济制裁和暴力手段来打压民权运动。随着种族隔离法被废除，其影响力大大减弱。

Margaret Mitchell (1900 –1949): an American author and journalist. One novel by Mitchell was published during her lifetime, the American Civil War-era novel, Gone with the Wind. For it she won the National Book Award for Most Distinguished Novel of 1936 and the Pulitzer Prize for Fiction in 1937.

玛格利特·米切尔：美国现代著名女作家，普利策奖和国家图书奖获得者。1949年，她不幸被车撞死。她短暂的一生并未留下太多的作品，但只一部《飘》足以奠定她在世界文学史中不可动摇的地位。

The Jim Crow laws: state and local laws in the United States enacted between 1876 and 1965. They mandated racial segregation in all public facilities in Southern states of the former Confederacy, with, starting in 1890, a "separate but equal" status for African Americans. The separation in practice led to conditions for African Americans that tended to be inferior to those provided for white Americans, systematizing a number of economic, educational and social disadvantages.

吉姆·克劳法：又被称作种族隔离法，泛指1876年至1965年间美国南部各州以及边境各州对有色人种（主要是非洲裔美国人，但同时也包含其他族群）实施种族隔离制度的法律。其核心原则是"隔离，但平等"，表面上不违反法律，本质上却是严重的种族歧视法。

Medgar Wiley Evers (1925 –1963): an African-American civil rights activist from Mississippi involved in efforts to overturn segregation at the University of Mississippi. He became active in the civil rights movement after returning from overseas service in World War II and completing secondary education; he became a field secretary for the NAACP. Evers was assassinated by Byron De La Beckwith, a member of the White Citizens' Council. As a veteran, Evers was buried with full military honors at Arlington National Cemetery. His murder and the resulting trials inspired civil rights protests, as well as numerous works of art, music, and film.

迈德加·艾佛斯：美国著名的黑人民权运动领袖。1963年6月12日，美国总统肯尼迪发表电视讲话支持民权运动，一个小时后，艾佛斯在回家途中被白人市民议会成员拜伦·德·拉·贝克维斯射杀。艾佛斯被葬在阿灵顿国家公墓。

Exodus: the second book of the Hebrew Bible. The book tells how the children of Israel leave slavery in Egypt through the strength of Yahweh, the god who has chosen Israel as his people. Led by their prophet Moses they journey through the wilderness to Mount Sinai, where Yahweh promises them the land of Canaan (the "Promised Land") in return for their faithfulness.

《出埃及记》：《圣经》经卷的第二册，讲述了以色列人在摩西的引领下走出埃及，摆脱奴役的过程。

Moses: a religious leader, lawgiver and prophet, who led the children of Israel leave slavery in Egypt，

摩西：公元前13世纪的犹太人先知，"旧约圣经"前五本书的执笔者，是带领在埃及过着奴隶生活的以色列人到达迦南（巴勒斯坦的古地名，在今天约旦河与死海的西岸一带）的犹太先知。

Social Security: in the United States, refers to the Old-Age, Survivors, and Disability Insurance (OASDI) federal program. The original Social Security Act (1935) and the current version of the Act, as amended, encompass several social welfare and social insurance programs.

美国的社会保障：主要依据"老年、遗属、残疾者保险"的联邦制度，由社会保险、社会福利、社会救济三部分组成。

The Ku Klux Klan (KKK): informally known as the Klan, is the name of three distinct past and present far-right organizations in the United States, which have advocated extremist reactionary currents such as white supremacy, white nationalism, and anti-immigration, historically expressed through terrorism.

三K党：美国历史上和现在依然存在的一个奉行白人至上主义的民间组织，也是美国种族主义的代表性组织。三K党是美国最悠久、最庞大的恐怖主义组织。

Fourth of July: commonly known as the Independence Day, is a federal holiday in the United States commemorating the adoption of the Declaration of Independence on July 4, 1776, declaring independence from the Kingdom of Great Britain. Independence Day is commonly associated with fireworks, parades, barbecues, carnivals, fairs, picnics, concerts, baseball games, family reunions, and political speeches and ceremonies, in addition to various other public and private events celebrating the history, government, and traditions of the United States.

独立日：美国的主要法定节日之一，日期为每年7月4日，以纪念1776年7月4日大陆会议在费城正式通过《独立宣言》。

Trivia 八卦一下

Costars Emma Stone and Bryce Dallas Howard have both played Gwen Stacy in a Spider-Man movie.

在影片中合作的艾玛·斯通和布莱丝·达拉斯·霍华德都在不同的"蜘蛛侠"电影中扮演过葛温·斯塔西（Gwen Stacy）这个角色。

The book store in the film, Avent & Clark Booksellers, was named after Avent Clark, a production assistant on the film from Greenwood, MS.

片中出现的Avent & Clark 书店是以来自密西西比州的助理制片人Avent Clark命名的。

Kathryn Stockett's book on which this film is based was rejected 60 times before it was eventually published.

本片改编自凯瑟琳·斯托科特的同名处女作。此小说在发表之前曾被出版商拒绝过60次。

Skeeter's bookshelf contains the following books: Ralph Ellison's *Invisible Man*, Harper Lee's *To Kill a Mockingbird*, and Margaret Mitchell's *Gone with the Wind*. All three of these books are discussed many times in the original novel.

斯基特的书架上摆着拉尔夫·埃里森的《隐形人》、哈珀·李的《杀死一只知更鸟》和玛格丽特·米切尔的《飘》。在小说原著中这三部著名的小说被多次提及。

Director Tate Taylor and the author of the book, Kathryn Stockett, were childhood friends in Jackson, Mississippi.
导演泰特·泰勒和小说作者凯瑟琳·斯托科特都来自密西西比州的杰克逊，并且两人从小一起长大。

Viola Davis appeared in two movies that were both nominated for the Best Picture Academy Award (Oscar) in 2012. Davis starred in both this movie and *Extremely Loud & Incredibly Close*. Jessica Chastain also appeared in two movies that were both nominated for the Best Picture Academy Award (Oscar) in 2012. Chastain also starred in both this movie and *The Tree of Life*.
维奥拉·戴维斯和杰西卡·查斯坦都同时在2012年两部奥斯卡最佳提名影片中扮演重要角色。

Part III. Extra Credit
美文品读

I Have a Dream
我有一个梦想
Martin Luther King, Jr. 马丁·路德·金

I am happy to join with you today in what will go down in history as the greatest demonstration for freedom in the history of our nation.

Five score years ago, a great American, in whose symbolic shadow we stand today, signed the Emancipation Proclamation. This momentous decree came as a great beacon light of hope to millions of Negro slaves, who had been seared in the flames of withering injustice. It came as a joyous daybreak to end the long night of their captivity.

But one hundred years later, the Negro still is not free. One hundred years later, the life of the Negro is still sadly crippled by the manacles of segregation and the chains of discrimination. One hundred years later, the Negro lives on a lonely island of poverty in the midst of a vast ocean of material prosperity. One hundred years later, the Negro is still languished in the corners of American society and finds himself an exile in his own land. And so we've come here today to dramatize a shameful condition.

In a sense we have come to our nation's capital to cash a check. When the architects of our republic wrote the magnificent words of the Constitution and the Declaration of Independence, they were signing a promissory note to which every American was to fall heir. This note was a promise that all men, yes, black men as well as white men, would be guaranteed the unalienable rights of life, liberty, and the pursuit of happiness. It is obvious today that America has defaulted on this promissory note, insofar as her citizens of color are concerned. Instead of honoring this sacred obligation, America has given the Negro people a bad check, a check which has come back marked "insufficient funds."

But we refuse to believe that the bank of justice is bankrupt. We refuse to believe that there are insufficient funds in the great vaults of opportunity of this nation. And so we have come to cash this check, a check that will give us upon demand the riches of freedom and the security of justice.

We have also come to this hallowed spot to remind America of the fierce urgency of Now. This is no time to engage in the luxury of cooling off or to take the tranquilizing drug of gradualism. Now is the time to make real the promises of democracy. Now is the time to rise from the dark and desolate valley of segregation to the sunlit path of racial justice. Now is the time to lift our nation from the quick sands of racial injustice to the solid rock of brotherhood. Now is the time to make justice a reality for all of God's children.

It would be fatal for the nation to overlook the urgency of the moment. This sweltering summer of the Negro's legitimate discontent will not pass until there is an invigorating autumn of freedom and equality. Nineteen sixty-three is not an end but a beginning. Those who hope that the Negro needed to blow off steam and will now be content will have a rude awakening if the nation returns to business as usual. There will be neither rest nor tranquility in America until the Negro is granted his citizenship rights. The whirlwinds of revolt will continue to shake the foundations of our nation until the bright day of justice emerges.

But there is something that I must say to my people who stand on the warm threshold which leads into the palace of justice. In the process of gaining our rightful place we must not be guilty of wrongful deeds. Let us not seek to satisfy our thirst for freedom by drinking from the cup of bitterness and hatred. We must ever conduct our struggle on the high plane of dignity and discipline. We must not allow our creative protest to degenerate into physical violence. Again and again we must rise to the majestic heights of meeting physical force with soul force.

The marvelous new militancy which has engulfed the Negro community must not lead us to a distrust of all white people, for many of our white brothers, as evidenced by their presence here today, have come to realize that their destiny is tied up with our destiny. And they have come to realize that their freedom is inextricably bound to our freedom. We cannot walk alone.

And as we walk, we must make the pledge that we shall always march ahead. We cannot turn back. There are those who are asking the devotees of civil rights, "When will you be satisfied?" We can never be satisfied as long as the Negro is the victim of the unspeakable horrors of police brutality. We can never be satisfied as long as our bodies, heavy with the fatigue of travel, cannot gain lodging in the motels of the highways and the hotels of the cities. We cannot be satisfied as long as a Negro in Mississippi cannot vote and a Negro in New York believes he has nothing for which to vote. No, no, we are not satisfied and we will not be satisfied until justice rolls down like waters and righteousness like a mighty stream.

I am not unmindful that some of you have come here out of great trials and tribulations. Some of you have come fresh from narrow jail cells. Some of you have come from areas where your quest for freedom left you battered by the storms of persecutions and staggered by the winds of police brutality. You have been the veterans of creative suffering. Continue to work with the faith that unearned suffering is redemptive. Go back to Mississippi, go back to Alabama, go back to South Carolina, go back to Georgia, go back to Louisiana, go back to the slums and ghettos of our northern cities, knowing that somehow this situation can and will be changed. Let us not wallow in the valley of despair, I say to you today, my friends. And so even though we face the difficulties of today and tomorrow, I still have a dream. It is a dream deeply rooted in the American dream.

I have a dream that one day this nation will rise up and live out the true meaning of its creed: We hold these truths to be self-evident that all men are created equal.

I have a dream that one day on the red hills of Georgia the sons of former slaves and the sons of former slave owners will be able to sit down together at the table of brotherhood.

I have a dream that one day even the state of Mississippi, a state sweltering with the heat of injustice, sweltering with the heat of oppression, will be transformed into an oasis of freedom and justice.

I have a dream that my four little children will one day live in a nation where they will not be judged by the color of their skin but by the content of their character. I have a dream today!

I have a dream that one day, down in Alabama, with its vicious racists, with its governor having his lips dripping with the words of interposition and nullification; one day right down in Alabama little black boys and black girls will be able to join hands with little white boys and white girls as sisters and brothers. I have a dream today!

I have a dream that one day every valley shall be exalted, and every hill and mountain shall be made low, the rough places will be made plain, and the crooked places will be made straight, and the glory of the Lord shall be revealed and all flesh shall see it together.

This is our hope. This is the faith that I will go back to the South with. With this faith we will be able to hew out of the mountain of despair a stone of hope. With this faith we will be able to transform the jangling discords of our nation into a beautiful symphony of brotherhood. With this faith we will be able to work together, to pray together, to struggle together, to go to jail together, to stand up for freedom together, knowing that we will be free one day. And this will be the day, this will be the day when all of God's children will be able to sing with new meaning, "My country 'tis of thee, sweet land of liberty, of thee I sing. Land where my fathers died, land of the Pilgrim's pride, from every mountainside, let freedom ring!" And if America is to be a great nation, this must become true.

And so let freedom ring – from the prodigious hilltops of New Hampshire.

Let freedom ring – from the mighty mountains of New York.

Let freedom ring – from the heightening Alleghenies of Pennsylvania.

Let freedom ring – from the snow-capped Rockies of Colorado.

Let freedom ring – from the curvaceous slopes of California.

But not only that.

Let freedom ring – from Stone Mountain of Georgia.

Let freedom ring – from Lookout Mountain of Tennessee.

Let freedom ring – from every hill and molehill of Mississippi,

from every mountainside, let freedom ring!

And when this happens, when we allow freedom to ring, when we let it ring from every village and every hamlet, from every state and every city, we will be able to speed up that day when all of God's children, black men and white men, Jews and Gentiles, Protestants and Catholics, will be able to join hands and sing in the words of the old Negro spiritual, "free at last, free at last."

Thank God Almighty, we are free at last.

Making Sense 解文说词

① Five score years ago, a great American, in whose symbolic shadow we stand today, signed the Emancipation Proclamation. (para. 1)

100年前，一位伟大的美国人签署了《解放黑奴宣言》，今天我们就是在他的象征性的影子之中。

② …the Negro lives on a lonely island of poverty in the midst of a vast ocean of material prosperity.. (para. 2)

这里的vast ocean和lonely island都是用比喻的手法衬托出了黑人在美国的生存状况。

③ This is no time to engage in the luxury of cooling off or to take the tranquilizing drug of gradualism. (para. 6)

再也没有时间允许我们慢条斯理地冷静下来，没有时间等待渐进主义的镇静剂发挥作用了。

④ We will not be satisfied until justice rolls down like waters and righteousness like a mighty stream. (para. 10)

在公平好像流水、正义好像激流一样滚滚而来之前，我们不会满足。

⑤ …the veterans of creative suffering (para. 11)

经历过创造性苦难的老斗士

⑥ We hold these truths to be self-evident that all men are created equal. (para. 12)

我们认为这些真理是不言而喻的：人人生而平等。

这是美国《独立宣言》中的最著名的一句话也是美国民主的信条。

⑦ …a state sweltering with the heat of injustice, sweltering with the heat of oppression, will be transformed into an oasis of freedom and justice.

……在不公平和压迫之下闷热不堪的沙漠之州，也会变成一个自由、公平的绿洲。

这里的heat和oasis还是用了比喻的手法揭示现状，期望未来。

⑧ …down in Alabama, with its vicious racists, with its governor having his lips dripping with the words of interposition and nullification.

……亚拉巴马州的州长还是满口反对、拒绝。

Background 文化大本营

Emancipation Proclamation: an order issued to all segments of the Executive branch (including the Army and Navy) of the United States by President Abraham Lincoln on January 1, 1863, during the American Civil War. It was based on the president's constitutional authority as commander in chief of the armed forces; it was not a law passed by Congress. It proclaimed all those enslaved in Confederate territory to be forever free, and ordered the Army (and all segments of the Executive branch) to treat as free all those enslaved in ten states that were still in rebellion, thus applying to 3.1 million of the 4 million slaves in the U.S.

《解放黑奴宣言》：一份由美国总统亚伯拉罕·林肯公布的宣言，主张所有美利坚邦联叛乱下的领土内的黑奴应享有自由，豁免的对象包含未脱离联邦的边境州，以及联邦掌控下的诸州。此宣言不仅立即解放了少部分奴隶，而且实质上强化联邦军掌控邦联的领土后这些黑奴自由的权威性，并为最终废除全美奴隶制度预先铺好了道路。

The Constitution of the United States: the supreme law of the United States of America. The first three Articles of the Constitution establish the rules and separate powers of the three branches of the federal government: a legislature, the bicameral Congress; an executive branch  led by the President; and a federal judiciary headed by the Supreme Court. The last four Articles frame the principle of federalism. The Tenth Amendment confirms its federal characteristics. The Constitution was adopted on September 17, 1787, by the Constitutional Convention in Philadelphia, Pennsylvania, and ratified by conventions in eleven states. It went into effect on March 4, 1789.

《美国宪法》：通称《美国联邦宪法》。它是美国的根本大法，奠定了美国政治制度的法律基础。《美国宪法》是世界上第一部成文宪法。1787年5月，美国各州（当时为13个）代表在费城（Philadelphia）召开制宪会议，同年9月15日制宪会议通过《美利坚合众国宪法》。1789年3月4日，该宪法正式生效。后来，《美国宪法》又附加了27条宪法修正案。

The American Dream: a national ethos of the United States, a set of ideals in which freedom includes the opportunity for prosperity and success, and an upward social mobility achieved through hard work. In the definition of the American Dream by James Truslow Adams in 1931, "life should be better and richer and fuller for everyone, with opportunity for each according to ability or achievement" regardless of social class or circumstances of birth

美国梦：自1776年以来，世世代代的美国人都深信不疑，只要经过努力不懈的奋斗便能获得更好的生活；也就是说人们必须通过自己的勤奋、勇气、创意和决心迈向繁荣，而非依赖于特定的社会阶级和他人的援助。

"My Country, 'Tis of Thee",: (also known as "America", is an American patriotic song. The song served as one of the de facto national anthems of the United States (along with songs like "Hail, Columbia") before the adoption of "The Star-Spangled Banner" as the official anthem in 1931.

《我的祖国，这是为了你》：这首歌曲也称为"America"，是美国的一首著名的爱国歌曲。在奥巴马2013年就职典礼上也曾由女歌手演唱此歌曲。在美国正式确认国歌前，它曾是默认的美国国歌。如果需要在中国找一个对等的例子，这首歌在美国的地位相当于《歌唱祖国》。

Pilgrim: a traveler (literally one who has come from afar) who is on a journey to a holy place. Since the first immigrants to the New Continent were 102 English Pilgrims who took the boat of *The Mayflower* in 1620, Americans often refer to themselves as the descendents of the pilgrims.

朝圣者（也叫香客）：由于1620年首批到达美洲大陆的英国移民是乘坐"五月花号"的102名英国香客，所以美国自称为"香客的国家"。

Alleghenies: part of the vast Appalachian Mountain Range of the eastern United States and Canada. It has a northeast-southwest orientation and runs for about 400 miles (640 km) from north-central Pennsylvania, through western Maryland and eastern West Virginia, to southwestern Virginia.

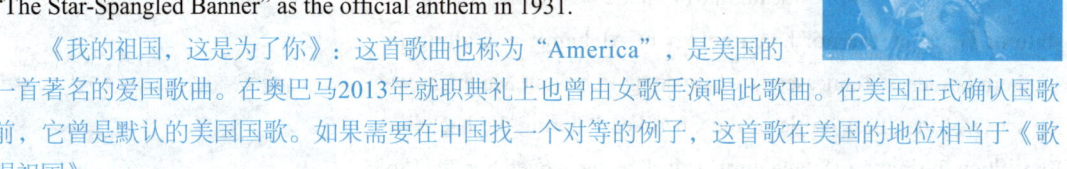

阿勒格尼山脉：北美阿巴拉契亚山系西北部的分支，延伸于美国宾夕法尼亚州、马里兰州、弗吉尼亚州和西弗吉尼亚州境内。它东侧隔着大谷地，与蓝岭山脉相平行，其连续不断的山峰海拔1000米左右，峻拔的东斜面称为"阿勒格尼峰"，陡落于大谷地中，是大西洋水系和墨西哥湾水系的分水岭，在开拓运动初期，它是向西移民的障碍。

The Rokies: known as the Rocky Mountains are a major mountain range in western North America. The Rocky Mountains stretch more than 3,000 miles (4,830 km) from the northernmost part of British Columbia, in western Canada, to New Mexico, in the southwestern United States.

落基山脉：美洲科迪勒拉山系在北美的主干，由许多小山脉组成，被称为北美洲的"脊骨"。从阿拉斯加到墨西哥，它南北纵贯4500多千米，广袤而缺乏植被，其名称源自印第安部落名。

Stone Mountain: a quartz monzonite dome monadnock in Stone Mountain, Georgia, United States. At its summit, the elevation is 1,686 feet (514 m) MSL and 825 feet (251 m) above the surrounding area. Stone Mountain is well-known not only for its geology, but also for the enormous bas-relief on its north face, the largest bas-relief in the world.

石头山：位于亚特兰大东郊，是一座天然花岗岩石山，也是亚特兰大市的著名景点之一。石头山享誉世界，号称"全世界八大奇景之一"的世界最大天然裸露花岗岩石。该山上有90英尺高、190英尺宽的巨大浮雕，上面雕刻着美国历史上三位南部邦联的著名人物：南部邦联总统杰弗逊·戴维斯、托玛斯·杰克逊将军和李将军。此雕像构思于1915年，历时55年的浩繁工程，在1970年被完整地展现于世人面前。

Lookout Mountain: located at the northwest corner of the US state of Georgia, the northeast corner of Alabama, and along the southern border of Tennessee at Chattanooga. Lookout Mountain was the scene of the "Last Battle of the Cherokees" during the Nickajack Expedition during the 18th century, as well as the November 24, 1863 Battle of Lookout Mountain during the American Civil War.

卢考特山：位于美国田纳西州，是阿帕拉契山脉的一部分。它是美国印第安人最后的战场，也是美国南北战争的重要战场之一。

South Carolina: a state in the Southeastern United States. It was the first of the 13 colonies that declared independence from the British Crown during the American Revolution. South Carolina is the 40th most extensive and the 24th most populous of the 50 United States. South Carolina comprises 46 counties. The capital and largest city of the state is Columbia.

南卡罗来纳州：美国东南部7州中的一个州，首府是哥伦比亚城。该州箴言为——"做好意志与策略的准备；当我活着时，我有信心"（"Prepared in mind and resources; While I breathe, I hope"．）。

Georgia: a state located in the southeastern United States. It was established in 1732, the last of the original Thirteen Colonies. Georgia is the 24th most extensive and the 8th most populous of the 50 United States. Georgia is known as the *Peach State and the Empire State of the South*. Atlanta is the state's capital and its most populous city.

佐治亚州：美国最南部诸州之一，名从英国国王乔治二世，为美国最初13州之一，别称有"桃州"、"南方帝国州"，其首府为亚特兰大。

Alabama: a southern US state, also called the Cotton State and the Heart of Dixie. The capital city is Montgomery and the largest city is Birmingham.

阿拉巴马州：美国南部一州，又被称为"棉花洲"和"美国南部各州的心脏"。阿拉巴马州名称来自印第安语，其意义为："披荆斩棘"（I clear the thicket），其州府是蒙哥马利，最大城市为伯明翰。

Tennessee: a US state located in the Southeastern United States. Tennessee has seen some of the nation's worst racial strife, from the formation of the Ku Klux Klan in Pulaski in 1866 to the assassination of Martin Luther King in Memphis in 1968. Tennessee has played a critical role in the development of many forms of American popular music, including rock and roll, blues, country, and rockabilly.

田纳西州：美国东南部的一个州，又称作"志愿者州"。田纳西州曾是美国种族歧视的灾难州，是3K党的所在地，马丁·路德·金正是在该州的孟菲斯被暗杀的。田纳西州又是美国乡村音乐、摇滚乐等的发源地。

New YorkL: a state in the Northeastern region of the United State，also nicknamed Empire State. New York is famous for New York City.

纽约州：美国东北部的一个州，是美国50州中最重要的一州，美国经济最发达的州之一，农业和制造业为该州的主要产业，别称"帝国州"。

Colorado: a western US state whose capital is Denver. It is popular with tourists and is famous for Aspen and other towns in the Rocky Mountains where people ski. The state's history includes the discovery of gold in 1858 and the cultural influences of Native Americans and Mexicans.

科罗拉多州：美国西部的一个州，首府为丹佛。该州深受旅游者喜欢，并因落基山脉的阿斯彭和其他城镇而著称。该州历史上曾发现黄金，文化受美洲印第安和墨西哥文化的影响。

 Writing Tips 写作秘笈

这是人类历史上著名的演讲之一。它之所以能够影响全世界，原因主要有二：一是内容丰富、思想深邃；二是它拥有诗一般的语言。作者马丁·路德·金就像一位修辞大师。整篇演讲，新颖贴切的比喻、气势磅礴的排比、反差强烈的对比、动人心魄的反复、恰到好处的引用，俯拾皆是。

Unit 9

Literature's marriage to movies: Yes, I do!
电影：文学经典的影像脚注

Part I. Get-go
给力起步

It's not always a novelist's dream to see their words come to life on the silver screen, but Hollywood inevitably takes a pass at any good book they can find. Literature is the art of the written word, and some of the best texts have also made some of the most successful movies. Take a look at 10 that made the grade both in print and at the box office.

> 文学作品从来都是电影人的灵感之源。无论是经典大作还是鲜为人知的铅字读物，好莱坞总能推陈出新地把纸质承载的震撼变成宽银幕的综合冲击。以下就是十部堪称典范的名著名片。

Out of Africa (1985)《走出非洲》

When Finecke decided to write her memoirs under the penname of Isak Dinesen, she probably didn't envision her life acted out by Academy Award-winning actress Meryl Streep or directed by Sydney Pollack. *Out of Africa*, originally penned in 1937, took home seven Academy Awards in 1985, including Best Picture, Director and Adapted Screenplay.

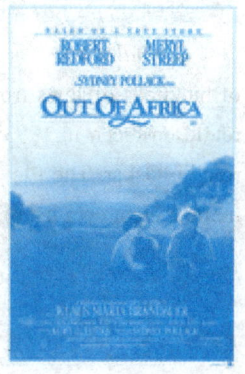

原著：《走出非洲》
作者：伊萨克·迪内森
电影导演：西德尼·波拉克
主演：梅丽尔·斯特里普、罗伯特·雷德福
经典台词：
Karen Blixen: I had a farm in Africa.
凯伦·布利森：我在非洲有一个农场。

当年，丹麦作家布利克森用笔名"迪内森"写出她的传奇自传体小说《走出非洲》时，她不曾预料到奥斯卡影后梅丽尔·斯特里普和导演西德尼·波拉克竟把它演绎成另外一个传奇：该片1985年荣获七项奥斯卡，包括最佳影片、最佳导演、最佳剧本改编奖等。

The Shawshank Redemption (1994)《肖申克的救赎》

The original work, a Stephen King novella, likely would have faded into obscurity had a movie of it never been made. The movie very nearly disappeared as well, making only $28 million at the box office despite a pair of releases. Critics, however, sang the praises of this prison drama starring Tim Robbins and Morgan Freeman, helping it to garner seven Oscar nominations. Alas, 1995 was Forrest Gump's year, and Shawshank won nothing. It was obscurity again, until the cable TV network TNT discovered it a couple years later and began airing it about once every two months, which its done ever since. Finally, a fine, inspirational film got the audience it deserved.

原著：《丽塔海华丝及肖申克监狱的救赎》收录于《不同的季节》
作者：斯蒂芬·金

电影导演：弗兰克·达拉邦特

主演：摩根·弗里曼、提姆·罗宾斯

经典台词：

Ellis Redding: I guess it comes down to a simple choice: get busy living or get busy dying.

雷德：生活可以归结为一种简单的选择：不是忙于真正的生活，就是一步步地走向死亡。

如果不是这部电影，也许斯蒂芬·金的这部不朽之作将永远鲜为人知。虽然当年"生不逢时"地碰上了"阿甘"，但是这部突破了牢狱类型片的希望之作，拍出了同类作品罕见的人情味和温馨感觉。时至今日，本片在国内外各大电影网站的电影排行中始终稳坐第一。

Schindler's List (1993)：《辛德勒的名单》

Schindler's Ark is the true story of industrialist Oskar Schindler's rescue of hundreds of Jews from the concentration camps of Germany. The story was retold onscreen in 1993 as *Schindler's List*, with Liam Nelson playing the lead role — Oskar. The film won seven Academy Awards, seven BAFTAs and rank number eight on a list of 100 best American films by the American Film Institute.

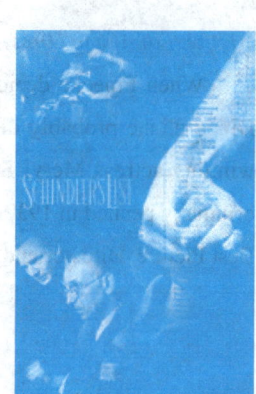

原著：《辛德勒方舟》

作者：托马斯·肯尼利

电影导演：史蒂文·斯皮尔伯格

主演：连姆·尼森

经典台词：

Schindler: Power is when we have every justification to kill, and we don't.

辛德勒：真正的权力是，我们有充足的理由去处死他，而我们却不去这样做。

澳大利亚作家托马斯·肯尼利讲述了一个人性的真实故事，大师斯皮尔伯格把它打造成磅礴的银幕史诗，七项奥斯卡奖的荣耀使其位列美国电影协会百部伟大影片的前十名之中。

To Kill a Mockingbird (1962) 《杀死一只知更鸟》

Published in 1960, this award-winning novel is loosely based on an incident that occurred in the author's hometown. In 1962, Gregory Peck brought the role of attorney-hero Atticus Finch to life in what would rank as the 25th Greatest American Movie of All-Time according to the American Film Institute.

原著：《杀死一只知更鸟》

作者：哈伯·李

电影导演：罗伯特·马利根

主演：格利高里·派克

经典台词：

Atticus Finch: You never really understand a person until you consider things from his point of view… until you climb inside of his skin and walk around in it.

艾蒂科斯·芬奇：除非你从别人的观点考虑问题——否则在你钻进别人的身体里四处游荡之前，你决不会真正了解他。

杀死一个没有犯罪的人就如同杀死了一只无辜的知更鸟，芬奇律师无疑是这场反种族歧视之战中的英雄。格利高里·派克用他自然、脱俗的演技将哈伯·李的普利策奖之作变成了一份珍贵的时代文物，为世人保存了希望与情感。

The English Patient (1996)《英国病人》

In adapting a book, by Michael Ondaatje, that was virtually impossible to imagine as a movie, filmmaker Anthony Minghella managed to win nine Academy Awards on 12 nominations, including Best Picture. Working closely with Ondaatje on the screenplay certainly helped. The editing is masterful, cutting between past and present storylines no less than 40 times without exhausting the audience. But most of all, Minghella showed a thorough understanding of the many shapes and colors love takes in the book, and effectively shared what he was able to comprehend with his cast. Every stage of the film's production was blessed and it shows a rare and remarkable feat.

原著：《英国病人》

作者：迈克尔·翁达杰

电影导演：安东尼·明格拉

主演：拉尔夫·费因斯、克里斯汀·斯科特·托马斯

经典台词：

Katharine：My darling, I am waiting for you. How long is a day in the dark? Or a week?

凯瑟琳：亲爱的，我在等你。不见天日的一天会有多长？一周吗？

若是将加拿大作家翁达杰的时空交错小说改变成电影，其本身就是一大挑战，安东尼·明格拉做到了，并且把现实与回忆融合成一幅绚丽的历史画卷，既气势磅礴又细腻动人。更让人赞叹的是本片获得奥斯卡最佳影片、最佳导演、最佳女配角、最佳摄影、最佳剪辑、最佳电影配乐、最佳音乐、最佳美术指导、最佳服装设计9项大奖。

Gone with the Wind (1939)《乱世佳人》

Gone with the Wind is an epic romance novel set in Georgia during the Civil War. The film garnered 10 Academy Awards and made number four on the America Film Institute's Top 100 American Films. The original celluloid is preserved in the archives of the National Film Registry. You may not give a damn, but *Gone with the Wind* was also one of the first films shot in Technicolor.

原著：《乱世佳人》

作者：玛格丽特·米切尔

电影导演：维克多·弗莱明

主演：费雯丽、克拉克·盖博

经典台词：

Scarlett O'Hara: Tomorrow is another day.

郝思嘉：明天又是新的一天。

玛格丽特·米切尔的浪漫史诗小说一经搬上银幕就成为影史上永远的经典，荣得10项奥斯卡大奖。当年的原版胶片被永久保存在美国国家电影登记局的档案馆中。你也许从没注意到，它还是世界上第一部彩色电影。

The Godfather (1972)《教父》

This novel published in 1969 covers the life and times of mob boss Vito Corleone and his family. The movie, directed by Francis Ford Coppola, starred prominent names such as Marlon Brando and Al Pacino as main characters. *The Godfather* won three Academy Awards including Best Picture and Writing. It was also followed by two equally successful sequels.

原著：《教父》

作者：马里奥·普佐

电影导演：弗朗西斯·福特·科波拉

主演：马龙·白兰度、阿尔·帕西诺

经典台词：

Vito Corleone: I'm gonna make him an offer he can't refuse.

维托·柯里昂：我准备向他提出一个他不可能拒绝的条件。

如果没有科波拉的电影《教父》，马里奥·普佐的小说不会再被人提起。这是一部众口称赞的超级经典，是反映美国文化的代表作之一。除了奥斯卡最佳影片、最佳改编剧本和最佳男主角奖之外，本片还摘得五项金球奖和一项格莱美奖。1990年，美国国会图书馆将本片列入国家电影目录。唐·维托道出的"我会给他提出一个他不会拒绝的条件"在美国电影学会评选的"电影百年百佳台词"排行榜上位居第二位。《教父》不但在评论、艺术和票房上取得了全胜，而且还为后人树立了典范。

The Wonderful Wizard of OZ (1939)《绿野仙踪》

The book was first published as part of a series in 1900 and the film version was initially a box office failure. *The Wizard of OZ* would wait years to get the public accolades it deserved. Today, this film starring Judy Garland is listed by the Library of Congress as the most watched movie of all time.

原著：《奥兹国的魔法师》

作者：弗兰克·鲍姆

电影导演：维克多·弗莱明

主演：朱迪·嘉兰

经典台词：

Dorothy: "Toto, I've got a feeling we're not in Kansas anymore."

桃乐丝：托托，我想我们再也回不去堪萨斯了。

《OZ国经典童话》是美国作家弗兰克·鲍姆(Frank Baum)在1900—1920年期间陆续创作发表的奇幻冒险童话故事集，是美国儿童文学协会(CLA)评选的"十部美国最伟大的儿童文学作品"之一，也是美国全国教育协会(NEA)推荐的"最佳童书之一"。1939年，导演维克多·弗莱明一年拍了两部经久不衰的电影，《绿野仙踪》和《乱世佳人》。美国国会图书馆将这两部电影都列为史上最受欢迎的电影之作。

The Lord of the Rings Trilogy (2001, 2002, 2003)《魔戒三部曲》

Director Peter Jackson brought the epic fantasy world of Tolkien alive not once, but three times. *The Fellowship of the Ring* and its two subsequent sequels followed the travels of the hobbit Frodo Baggins as he trekked across Middle-Earth trying to rid himself of the ring that threatened to possess his body and soul. Tolkien spent more than 10 years writing the story that has now sold over 150 million copies worldwide.

原著：《指环王》

作者：约翰·罗纳德·鲁埃尔·托尔金

电影导演：彼得·杰克逊

主演：伊利亚·伍德

经典台词：

Galadriel: The world is changed. I feel it in the water, I feel it in the earth, I smell it in the air.

盖拉德丽尔：世界发生了变化。我在水中能感觉到，我在地上能看到，我在空中能嗅到。

彼得·杰克逊将英国作家约翰·罗纳德·鲁埃尔·托尔金的史诗奇幻小说成功地搬上了银幕，而且不是一次，是三次。《魔戒三部曲》被视为最宏大的电影之一，名列许多"十大"电影名单中。2007年，《今日美国》认为《魔戒三部曲》是25年来最重要的电影。三部电影分别名列最高电影票房收入的第27位、第20位及第6位。它们在30项奥斯卡金像奖提名里赢得了17项，而该系列的终结片《王者归来》则获得十一项奥斯卡奖，成为继《泰坦尼克》和《宾虚》外，第三部获得十一项奥斯卡大奖的电影。

Harry Potter (2001,2002,2004,2005,2007,2009,2010,2011)《哈利波特系列》

In seven fantasy novels, Rowling chronicled the adventures of Harry Potter and his friends at the Hogwarts School of Witchcraft and Wizardry. Warner Bros took the stories of J.K. Rowling and turned them into a franchise of eight films that made them over seven billion dollars at the box office. In 2011, the author, directors and stars of the Harry Potter films collectively accepted the Michael Balcon Award for Outstanding British Contribution to Cinema for the film series.

原著：《哈利波特》

作者：J.K.罗琳

电影导演：克里斯·哥伦布，大卫·耶茨 等

主演：丹尼尔·雷德克里夫

经典台词：

Prof. McGonagall: This boy will be famous. There won't be a child in our world who doesn't know his name.

麦格教授：这个孩子会非常有名，我们世界里的每一个人都会知道他的名字。

英国女作家J.K.罗琳的七部系列小说《哈利·波特》位列史上非宗教、市场销售类图书首位。此系列分别被不同的导演拍成了八部电影，风靡全世界。哈利·波特这个人物惊诧了文学和电影江湖，让数不清的读者和观众为之倾倒，这不得不说是文学史上和电影史上的一个奇迹。《哈利·波特》系列电影的原作者、导演和演员荣获2011年英国影艺学院奖的"英国杰出电影贡献奖"（迈克尔巴尔康奖）。

Part II. cineWatch
光影星荟萃

Gone With The Wind 《乱世佳人》

史诗般的爱情，经典中的经典……

This story happened during the American Civil War. Hot-tempered, self-centered, part-Irish Southern beauty Scarlett O'Hara loves the gentleman Ashley Wilkes. Smug, rebellious, honest blockade-running profiteer Rhett Butler loves Scarlett. Ashley, who is also in love with Scarlett, marries his genteel cousin Melanie because he believes that their quiet similarities will create a better marriage than Scarlett's passion. Meanwhile, sparks fly between Rhett and Scarlett at their first encounter and continue throughout Scarlett's first two marriages. Scarlett and Rhett finally wed. but things go sour and really tank when their daughter is killed in a riding accident. After Melanie dies while giving birth, Scarlett thinks Ashley might finally be hers — but she learns quickly she's been deluding herself all this time. She tries to reconcile with Rhett, but it's too late. Rhett leaves, and Scarlett is now alone, with only one thing to keep her going: her family plantation —Tara.

美国南北战争前夕，南方农场塔拉庄园的千金郝思嘉（费•雯丽Vivien Leigh 饰）爱上了另一个农场主的儿子艾希礼（李斯利•霍华德 Leslie Howard饰），但遭到了拒绝。为了报复，她嫁给了自己不爱的男人，艾希礼妻子梅兰妮（奥莉薇•黛•哈佛兰Olivia de Havilland 饰）的弟弟查尔斯。战争期间，郝思嘉成为寡妇，失去母亲，挑起生活的重担，不再是当初的千金小姐；战争结束后，她又两度为人妻，嫁给了爱她多年的投机商人白瑞德（克拉克•盖博 Clark Gable 饰）。然而，纵使经历了生活的艰苦，郝思嘉对艾希礼的感情仍然没有改变。艾希礼妻子梅兰妮的去世，给了郝思嘉一个机会，一边是深爱自己的丈夫白瑞德，一边是心中惦念多年的艾希礼，郝思嘉会何去何从？会给自己怎样一个不一样的明天？

⭐ Cast 星光闪烁

George Cukor ... Director   奥斯卡最佳导演奖、终身成就奖

Clark Gable ... Rhett Butler   奥斯卡最佳男主角

 Vivien Leigh ... Scarlett O'Hara   奥斯卡影后、金球奖提名

 Memorable quotes 余音绕梁

Rhett Butler: I'm not asking you to forgive me. I'll never understand or forgive myself. And if a bullet gets me, so help me, I'll laugh at myself for being an idiot. There's one thing I do know… and that is that I love you, Scarlett. In spite of you and me and the whole silly world going to pieces around us, I love you, because we're alike.

Rhett Butler: Scarlett! Look at me! I've love you more than I've ever loved any woman and I've waited for you longer than I've ever waited for any woman.

Rhett Butler: Here's a soldier of the South who loves you, Scarlett. Wants to feel your arms around him, wants to carry the memory of your kisses into battle with him. Never mind about loving me, you're a woman sending a soldier to his death with a beautiful memory. Scarlett! Kiss me! Kiss me... once...

Scarlett: Oh, no! No, you're wrong, terribly wrong! I don't want a divorce. Oh Rhett, but I knew tonight, when I… when I knew I loved you, I ran home to tell you, oh darling, darling!

Scarlett: I wanted you. I wanted you desperately but I didn't think you wanted me.

Rhett Butler: It seems we've been at cross purposes, doesn't it? But it's no use now. As long as there was Bonnie, there was a chance that we might be happy. I liked to think that Bonnie was you, a little girl again, before the war, and poverty had done things to you. She was so like you, and I could pet her, and spoil her, as I wanted to spoil you. But when she went, she took everything.

Rhett Butler: My darling, you're such a child. You think that by saying, "I'm sorry," all the past can be corrected. Here, take my handkerchief. Never, at any crisis of your life, have I known you to have a handkerchief.

Rhett Butler: No. I'm through with everything here. I want peace… I want to see if somewhere there isn't something left in life of charm and grace… Do you know what I'm talking about?

Scarlett: As God is my witness, as God is my witness they're not going to lick me. I'm going to live through this and when it's all over, I'll never be hungry again. No, nor any of my folk. If I have to lie, steal, cheat or kill. As God is my witness, I'll never be hungry again.

Scarlett: I can't let him go! I can't! I won't think about losing him now! I'll go crazy if I do!… I'll think about that tomorrow… After all, tomorrow is another day!

Scarlett: Tara! Home. I'll go home. And I'll think of some way to get him back. After all… tomorrow is another day.

Culture inside 文化反光镜

General Sherman (1820 – 1891)(William Tecumseh Sherman): a US military leader during the Civil War. General Sherman commanded the US Army in the West. He is best remembered for his march through Georgia with 60,000 soldiers, destroying anything that might be useful to the South in the war. After the war, in 1879, he made his famous statement that "War is Hell."

威廉·特库姆塞·舍曼（又译谢尔曼）：美国南北战争时期的军事将领。舍曼将军指挥西部地区的美国军队。他最出名的战役是统领6万士兵行军通过佐治亚州时摧毁了任何可能在战争中对南方有用的东西。战后，他发表了著名的言论"战争是灾难。"

Bull Run: The first Battle of Manassas (the first Bull Run Battle) occurred on July 21, 1861 near Manassas in Virginia and the Bull Run River. It is the first important battle of the Civil War. The South Army acted so fast that broke the Yankee army's plan of capturing Richmond. The North Army, with Commander Owen McDowell, is about 28,000; And the South Army has Pierre Bray Gardner and Joseph Johnston as its officers as well as more than 30,000 soldiers. Failed in the first Battle of Manassas, the North Army stopped underestimating the enemy and began to prepare for a long and arduous full-scale war.

第一次马纳沙斯之役(第一次牛奔河之役，第一次布尔渊战役)：该战役于1861年7月21日发生在维吉尼亚的马纳沙斯和牛奔河附近，是南北战争中的第一场重要战役。南军表现优异，打破了北军进攻里士满的计划。北军军官为欧文·麦克道尔，士兵人数约为28,000；南军则由皮埃尔·博雷加德和约瑟夫·约翰斯顿率领，士兵人数超过30,000。

Second battle of Manassas (known as the second Bull Run Battle): broken out on the 29th and 30th of August, 1862. The victory of this battle inspired the South to invade to the north and led in the Maryland Campaign.

第二次马纳沙斯之役(又名第二次牛奔河之役)：爆发于1862年8月29日及30日，此战役的胜利鼓舞南军主动向北方发动侵略，不久便展开马里兰会战。

The United States Military Academy: at West Point always referred as West Point Military School. West Point Military School, the first military school of United States, located in the west bank of Hudson River about 80 km from New York city. "Duty, Honor, Country" is well known as its motto and the school is one of the oldest American military academy. With the British Royal Military College, Sandhurst Russian Frunze military academy and the French Saint-Cyr military academy, it is called "the four major world".

美国西点军事学院：常被称为"西点军校"，是美国第一所军事学校，位于纽约州西点（哈德逊河西岸），距离纽约市约80公里。学校占地1万6千英亩（约6千5百公亩）。西点军校的校训是"责任、荣誉、国家"，该校是美国历史最悠久的军事学院之一。它曾与英国桑赫斯特皇家军事学院、俄罗斯伏龙芝军事学院以及法国圣西尔军校并称世界"四大军校"。

General Lee (1807–1870)(Robert Edward Lee): the leader of the armies of the Confederate States during the American Civil War. He was respected for his honour and kindness. General Lee won many battles against the larger Union armies, but lost at Gettysburg, however. After the war, he became President of Washington College, later named Washington and Lee College.

罗伯特·爱德华·李：美国职业军人，著名军事家，为南北战争期间南方邦联最出色的将军，曾在1859年平息了约翰·布朗的骚乱。在美国南北战争中，他是美国南方邦联的总司令。南北战争后，他积极从事教育事业，任华盛顿大学的校长。

Spotsylvania: a small town which lies in the central area of Virginia. As there was once a war , it can also refer to this battle. The battle was broken on 8th of May and is the second land campaign declared by General Grant. There are over 150,000 American soldiers who took part in this war and about 30,000 were dead or wounded.

史波特斯凡尼亚郡府之役：又名史波特斯凡尼亚之役，爆发于1864年5月8日至5月21日，是格兰特将军上任东部战场的总司令后发动的陆路会战的第二场战役，参与的兵士达15万，死伤者约30000人。史波特斯凡尼亚是位于维吉尼亚州中部的一个小城镇。

Yankee: the term Yankee (sometimes shortened to Yank) has several interrelated meanings, referring to people from the United States. Within the US it refers to people originating in the northeastern US, or still more narrowly New England, where application of the term is largely restricted to the descendants of colonial English settlers in the region.

美国公民，美国佬：主要是指美国北方诸州的人，（美国南北战争时期）北军士兵，又或者仅指新英格兰地区的美国人，而在美国领土之外，常常用这个词来范指美国人。

Trivia 八卦一下

When Gary Cooper turned down the role for Rhett Butler, he was passionately against it. He is quoted saying both, "*Gone with the Wind* is going to be the biggest flop in Hollywood history," and, "I'm just glad it'll be Clark Gable who's falling on his face and not Gary Cooper."

加里·库柏拒绝扮演片中的巴特勒（白瑞德），而且十分反感本片。

The movie ranked 4 on the American Film Institute's list of the 10 greatest films in the genre "Epic".

本片在1998年美国电影协会评选的"20世纪最伟大100部电影"中排名第四。

The movie's line "Frankly, my dear, I don't give a damn." was voted as the first movie quote by the American Film Institute (out of 100).

克拉克·盖伯的台词"Frankly, my dear, I don't give a damn"在美国电影协会评选的"百佳电影台词"排行榜上名列榜首。

For the premiere in Atlanta in December 15, 1939, the governor declared a state holiday. Ticket prices for the premiere were 40 times the usual going rate.

影片在亚特兰大的首映日期是1939年12月15日。州政府宣告当日全州放假，而影片的票价是平时的40倍。

First color film to win the Best Picture Oscar.

本电影拍摄中使用了特艺七彩技术，赢得了此类彩色电影中的第一个奥斯卡最佳摄影奖。

There are more than 50 speaking roles and 2,400 extras in the film.

片中有台词的演员超过50名，临时演员多达2400名。

The first rough cut in July 1939 ran four and a half hours — 48 minutes longer than the final release.

影片的初剪版本长4个半小时，比上映版本长48分钟。

Vivien Leigh worked for 125 days and received about $25,000. Clark Gable worked for 71 days and received over $120,000.

费雯·丽共工作了125天，片酬为25000美元；克拉克·盖伯只工作了71天，片酬高达12万美元。

Hattie McDaniel became the first African-American to be nominated for, and win, an Academy Award.

海蒂·麦克丹尼尔凭借本片成为第一位获奥斯卡提名的非裔美国人。

If box office receipts for the movie were adjusted for inflation, it would be the top grossing movie of all time; Star Wars would only be the second most successful movie of all time. According to the Guinness World Records homepage the total gross in 2005 figures would be $3,785,107,801.

在商业上，本片是美国史上售出票数最多者。有许多研究指出如在计算中考虑通货膨胀的话，这是美国史上票房最高的电影。

Part III. Extra Credit
美文品读

When the ordinary becomes universal
当平凡成为真理

When she wrote the line "It is a truth universally acknowledged that a single man in possession of a good fortune must be in want of a wife", Jane Austen could scarcely have imagined that two hundred years later her novel would be adapted for a Bollywood film in India. But why is *Pride and Prejudice* so enduringly popular?

Austen wasn't always such a big hit. The 19th century novelist Mark Twain thought her work was "unreadable". Victorian readers preferred Charles Dickens and George Eliot with their panoramic views of English society. Authors like Leo Tolstoy tried to depict the whole range of human life in their works.

Austen was, and still is, very different. Her work is not about the big picture, but focuses on a very small part of English life — the "drawing room" culture of rich families in the early 19th century. In this world, women's lives were controlled by men.

"Admiration, love and matrimony were, for many men, the sum total of a woman's life: they admired men, loved them, and then married them," wrote professors Sandra Gilbert and Susan Gubar in their critique *The Madwoman in the Attic*, published in 1979. "In all her novels Austen examines the female powerlessness."

Many academics believe that Austen's work, by describing injustice and sexism, helped with female empowerment. This is a key reason for the novel's popularity today.

Pride and Prejudice has been adapted a great deal for film and television. Movies like *Bridget Jones' Diary* took the novel's tensions and rewrote them for modern audiences. The 2004 Bollywood movie *Bride and Prejudice* transferred the cultural explorations of the novel into the complex marriage traditions of India. *Aisha* (2010), is a Hindi-language movie loosely based on Austen's novel *Emma*. The ease with which it fits into other cultures shows how the story, in some sense, is universal.

James Joyce, a 20th century novelist, once wrote, "It is in the local that we find the universal." The highly local world Austen creates reflects the limited lives of women at the time, but it's also home to some resonating universal truths.

American author Anna Quindlen wrote in an introduction to the novel, "*Pride and Prejudice* is also about that thing that all great novels consider, the search for self. And it is the first great novel to teach us that that search is as surely undertaken in the drawing room making small talk as in the pursuit of a great white whale or the public punishment of adultery. " The novel remains popular because it teaches us that the largest truths don't need a huge backdrop—they can be found in the most ordinary of places.

（From *21ˢᵗ Century* , Jan.16, 2013）

Making Sense 解文说词

① "It is a truth universally acknowledged that a single man in possession of a good fortune must be in want of a wife". (para. 1)

"凡是富有的单身汉，肯定需要一位夫人，这已经成了举世公认的真理。"

② The 19th century novelist Mark Twain thought her work was "unreadable". (para.2)

19世纪著名作家马克·吐温认为简·奥斯汀的作品简直不值得一读。他曾说："每次读《傲慢与偏见》，我都想把简·奥斯汀从坟墓里挖出来，然后用她的胫骨打她的头盖骨。"

③ Victorian readers preferred Charles Dickens and George Eliot with their panoramic views of English society. (Para.2)

在英国维多利亚时期，读者们更偏爱查尔斯·狄更斯和乔治·艾略特的作品，因为从中能了解到英国社会全貌。从勃朗特姐妹奔放地想象到盖斯凯尔忠实朴素的描摹，从狄更斯的夸张与象征到萨克雷、艾略特的心理分析，总之，从狄更斯到埃略特的一代小说家谱写了英国小说史上最辉煌的一页。

④ Her work is not about the big picture, but focuses on a very small part of English life - the "drawing room" culture of rich families in the early 19th century. In this world, women's lives were controlled by men. (Para.3)

简·奥斯汀的作品主要关注英国乡绅家庭女性的婚姻和生活,以女性特有的细致入微的观察力和活泼风趣的文字真实地描绘了她周围世界的小天地。而在这片小天地里,女性的生活往往是由男性来操控的。

⑤"Admiration, love and matrimony were, for many men, the sum total of a woman's life: they admired men, loved them, and then married them," wrote professors Sandra Gilbert and Susan Gubar in their critique *The Madwoman in the Attic*, published in 1979. In all her novels Austen examines the female powerlessness." (Para.4)

"对于大多数男性而言,钦美、爱慕和婚姻构成了女性的全部生活。"女权主义批评家桑德拉·吉尔伯特和苏珊·古芭在1979年出版的《阁楼里的疯女人》论著中曾这样写到。

Background 文化大本营

Jane Austen (1775 –1817): an English novelist whose works of romantic fiction, set among the landed gentry, earned her a place as one of the most widely read writers in English literature. Her realism and biting social commentary have gained her historical importance among scholars and critics.

简·奥斯汀:19世纪英国小说家,世界文学史上最具影响力的女性文学家之一,其最著名的作品是《傲慢与偏见》和《理智与情感》,以细致入微的观察和活泼风趣的文字著称。她的作品主要关注乡绅家庭女性的婚姻和生活,以女性特有的细致入微的观察力和活泼风趣的文字真实地描绘了她周围世界的小天地。

Bollywood: the informal term popularly used for the Hindi-language film industry based in Mumbai, India. The term is often incorrectly used to refer to the whole of Indian cinema; however, it is only a part of the total Indian film industry, which includes other production centres producing films in multiple languages. Bollywood is the largest film producer in India and one of the largest centres of film production in the world.

宝莱坞:对位于印度孟买电影基地的印地语电影产业的别称,和印度其他几个主要影视基地一起构成了印度的庞大电影业,每年出产的电影数量和售出的电影票数量居全世界第一。"Bollywood(宝莱坞)"这个词是由"Bombay(孟买)"和美国电影产业中心"Hollywood"这两个词组合而成的。影城以印度电影之父巴尔吉的名字命名。宝莱坞对印度以至整个印度次大陆、中东以及非洲和东南亚一部分流行文化都有重要的影响,并通过南亚的移民输出传播到整个世界。

Pride and Prejudice: a novel by Jane Austen, first published in 1813. The story follows the main character Elizabeth Bennet as she deals with issues of manners, upbringing, morality, education, and marriage in the society of the landed gentry of early 19th century England. Though the story is set at the turn of the 19th century, it retains a fascination for modern readers, continuing near the top of lists of "most loved books" such as The Big Read. It has become one of the most popular novels in English literature and receives considerable attention from literary scholars. Modern interest in the book has resulted in a number of dramatic adaptations and an abundance of novels and stories imitating Austen's memorable characters or themes. To date, the book has sold some 20 million copies worldwide.

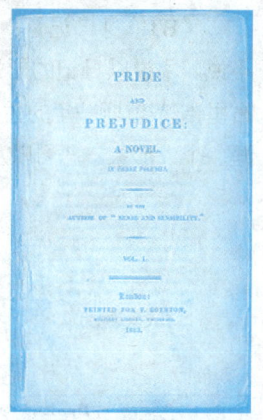

《傲慢与偏见》：世界文学名著之一，19世纪英国小说家简·奥斯丁最著名的小说。核心主题是围绕着18世纪末19世纪初，英国地主乡绅贵族的情感和婚姻问题。简·奥斯丁1796年至1797年间写成此著，写作地点都是在英国汉普郡的史蒂文顿。1811年，奥斯汀校正，原书名叫《第一印象》，不过后来改名为《傲慢与偏见》。1813年，由白丘的军方图书馆出版社的艾格顿先生出版。此出版社在1811年出版了简·奥斯丁的著名小说《理智与情感》，口碑不错，因此决定出版《傲慢与偏见》。

George Eliot (1819–1880): an English novelist, journalist and translator, and one of the leading writers of the Victorian Period. She is the author of seven novels, including Adam Bede (1859), The Mill on the Floss (1860), Silas Marner (1861), Middlemarch (1871–1872), and Daniel Deronda (1876), most of them set in provincial England and known for their realism and psychological insight.

乔治·艾略特：英国小说家，与狄更斯和萨克雷齐名，其主要作品有《弗洛斯河上的磨坊》、《米德尔马契》等。

Leo Tolstoy: a Russian writer who primarily wrote novels and short stories. Later in life, he also wrote plays and essays. Tolstoy is equally known for his complicated and paradoxical persona and for his extreme moralistic and ascetic views, which he adopted after a moral crisis and spiritual awakening in the 1870s, after which he also became noted as a moral thinker and social reformer.

列夫·托尔斯泰：俄国小说家、评论家、剧作家和哲学家，同时也是非暴力的基督教无政府主义者和教育改革家。托尔斯泰著有《战争与和平》、《安娜·卡列尼娜》和《复活》这几部被视作经典的长篇小说，被认为是世界最伟大的作家之一。

The Madwoman in the Attic: published in 1979, examines Victorian literature from a feminist perspective. Authors Sandra Gilbert and Susan Gubar draw their title from Charlotte Bronte's Jane Eyre, in which Rochester's wife Bertha Mason is kept locked in the attic by her husband.

《阁楼里的疯女人》：由桑德拉·吉尔伯与苏珊·古芭合著。探讨女作家笔下的女性人物，并挖掘遭受传统文学史忽略的女作家和作品，以期建构女性文学史。书名取自《简·爱》中被男主人公锁在阁楼上的疯女人。

Bridget Jones' Diary: a 2001 British romantic comedy film based on Helen Fielding's novel of the same name which is a reinterpretation of Austen's *Pride and Prejudice*. The adaptation stars Renée Zellweger as Bridget, Hugh Grant as the caddish Daniel Cleaver and Colin Firth as Bridget's "true love", Mark Darcy. *A sequel, Bridget Jones: The Edge of Reason*, was released in 2004.

《BJ单身日记》：英国女作家海伦·菲尔丁在1996年发行的一部畅销小说。小说以日记的形式，描绘了一个30岁左右的伦敦单身职业女性——布里吉特·琼斯一年的生活。在日记中，她以幽默的口吻写出了她的职业生涯、个人形象、恶习以及她与家人、朋友的关系。

Bride and Prejudice: a Bollywood-style adaptation of Pride and Prejudice by Jane Austen， is a 2004 romantic musical film directed by Gurinder Chadha. It was well received by film critics.

《爱斗气爱上你》：2004年的印度喜剧歌舞片，由古林德·乍得哈导演。可以说它是一部爱情歌舞片，也是1813年简·奥斯汀的小说《傲慢与偏见》的歌舞杂烩版。

Aisha: a 2010 Hindi romantic comedy film directed by Rajshree Ojha, starring Sonam Kapoor and Abhay Deol . The movie is a modern day adaptation of the 1815 British novel, *Emma* by Jane Austen, a "comedy of manners" set in the upper class society of Delhi, India.

《爱莎》：这部印度浪漫喜剧电影，改编自1815年简·奥斯汀的小说《爱玛》。该片于2010年8月6日放映，虽然广受好评，但票房不佳。

Emma: a novel by Jane Austen, about youthful hubris and the perils of misconstrued romance. The novel was first published in December 1815. As in her other novels, Austen explores the concerns and difficulties of genteel women living in Georgian-Regency England; she also creates a lively comedy of manners among her characters.

《爱玛》：英国小说家简·奥斯丁的喜剧小说，1816年出版，是奥斯丁最受欢迎、评价最高的小说之一。

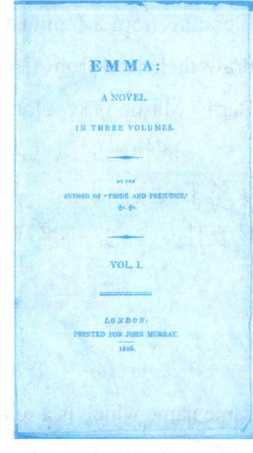

James Joyce (1882–1941): an Irish novelist and poet, considered to be one of the most influential writers in the modernist avant-garde of the early 20th century. Joyce is best known for *Ulysses* (1922), a landmark work in which the episodes of Homer's *Odyssey* are paralleled in an array of contrasting literary styles, perhaps most prominent among these the stream of consciousness technique he perfected. Other major works are the short-story collection *Dubliners* (1914), and the novels *A Portrait of the Artist as a Young Man* (1916) and *Finnegans Wake* (1939).

詹姆斯·乔伊斯：爱尔兰作家和诗人，20世纪最重要的作家之一，代表作包括短篇小说集《都柏林人》（1914）、长篇小说《一个青年艺术家的画像》（1916）、《尤利西斯》（1922）以及《芬尼根的苏醒》（1939）。乔伊斯的著作几乎穷尽了20世纪所有的小说表现艺术。他不断拓宽小说创作的实验领地，开创全新的文学模式，为现代小说艺术形式的探索做出了极大的贡献。

Anna Quindlen (1952 –): an American author, journalist, and opinion columnist whose New York Times column, Public and Private, won the Pulitzer Prize for Commentary in 1992.

安娜·昆德兰：《纽约时报》著名专栏作家、记者和小说家，普利策评论奖得主。

Writing Tips 写作秘笈

一篇好的文章开头的段落要引人入胜，要能够激起读者对本文内容的兴趣或好奇心，同时提供必要的背景知识。本文作者以引用简·奥斯丁小说《傲慢与偏见》中的第一句话开始了全篇叙述。文章的开头并非千篇一律，写作时可学习本文作者使用引言。除此之外，还可使用如下方法：使用问句，使用定义，叙述事件发生的时间与地点，使用统计数字，提供有关的背景资料，也可使用对话或讲述一件奇闻轶事。

Unit 10

Not of an Age, but All Time
一路光芒：英雄与时间同在

Part I. Get-go
给力起步

The most renowned magazine *The Atlantic* released "The 100 most influential Americans". They are the people who inspire us, entertain us, challenge us and change our world. They are listed belew.

> 2006 年，美国知名杂志《大西洋月刊》邀请 10 名著名的历史学家（其中四位普利策奖获得者），评出他们心目中对美国历史影响最大的一百名美国人。结果，美国前总统林肯名列第一。

Abraham Lincoln

He saved the Union, freed the slaves, and presided over America's second founding.

> 亚伯拉罕·林肯：他拯救了联邦，解放了黑奴，第二次缔造了美利坚合众国。

George Washington

He made the United States possible—not only by defeating a king, but by declining to become one himself.

> 乔治·华盛顿：有了他人类历史上才有了一个美利坚合众国，他不仅打败了强大的英王，更重要的是他拒绝成为另一个国王。

Thomas Jefferson

The author of the five most important words in American history: "All men are created equal."

> 托马斯·杰佛逊：他写下的五个字永远镌刻在美国的历史"人生来平等"。

Franklin Delano Roosevelt

He said, "The only thing we have to fear is fear itself," and then he proved it.

> 富兰克林·D·罗斯福：他说"我们唯一害怕的是害怕本身"，而正是他带领美国人战胜了自己的恐惧。

Alexander Hamilton

Soldier, banker and political scientist, he set in motion an agrarian nation's transformation into an industrial power.

> 亚历山大·汉密尔顿：他是士兵、银行家、政治家，他让一个农业的美国走上了工业之路。

Benjamin Franklin

The Founder-of-all-trades— scientist, printer, writer, diplomat, inventor, and more; like his country, he contained multitudes.

> 本杰明·富兰克林：他是个七十二行，行行精通的大家，他是科学家、印刷家、作家、外交家、发明家等。如同它的祖国，他擅长的领域包罗万象。

John Marshall

The defining chief justice, he established the Supreme Court as the equal of the other two federal branches.

> 约翰·马歇尔：他是举足轻重的大法官，他是美国最高法院的掌门人，他使最高法院成为与行政、立法并列的联邦三大权力之一。

Martin Luther King Jr.

His dream of racial equality is still elusive, but no one did more to make it real.

> 马丁·路德·金：他是最勇敢的追梦人，他的种族平等的梦想也许还没有完全实现，但是没有第二个人使这个梦想更接近现实。

Thomas Edison

It wasn't just the lightbulb; the Wizard of Menlo Park was the most prolific inventor in American history.

> 托马斯·爱迪生：他不仅仅发明了钨丝灯泡，更是门洛帕克（爱迪生的实验室）的奇才，美国历史上拥有最多专利的发明大王。

Woodrow Wilson

He made the world safe for U.S. interventionism, if not for democracy.

> 伍德罗·威尔逊：即便他不是为了民主，就是为了美国的干涉主义，他也使世界变得安全了。

John D. Rockefeller

The man behind Standard Oil set the mold for our tycoons—first by making money, then by giving it away.

> 约翰·D·洛克菲勒：美孚石油公司的掌门人，创立了一种富豪模式——先挣后捐。

Ulysses S. Grant

He was a poor president, but he was the general Lincoln needed; he also wrote the greatest political memoir in American history.

> 尤利西斯·S·格兰特：他是个平平的总统，但是他是林肯总统不可多得的常胜司令；他写的政治回忆录在美国历史上排名第一。

James Madison

He fathered the Constitution and wrote the *Bill of Rights*.

> 詹姆斯·麦迪逊：他是美利坚合众国宪法的制宪人，他是美国《民权法案》的执笔者。

Henry Ford

He gave us the assembly line and the Model T, and sparked America's love affair with the automobile.

> 亨利·福特：他是T型车和汽车装配线之父，他使美国人从此恋上了汽车。

Theodore Roosevelt

Whether busting trusts or building canals, he embodied the "strenuous life" and blazed a trail for twentieth-century America.

> 西奥多·罗斯福：无论是解散托拉斯还是开凿运河，他是美国活力的体现，是美国20世纪的领路人。

Mark Twain

Author of our national epic, he was the most unsentimental observer of our national life.

> 马克·吐温：美国国家史诗的作者，美国生活的冷静观察者。

Ronald Reagan

The amiable architect of both the conservative realignment and the Cold War's end.

> 罗纳德·里根：和蔼的设计大师，让保守重归，让冷战结束。

Andrew Jackson

The first great populist: he found America a republic and left it a democracy.

> 安德鲁·杰克逊：他是第一个伟大的平民总统，他把美利坚合众国带向了民主之路。

Thomas Paine

The voice of the American Revolution, and our first great radical.

> 托马斯·潘恩：美国革命之声，美国的第一个激进者。

Andrew Carnegie

The original self-made man forged America's industrial might and became one of the nation's greatest philanthropists.

> 安德鲁·卡耐基：这个白手起家的人缔造了美国的工业国力，又被称为美国最伟大的慈善家。

Harry Truman

An accidental president, this machine politician ushered in the Atomic Age and then the Cold War.

> 哈里·杜鲁门：一个偶然的总统，这个勤奋的政治家带领美国进入原子弹时代和冷战时代。

Walt Whitman

He sang of America and shaped the country's conception of itself.

> 瓦特·惠特曼：他歌颂美国，他塑造了一个国家意识。

Wright Brothers

They got us all off the ground.

> 莱特兄弟：他们带我们起飞。

Alexander Graham Bell

By inventing the telephone, he opened the age of telecommunications and shrank the world.

亚历山大·贝尔：他发明了电话，开创了一个电信新时代，他使世界变小。

John Adams

His leadership made the American Revolution possible; his devotion to republicanism made it succeed.

约翰·亚当斯：因为有了他的领导，美国革命才有可能；又因为有了他对共和的执着，美国革命才能成功。

Walt Disney

The quintessential entertainer-entrepreneur, he wielded unmatched influence over our childhood.

沃尔特·迪士尼：他是娱乐人和企业家的成功融合体，他对美国人童年的影响不可撼动。

Eli Whitney

His gin made cotton king and sustained an empire for slavery.

伊莱·惠特尼：他发明的轧花机使棉花大派用场，使南方蓄奴制经济更加巩固。

Dwight Eisenhower

He won a war and two elections, and made everybody like Ike.

德怀特·艾森豪威尔：他赢了一场大战和两次大选，他让所有人爱上了 Ike（艾森豪威尔的名字）。

Earl Warren

His Supreme Court transformed American society and bequeathed to us the culture wars.

> 厄尔·沃伦：他的最高法院改变了美国社会，也把文化战留给我们。

Elizabeth Cady Stanton

One of the first great American feminists, she fought for social reform and women's right to vote.

> 伊丽莎白·凯迪·斯坦顿：她是美国最早的一批女权主义积极分子，她全力争取社会改革，为美国妇女争取到了选举权。

Henry Clay

One of America's greatest legislators and orators, he forged compromises that held off civil war for decades.

> 亨利·克莱：美国最伟大的立法家和演讲家，他的调解使南北战争推后了几十年。

Albert Einstein

His greatest scientific work was done in Europe, but his humanity earned him undying fame in America.

> 阿尔伯特·爱因斯坦：他的伟大成就来自欧洲，他在美国留下不朽的盛名。

Ralph Waldo Emerson

The bard of individualism, he relied on himself—and told us all to do the same.

> 拉尔夫·瓦尔多·爱默生：他是个性主义的诗神，他自力更生，他也教我们这样做。

Jonas Salk

His vaccine for polio eradicated one of the world's worst plagues.

> 乔纳斯·萨尔克：他发明的小儿麻痹疫苗根除了世界上最严重的顽症。

Jackie Robinson

He broke baseball's color barrier and embodied integration's promise.

> 杰基·罗宾森：他打破了棒球界的肤色界限，他是种族融合的最好印证。

William Jennings Bryan

"The Great Commoner" lost three presidential elections, but his populism transformed the country.

> 威廉·詹宁斯·布赖恩：他是最伟大的平民领袖，他三次与总统宝座失之交臂，但是他的平民做派改变了一个国家。

J. P. Morgan

The great financier and banker was the prototype for all the Wall Street barons who followed.

> J. P. 摩根：伟大的金融家和银行家，他是华尔街的领路人。

Susan B. Anthony

She was the country's most eloquent voice for women's equality under the law.

> 苏珊.B.安东尼：她发出了这个国家最强悍的女权之声。

Rachel Carson

The author of *Silent Spring* was godmother to the environmental movement.

> 蕾切尔·卡尔森：《寂静的春天》的作者，环保运动的教母。

John Dewey

He sought to make the public school a training ground for democratic life.

> 约翰·杜威：他努力使公立学校成为民主的见证。

Harriet Beecher Stowe

Her *Uncle Tom's Cabin* inspired a generation of abolitionists and set the stage for civil war.

> 哈丽叶特·比切·斯托夫人：她的《汤姆叔叔的小屋》激励了一代废奴主义战士，也点燃了美国内战之火。

Eleanor Roosevelt

She used the first lady's office and the mass media to become "first lady of the world."

> 埃莉诺·罗斯福：她用第一夫人办公室和大众媒体创造了一个"全球的第一夫人。"

W. E. B. DuBois

One of America's great intellectuals, he made the "problem of the color line" his life's work.

> W.E.B. 杜波依斯：美国最伟大的学者之一，他把"肤色界限问题"当成自己毕生的工作。

Lyndon Baines Johnson

His brilliance gave us civil-rights laws; his stubbornness gave us Vietnam.

> 林登·贝恩斯·约翰逊：他的才华使我们享有民权法案；他的固执也把我们卷入越南。

Samuel F. B. Morse

Before the Internet, there was Morse code.

> 塞缪尔 F·B 摩斯：在互联网之前，我们的通信靠的全是摩斯电码。

William Lloyd Garrison

Through his newspaper, *The Liberator*, he became the voice of abolition.

> 威廉·劳埃德·加里森：他的报纸《解放者》是废奴主义的咽喉。

Frederick Douglass

After escaping from slavery, he pricked the nation's conscience with an eloquent accounting of its crimes.

> 弗雷德里克·道格拉斯：他逃出了奴役，他更是用自己超群的文笔控诉了蓄奴的罪恶，唤起了一个国家的良知。

Robert Oppenheimer

The father of the atomic bomb and the regretful midwife of the nuclear era.

> 罗伯特·奥本海默：原子弹之父，令人惋惜的核武器时代的"助产士"。

Frederick Law Olmsted

The genius behind New York's Central Park, he inspired the greening of America's cities.

弗雷德里克·劳·奥姆斯特德：天才的纽约中央公园景观大师，他推动了美国的城市绿化。

James K. Polk

This one-term president's Mexican War landgrab gave us California, Texas, and the Southwest.

詹姆斯·K·波尔克：虽说只当了一届总统，但是他在墨西哥战争中的夺地之举给美国领土增添了加利福尼亚州、得克萨斯州以及美国的西南部。

Margaret Sanger

The ardent champion of birth control—and of the sexual freedom that came with it.

玛格丽特·桑格：节育和性自由的英勇战士。

Joseph Smith

The founder of Mormonism, America's most famous homegrown faith.

约瑟夫·史密斯：美国土生土长的信仰——摩门教的创始人。

Oliver Wendell Holmes Jr.

Known as "The Great Dissenter," he wrote Supreme Court opinions that continue to shape American jurisprudence.

奥利弗·温德尔·霍姆斯："伟大的异议者"，他写的最高法院意见至今影响着美国的法学。

Bill Gates
The Rockefeller of the Information Age, in business and philanthropy alike.

> 比尔·盖茨：他是信息时代的洛克菲勒，无论是商业还是慈善。

John Quincy Adams
The Monroe Doctrine's real author, he set nineteenth-century America's diplomatic course.

> 约翰·昆西·亚当斯：他是"门罗宣言"的实际作者，是他奠定了美国19世纪的外交历程。

Horace Mann
His tireless advocacy of universal public schooling earned him the title "The Father of American Education."

> 霍瑞思·曼：他是"美国教育之父"，他毕生都在不知疲倦地倡导全面公立教育。

Robert E. Lee
He was a good general but a better symbol, embodying conciliation in defeat.

> 罗伯特·E·李：他是一个好司令，他更是一个战败后善于调整的好楷模。

John C. Calhoun
The voice of the antebellum South, he was slavery's most ardent defender.

> 约翰·凯尔宏：美国南北战争前南方的代言人，他是奴隶制的忠实捍卫者。

Louis Sullivan

The father of architectural modernism, he shaped the defining American building: the skyscraper.

路易斯·萨利文：现代建筑之父，他缔造了美国式的建筑——摩天大楼。

William Faulkner

The most gifted chronicler of America's tormented and fascinating South.

威廉·福克纳：他是迷人又让人痛苦的美国南方生活的天才记录者。

Samuel Gompers

The country's greatest labor organizer, he made the golden age of unions possible.

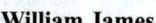

萨缪尔·龚帕斯：美国最伟大的劳工组织者，他开创了工会的黄金时代。

William James

The mind behind Pragmatism, America's most important philosophical school.

威廉·詹姆斯：美国本土最重要的哲学流派——实用主义哲学的创始者。

George Marshall

As a general, he organized the American effort in World War II; as a statesman, he rebuilt Western Europe.

乔治·马歇尔：作为将军，他是美国在第二次世界大战中的战略灵魂；作为政治家，他重新缔造了西欧。

Jane Addams
The founder of Hull House, she became the secular saint of social work.

简·亚当斯：霍尔馆的创始人，她是社会工作的现世圣人。

Henry David Thoreau
The original American dropout, he has inspired seekers of authenticity for 150 years.

亨利·戴维·梭罗：美国最早的循世者，150年来他激励人们追求真实。

Elvis Presley
The king of rock and roll. Enough said.

埃尔维斯·普里斯雷：猫王，摇滚之王。

P. T. Barnum
The circus impresario's taste for spectacle paved the way for blockbuster movies and reality TV.

P·T·巴纳姆：马戏团老板的创举奠定了大片和真人秀节目之路。

James D. Watson
He codiscovered DNA's double helix, revealing the code of life to scientists and entrepreneurs alike.

詹姆斯·D·沃森：他与人共同发现了DNA的双螺旋结构，给科学家也给企业家揭示了生命的密码。

James Gordon Bennett

As the founding publisher of *The New York Herald*, he invented the modern American newspaper.

> 詹姆斯·戈登·本纳特:《纽约先驱报》的创办者,美国现代报业的打造者。

Lewis and Clark

They went west to explore, and millions followed in their wake.

> 路易斯和克拉克:他们去西部拓荒,成千上万的人追随了他们的脚印。

Noah Webster

He didn't create American English, but his dictionary defined it.

> 诺亚·韦伯斯特:他没有发明美国英语,但他的韦氏字典给美国英语下了定义。

Sam Walton

He promised us "Every Day Low Prices", and we took him up on the offer.

> 山姆·沃尔顿:他承诺我们"天天低价",我们欣然接受。

Cyrus McCormick

His mechanical reaper spelled the end of traditional farming, and the beginning of industrial agriculture.

> 赛勒斯·麦考密克:他的机械收割机结束了传统的手工农业时代,开辟了工业化的农业时代。

George Herman "Babe" Ruth

He saved the national pastime in the wake of the Black Sox scandal—and permanently linked sports and celebrity.

> 乔治·赫曼·"贝比"·鲁斯：在棒球声势跌入"黑袜丑闻"的低谷时，他填补了美国人的娱乐空间，从此开创了体育界名人的先河。

Frank Lloyd Wright

America's most significant architect, he was the archetype of the visionary artist at odds with capitalism.

> 弗兰克·劳埃德·赖特：全美最出众的建筑师，他是与资本主义格格不入的视觉艺术家的典范。

Betty Friedan

She spoke to the discontent of housewives everywhere—and inspired a revolution in gender roles.

> 贝蒂·弗里丹：她和各地不满的家庭主妇交谈，激发了一场性别地位的革命。

John Brown

Whether a hero, a fanatic, or both, he provided the spark for the Civil War.

> 约翰·布朗：不论是英雄、狂热分子或两者兼而有之，他都为日后的内战埋下了一颗种子。

Louis Armstrong

His talent and charisma took jazz from the cathouses of Storyville to Broadway, television, and beyond.

> 路易斯·阿姆斯特朗：他的才华和魅力把爵士乐从新奥尔良的妓院带到了百老汇，带到了电视里以及更广阔的天地。

William Randolph Hearst
The press baron who perfected yellow journalism and helped start the Spanish-American War.

> 威廉·伦道夫·赫斯特：他是出版界巨头，他把耸人听闻的办报风格发挥得淋漓尽致，他也间接促成了美西战争的爆发。

Margaret Mead
With *Coming of Age in Samoa*, she made anthropology relevant—and controversial.

> 玛格丽特·米德：她的著作《萨摩亚人的成年》使人类学显出了它的意义，也引起了人们的争论。

George Horace Gallup
He asked Americans what they thought, and the politicians listened.

> 乔治·盖洛普：他询问美国人在想什么，政治家则倾听他的调查结果。

James Fenimore Cooper
The novels are unreadable, but he was the first great mythologizer of the frontier.

> 詹姆斯·费尼莫·库珀：他的小说虽然难懂，但他是第一个描写边疆的传奇作家。

Thurgood Marshall
As a lawyer and a Supreme Court justice, he was the legal architect of the civil-rights revolution.

> 瑟古德·马歇尔：作为律师和最高法院大法官，他是民权革命的法律推动者。

Ernest Hemingway

His spare style defined American modernism, and his life made machismo a cliché.

> 欧内斯特·海明威：他简洁的风格定义了美国的现代主义文学，生活中他依然是传统的大男子主义者。

Mary Baker Eddy

She got off her sickbed and founded Christian Science, which promised spiritual healing to all.

> 玛丽·贝克·埃迪：她离开病床，创建了基督教科学派，许诺说宗教信仰能治愈一切。

Benjamin Spock

With a single book—and a singular approach—he changed American parenting.

> 本杰明·斯伯克：用一本书和一种不寻常的方法，他改变了美国的育儿术。

Enrico Fermi

A giant of physics, he helped develop quantum theory and was instrumental in building the atomic bomb.

> 恩里科·费米：他是物理学巨人，他发展了量子理论，并在原子弹的制造中起了重要作用。

Walter Lippmann

The last man who could swing an election with a newspaper column.

> 沃尔特·李普曼：最后一个能用报纸专栏影响选举的人。

Jonathan Edwards

Forget the fire and brimstone: his subtle eloquence made him the country's most influential theologian.

> 乔纳森·爱德华兹：忘记地狱之火吧，他那了不起的口才使他成为这个国家最有影响力的神学家。

Lyman Beecher

Harriet Beecher Stowe's clergyman father earned fame as an abolitionist and an evangelist.

> 莱曼·比彻：哈丽特·比彻·斯托的牧师父亲，以废奴主义者和福音传教士而闻名。

John Steinbeck

As the creator of Tom Joad, he chronicled Depression-era misery.

> 约翰·斯坦贝克：作为汤姆·约德的创造者，他记录了大萧条中的苦难生活。

Nat Turner

He was the most successful rebel slave; his specter would stalk the white South for a century.

> 纳特·特纳：他是最成功的反叛的奴隶，他的幽灵在白人至上的南方徘徊了一个世纪。

George Eastman

The founder of Kodak democratized photography with his handy rolls of film.

> 乔治·伊斯曼：他是柯达的创始人，他用简单易用的胶卷使照相机在普通人中流行开来。

Sam Goldwyn

A producer for forty years, he was the first great Hollywood mogul.

塞缪尔·戈德温：有着40年制片生涯的他是第一个好莱坞巨头。

Ralph Nader

He made the cars we drive safer; thirty years later, he made George W. Bush the president.

拉尔夫·纳德：他使我们的汽车更安全。30年后，他"帮助"乔治·W·布什成为总统。

Stephen Foster

America's first great songwriter, he brought us "O! Susanna" and "My Old Kentucky Home."

史蒂芬·福斯特：美国第一个伟大的歌曲作家，他带给了我们《哦！苏珊娜》和《我的肯塔基老家》。

Booker T. Washington

As an educator and a champion of self-help, he tried to lead black America up from slavery.

布克·T·华盛顿：他是教师，同时作为自助的倡导者，他努力引领黑人挣脱奴役。

Richard Nixon

He broke the New Deal majority, and then broke his presidency on a scandal that still haunts America.

理查德·尼克松：他废除了自罗斯福总统以来实行的大多数新政，接着他用一个至今仍在美国人心中挥之不去的丑闻毁掉了自己的总统生涯。

Herman Melville

Moby Dick was a flop at the time, but Melville is remembered as the American Shakespeare.

> 赫尔曼·麦尔维尔:《白鲸》在当时是部失败之作,但麦尔维尔现在被认为是美国的莎士比亚。

 **NOTES**

The Atlantic Monthly: an American magazine founded in 1857 in Boston, Massachusetts. It was created as a literary and cultural commentary magazine. It quickly achieved a national reputation, which it has held for more than 150 years. It was important for recognizing and publishing new writers and poets, and encouraging major careers. It published leading writers' commentary on abolition, education, and other major issues in contemporary political affairs.

《大西洋月刊》:1857年11月,第一期《大西洋月刊》出版。它称自己为"一本有关文学、政治、科学与艺术的杂志"。它在创刊宣言中这样写道:"在政治领域,《大西洋月刊》将坚持无党派、无偏见原则,但不管如何,人们都将确信它是美国理想的代言人。《大西洋月刊》已经成为美国最受尊敬的杂志。

Union: during the American Civil War, the Union was a name used to refer to the federal government of the United States, which was supported by the 20 free states and five border slave states. It was opposed by 11 southern slave states that had declared a secession to join together to form the Confederacy. The Union has often been referred to as "the North", both then and now.

联邦:美国内战期间指美国联邦政府,或称北军,得到20个自由州和5个边界州的支持,与此同时南部11个奴隶州脱离联邦,成立邦联,而引起内战。此战不但改变当时美国的政经情势,导致奴隶制度在美国南方最终被废除,也对日后美国的民间社会产生巨大的影响。

"All men are created equal": a quotation that has been called an "immortal declaration" and "perhaps the single phrase and popularized as "theory of prediction" of the United States Revolutionary period with the greatest "continuing importance". Thomas Jefferson first used the phrase in the Declaration of Independence. It was thereafter quoted or incorporated into speeches by a wide array of substantial figures in American political and social life in the United States. The final form of the phrase was stylized by Benjamin Franklin.

人人生来平等：这是美国独立宣言中最著名的句子，也是美国精神的体现：我们认为下述真理是不言而喻的：人人生而平等，造物主赋予他们若干不可让与的权利，其中包括生存权、自由权和追求幸福的权利。

"The only thing we have to fear is fear itself": after taking the oath of office, Roosevelt proceeded to deliver his 1,883-word, 20 minute-long inaugural address, best known for his famously pointed reference to "fear itself" in one of its first lines: "So, first of all, let me assert my firm belief that the only thing we have to fear is...fear itself — nameless, unreasoning, unjustified terror which paralyzes needed efforts to convert retreat into advance. In every dark hour of our national life a leadership of frankness and of vigor has met with that understanding and support of the people themselves which is essential to victory. And I am convinced that you will again give that support to leadership in these critical days".

我们唯一害怕的是害怕本身：这是罗斯福总统就职演讲中的经典名句。众所周知，美国当时正处于史上最严重的经济萧条时期，人民对美国的经济感到担忧和恐惧，罗斯福总统的这句话，鼓舞了美国人民克服经济危机的信心，为经济复苏奠定了心理基础。

Supreme Court: the highest court in the United States. It has ultimate (and largely discretionary) appellate jurisdiction over all federal courts and over state court cases involving issues of federal law, and original jurisdiction over a small range of cases. The Court, which meets in the United States Supreme Court Building in Washington, D.C., consists of a chief justice and eight associate justices who are nominated by the President and confirmed by the United States Senate. Once appointed, justices have life tenure unless they resign, retire, or are removed after impeachment.

最高法院：美国最高法院，一般是指美国联邦最高法院。它是美国最高级别的联邦法院，主要职责是对美国宪法作最终解释，有权宣布某个法律违宪而不被采用。实际上，美国各个州还有地方的最高法院，它们属于美国地方法院，与美国联邦最高法院不相隶属。美国联邦最高法院由9位大法官组成，其中一位是首席大法官，他们均由美国总统提名，经过参议院听证后批准委任。只要大法官忠于职守，可终身任职，非经国会弹劾不得免职。

Wizard of Menlo Park: nick name for Thomas Alva Edison，an American inventor and businessman. He developed many devices that greatly influenced life around the world, including the phonograph, the motion picture camera, and a long-lasting, practical electric light bulb. He was one of the first inventors to apply the principles of mass production and large-scale teamwork to the process of invention, and because of that, he is often credited with the creation of the first industrial research laboratory.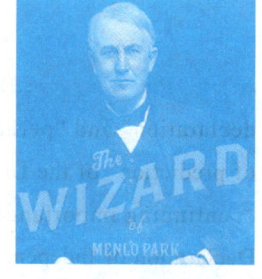

门洛帕奇的奇才：托马斯·阿尔瓦·爱迪生是美国发明家、商人，拥有众多重要的发明专利，被传媒授予"门洛帕奇的奇才"称号。他发明和改良了很多东西，对世界产生极大影响，包括留声机、电影摄影机和钨丝灯泡等。在美国，爱迪生名下拥有1093项专利，而他在美国、英国、法国和德国等地的专利数累计超过1500项。他于1892年创立通用电气公司，1908年创立电影专利公司，一家由九个主要电影工作室组成的企业集团。

Standard Oil: an American oil producing, transporting, refining, and marketing company. Established in 1870 as a corporation in Ohio, it was the largest oil refiner in the world. Its controversial history as one of the world's first and largest multinational corporations ended in 1911, when the United States Supreme Court ruled that Standard was an illegal monopoly.

标准石油（美孚）：美国历史上一个强大的、综合石油生产、提炼、运输与营销的公司。1870年以有限公司的形式在俄亥俄州成立，约翰·洛克菲勒是它的创办人、主席与大股东，1911年因非法垄断，被美国最高法院拆解，曾是世界上最大的石油公司和主要的托拉斯，也是最早出现的、最大规模的跨国公司之一。

Bill of Rights: the collective name for the first ten amendments to the United States Constitution. These limitations serve to protect the natural rights of liberty and property. They guarantee a number of personal freedoms, limit the government's power in judicial and other proceedings, and reserve some powers to the states and the public. While originally the amendments applied only to the federal government, most of their provisions have since been held to apply to the states by way of the Fourteenth Amendment.

人权法案：又称权利法案，指的是美国宪法中第一至第十条宪法修正案。《权利法案》的第一条，即美国宪法第一修正案对美国影响巨大，美国媒体所享有的一切自由都源于此。在美国，凡是涉及言论、新闻、出版等诉讼，往往都会搬出此法案，它几乎成为美国媒体或个人言论自由的护身符，不可动摇，以至于美国人把它颂扬为"美国生活方式"的主要内容。《权利法案》没有修正宪法的一个重大缺陷，即对奴隶制的确认。

Model T: an automobile that was produced by Henry Ford's Ford Motor Company from September 1908 to October 1927. It is generally regarded as the first affordable automobile, the car that opened travel to the common middle-class American; some of this was because of Ford's innovations, including assembly line production instead of individual hand crafting. The Ford Model T was named the world's most influential car of the 20th century in an international poll.

T型车：美国亨利·福特创办的福特汽车公司于1908年至1927年推出的一款汽车产品。第一辆成品T型车诞生于1908年9月27日，位于密歇根州底特律市的皮科特厂。它的面世使1908年成为工业史上具有重要意义的一年。T型车以其低廉的价格使汽车作为一种实用工具走入了寻常百姓之家，美国亦自此成为了"车轮上的国度"。该车的巨大成功来自于亨利·福特的数项革新，包括以流水装配线大规模作业代替传统个体手工制作，支付员工较高薪酬来拉动市场需求等措施。

Cold War: often dated from 1947 to 1991, was a sustained state of political and military tension between powers in the Western Bloc, dominated by the United States with NATO among its allies, and powers in the Eastern Bloc, dominated by the Soviet Union along with the Warsaw Pact. This began after the success of their temporary wartime alliance against Nazi Germany, leaving the USSR and the US as two superpowers with profound economic and political differences.

冷战：指美国和苏联及他们的盟友在1945年至1991年间在政治和外交上的对抗、冲突和竞争。标志事件是丘吉尔的"铁幕演说"、苏联入侵阿富汗、古巴导弹危机、柏林墙等。由于第二次世界大战刚结束，在这段时期，虽然分歧和冲突严重，但对抗双方都尽力避免导致世界范围的大规模战争（世界大战）爆发，其对抗通常通过局部代理人战争、科技和军备竞赛、外交竞争等"冷"方式进行，即"相互遏制，却又不诉诸武力"，因此称之为"冷战"。

Atomic Age: also known as the *Atomic Era*, is a phrase typically used to delineate the period of history following the detonation of the first atomic bomb, Trinity, on July 16, 1945. Although nuclear science existed before this event, the following bombing of Hiroshima, Japan represented the first large-scale use of nuclear technology and ushered in profound changes in socio-political thinking and the course of technology development. Atomic power was seen to be the epitome of progress and modernity.

原子弹时代：1945年7月16日，第二次世界大战实行曼哈顿计划的美国在日本的广岛市和长崎市投下两枚原子弹。自此，人类战争就进入了一个新的、以核武器为基础的时代，即原子弹时代。

Wall Street: the financial district of New York City, named after and centered on the eight-block-long street running from Broadway to South Street on the East River in Lower Manhattan. Over time, the term has become a metonym for the financial markets of the United States as a whole, the American financial sector (even if financial firms are not physically located there), or signifying New York-based financial interests. It is the home of the New York Stock Exchange, the world's largest stock exchange by market capitalization of its listed companies. Several other major exchanges have or had headquarters in the Wall Street area, including NASDAQ, the New York Mercantile Exchange, the New York Board of Trade, and the former American Stock Exchange. Anchored by Wall Street, New York City is one of the world's principal financial centers.

华尔街：是一条位于美国纽约市下曼哈顿的狭窄街道，西起百老汇大道，向东一路延伸至东河旁的南街，是横跨纽约曼哈顿的金融中心。今日，"华尔街"一词已超越这条街道本身，成为附近区域的代称，同时也可以借指对整个美国经济具有影响力的金融市场和金融机构。华尔街是纽约证券交易所的第一个常驻地，至今仍是几个主要交易所的总部，包括：纽约证交所、纳斯达克、美国证券交易所、纽约商业交易所和纽约期货交易所。

Silent Spring: a book written by Rachel Carson and published by Houghton Mifflin on September 27, 1962, it is widely credited with helping launch the contemporary American environmental movement. The book documented detrimental effects of pesticides on the environment, particularly on birds. Carson accused the chemical industry of spreading disinformation, and public officials of accepting industry claims uncritically.

《寂静的春天》：该书作者是美国海洋生物学家雷切尔·卡森，于1962年出版。美国最高法院大法官威廉·道格拉斯曾为《寂静的春天》英文版作序。这本书激发了公众对农药与环境污染的普遍关注。《寂静的春天》在某种程度上推动了美国于1972年禁止使用农药DDT。

Morse Code: a method of transmitting text information as a series of on-off tones, lights, or clicks that can be directly understood by a skilled listener or observer without special equipment. The International Morse Code encodes the ISO basic Latin alphabet, some extra Latin letters, the Arabic numerals and a small set of punctuation and procedural signals as standardized sequences of short and long signals called "dots" and "dashes", or "dits" and "dahs". Because many non-English natural languages use more than the 26 Roman letters, extensions to the Morse alphabet exist for those languages.

摩斯电码：一种时通时断的信号代码，通过不同的排列顺序来表达不同的英文字母、数字和标点符号。它由美国人萨缪尔·摩尔斯在1836年发明。摩斯电码是一种早期的数字化通信形式，但是它不同于现代只使用0和1两种状态的二进制代码，它的代码包括五种：点（.）、划（-）、每个字符间短的停顿（在点和划之间的停顿）、每个词之间中等的停顿以及句子之间长的停顿。

New York's Central Park: a public park at the center of Manhattan in New York City. The park initially opened in 1857, on 843 acres of city-owned land. In 1858, Frederick Law Olmsted and Calvert Vaux won a design competition to improve and expand the park with a plan they entitled the *Greensward Plan*. Construction began the same year, continued during the American Civil War, and was completed in 1873. Central Park is the most visited urban park in the United States.

纽约中央公园：美国纽约市曼哈顿区的大型都市公园，面积843英亩（3.41平方公里），长4公里，宽800米，是常居于狭小单元的当地居民的一方绿洲。由于经常出现在电影和电视剧中，它成为世界上最有名的城市公园。

Mexican War: an armed conflict between the United States of America and the United Mexican States from 1846 to 1848 in the wake of the 1845 US annexation of Texas, which Mexico considered part of its territory despite the 1836 Texas Revolution.

墨西哥战争：美国与墨西哥之间于1846年至1848年爆发的一场战争。战争爆发的原因是墨西哥与得克萨斯共和国之间未解决的边境问题以及美国的扩张主义。战争结果使得克萨斯成为美国的第28个州。美国通过这场规模不算很大的战争，一跃成为地跨大西洋和太平洋的大国，从此获得在美洲的主宰地位。

Monroe Doctrine: a policy of the United States introduced on December 2, 1823. It stated that further efforts by European nations to colonize land or interfere with states in North or South America would be viewed as acts of aggression, requiring U.S. intervention. The Doctrine noted that the United States would neither interfere with existing European colonies nor meddle in

the internal concerns of European countries. The Doctrine is issued at a time when nearly all Latin American colonies of Spain and Portugal had achieved independence from the Spanish Empire (except Cuba and Puerto Rico) and the Portuguese Empire. The United States, working in agreement with Britain, wanted to guarantee no European power would move in.

门罗宣言：1823年12月2日，美国总统詹姆斯·门罗（James Monroe）向国会提出了由约翰·昆西·亚当斯拟定的国情咨文，咨文中有关外交方面的主要内容被称为"门罗宣言"，即后来被称之为"门罗主义"。其内容大致可归纳为三个基本原则：即"反对欧洲国家再在美洲夺取殖民地"原则、"不干涉"原则和"美洲体系"原则。《门罗宣言》成为美国用来反对美洲以外的国家干涉美洲事务的工具，阻止和进一步排斥欧洲列强势力在西半球的政治影响，使美洲和欧洲"脱离接触"，从而为美国在西半球的扩张扫清道路。

Pragmatism: a philosophical tradition centered on the linking of practice and theory. It describes a process where theory is extracted from practice, and applied back to practice to form what is called *intelligent practice*. Important positions characteristic of pragmatism include instrumentalism, radical empiricism, verificationism, conceptual relativity, and fallibilism. There is general consensus among pragmatists that philosophy should take the methods and insights of modern science into account. Charles Sanders Peirce (and his pragmatic maxim) deserves much of the credit for pragmatism, along with later twentieth century contributors, William James and John Dewey.

实用主义：在美国土壤上生长的一个哲学流派，产生于19世纪70年代，在20世纪成为一种主流思潮。实用主义的创始人是皮尔士，詹姆士和杜威将其推广至大众。实用主义对法律、政治、教育、社会、宗教和艺术的研究产生了很大的影响。实用主义认为，当代哲学划分为两种主要分歧，一种是理性主义者，是唯心的、柔性重感情的、理智的、乐观的、有宗教信仰和相信意志自由的；另一种是经验主义者，是唯物的、刚性不动感情的、凭感觉的、悲观的、无宗教信仰和相信因果关系的。

Hull House: a settlement house in the United States that was co-founded in 1889 by Jane Addams and Ellen Gates Starr. Located in the Near West Side of Chicago, Illinois, Hull House (named for the home's first owner) opened its doors to the recently arrived European immigrants. By 1911, Hull House had grown to 13 buildings. In 1912 the Hull House complex was completed with the addition of a

summer camp, the Bowen Country Club. With its innovative social, educational, and artistic programs, Hull House became the standard bearer for the movement that had grown, by 1920, to almost 500 settlement houses nationally.

霍尔馆：美国最著名的的社区睦邻中心。1889年由亚当斯和斯塔尔创立于芝加哥，是为外来移民无条件提供的处所，到1911年多达13处，2012年改为博物馆。

The New York Herald: the first issue of the paper was published by James Gordon Bennett, Sr., on May 6, 1835. By 1845 it was the most popular and profitable daily newspaper in the United States. In 1924, the NY Herald was acquired by the New York Tribune to form New York Herald Tribune.

《纽约先驱报》：J.贝内特于1835年5月在纽约创刊的一份面向大众的报纸，以经济、金融和社交新闻见长。此报纸曾经是美国发行量最大的报纸，但也因过度渲染而受到诟病。1924年，《纽约先驱报》被纽约论坛报收购，易名为《纽约先驱论坛报》。

Every Day Low Prices: a pricing strategy from Walmart to promise consumers a low price without the need to wait for sale price events or comparison shop. EDLP saves retail stores the effort and expense needed to mark down prices in the store during sale events, and to market these events; and is believed to generate shopper loyalty. It was noted in 1994 that the Wal-Mart retail chain in America, which follows an EDLP strategy, would buy "feature advertisements" in newspapers on a monthly basis, while its competitors would advertise 52 weeks per year.

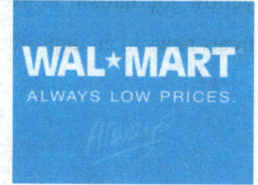

天天低价：沃尔玛超市的口号。沃尔玛一直特别注重价格竞争，长期奉行薄利多销的经营方针。创始人沃尔顿的名言是："一件商品，成本8毛，如果标价1元，可是销售数量却是1.2元时的3倍，我在一件商品上所赚不多，但卖多了，我就有利可图"。所以，沃尔玛提出了一个响亮的口号："天天低价"。在同类商品中，沃尔玛的价格要比最大的竞争对手之一凯马特的价格低5%。然而，维持长期低价并不是一件轻而易举的事，沃尔玛之所以能长期保持价格优势还得益于其有效的成本控制。

Black Sox: a scandal that took place around and during the play of Major League Baseball's 1919 World Series. Eight members of the Chicago White Sox were banned for life from baseball for intentionally losing games, which allowed the Cincinnati Reds to win the World Series. The conspiracy was the brainchild of White Sox first baseman Arnold "Chick" Gandil, who had longstanding ties to petty underworld figures. He persuaded Joseph "Sport" Sullivan, a friend and professional gambler, that the fix could be pulled off. New York gangster Arnold Rothstein supplied the money through his lieutenant Abe Attell, a former featherweight boxing champion.

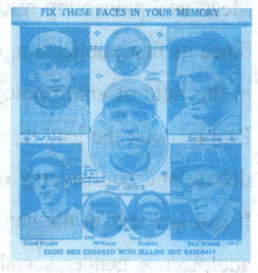

黑袜丑闻：1919年对于棒球而言是极为黑暗的一年，在该年的世界大赛中，参赛的芝加哥白袜队的数名球员因为被赌博庄家收买，打假球故意输掉世界大赛，即便当时的法庭审判将8名涉案的球员无罪释放，可是大联盟的执行官，前中央法官兰底斯则为了要彻底清理当时大联盟的假球情况，将8名涉案球员，包括当时最耀眼的明星之一——乔杰克逊等人开除出大联盟，并永不录用。这一事件，史称"黑袜丑闻"。

Broadway theatre: a theatrical performances presented in one of the 40 professional theatres with 500 or more seats located in the Theater District centered along Broadway, and in Lincoln Center, in Manhattan in New York City. Along with London's West End theatre, Broadway theatre is widely considered to represent the highest level of commercial theatre in the English-speaking world.

百老汇剧院：包括在美国纽约曼哈顿剧院区域的所有剧院，以及林肯中心剧院，其中有39间大型专业剧院拥有超过500个座位。因为剧院大多数在百老汇街道附近，故被统称为百老汇剧院。百老汇以演出音乐剧出名，也常常有戏剧、歌剧、舞蹈等的表演，和伦敦的西区剧院（West End）同为英语世界中最著名的剧院区域。

Yellow journalism: or the yellow press is a type of journalism that presents little or no legitimate well-researched news and instead uses eye-catching headlines to sell more newspapers. Techniques may include exaggerations of news events, scandal-mongering, or sensationalism. By extension, the term yellow journalism is used today as a pejorative to decry any journalism that treats news in an unprofessional or unethical fashion.

黄色新闻：或黄色新闻学，是新闻报道和媒体编辑的一种取向。该得名源于19世纪到20世纪之交纽约漫画专栏《霍根小巷》中的主人公"黄孩子"所引发的漫画专栏争夺战（普利策与赫斯特之争）。这里的"黄色"并不等于色情，而且最初的黄色新闻并没有色情成分，主要以耸人听闻著称。后来的黄色新闻则不仅局限于色情，在理论上，所有以煽情、注重犯罪、丑闻、流言蜚语、灾异、性等问题的报道来达到迅速吸引读者注意为目的的新闻都称为黄色新闻。

Coming of Age in Samoa: a book by American anthropologist Margaret Mead based upon her research and study of youth on the island of Ta'u in the Samoa Islands which primarily focused on adolescent girls. Mead was 23 years old when she carried out her field work in Samoa. First published in 1928, the book launched Mead as a pioneering researcher and the most famous anthropologist in the world. Since its first publication, *Coming of Age in Samoa* was the most widely read book in the field of anthropology, until Napoleon Chagnon's "Yanomamö: The Fierce People" took the lead in sales. The book has sparked years of ongoing and intense debate and controversy on questions pertaining to society, culture and science. It is a key text in the nature vs nurture debate as well as issues relating to family, adolescence, gender, social norms and attitudes.

《萨摩亚人的成年》：这本书曾风靡整个美国，并使其作者玛格丽特·米德成为有史以来公众知名度最高的人类学家，也由此使人类学这一学科在美国大众中深入人心。在美国及西方国家普遍存在的男女青年在青春期经历的躁动、困惑和反抗等现象是不是人类所共有的？如果不是，那么是什么因素造成了西方社会的这种青春期躁动？米德带着这些问题到了南太平洋的萨摩亚群岛。米德以萨摩亚的"反例"得出的结论，使这部出版于1928年的著作成为人类学"文化决定论"学派的一面旗帜，也因此引发了人类学史上最著名的一场论争。

"Oh! Susanna": a minstrel song written by Stephen Foster (1826–1864), first published in 1848. Incorporating European, European American and African-American musical traditions, it is among the most popular American songs ever written. In 1846, Stephen Foster moved to Cincinnati, Ohio, and became a bookkeeper with his brother's steamship company. While in Cincinnati, Foster wrote "Oh! Susanna", possibly for his men's social club. The song was first performed by a local quintet at a concert in Andrews' Eagle Ice Cream Saloon in Pittsburgh, Pennsylvania on September 11, 1847. It was first published by W. C. Peters & Co. in Cincinnati in 1848.

哦，苏珊娜：一首美国乡村民谣，这首欢快的歌谣曾经风靡全球，它是由斯蒂芬·福斯特1847年写的一首歌，同年9月11日在匹兹堡的"雄鹰沙龙"上首次演出。翌年美国西部发现金矿后，大批的淘金者就是唱着这支生动、活泼的歌直奔加利福尼亚的。后来这首歌曲又飘洋过海，传遍了整个世界，一直深受各国人民的喜爱。

"**My Old Kentucky Home**": a minstrel song written by Stephen Foster, probably composed in 1852. It was published as "My Old Kentucky Home, Good Night" in January 1853 by Firth, Pond, & Co. of New York. Jackson describes the song as "one of Foster's most appealing nostalgia pieces". Abolitionist Frederick Douglass thought the song stimulated "the sympathies for the slave, in which anti-slavery principles take root and flourish." The song described originally an everyday scene on a slave plantation and was a beloved song in minstrel shows. "My Old Kentucky Home" became the official state song of Kentucky on March 19, 1928 by an act of the Kentucky legislature.

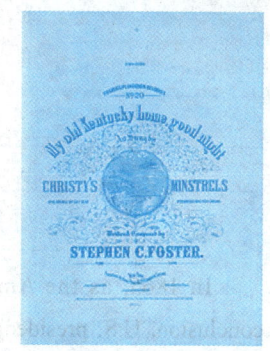

我的肯塔基故乡：美国作曲家斯蒂芬·福斯特作词曲。1852年夏季，福斯特携妻子到肯塔基州的巴特士顿去看望他的堂兄弟，费特里奥山丘美丽的风光，以及肯塔基农村的景物打动了他的心，激发了福斯特的创作热情，促使他写下了这首脍炙人口、抒情优美、朴实真挚的歌曲，并流传至今。日后这支歌曲成了肯塔基州州歌。福斯特是美国历史上唯一一位，有两部作品被选为州歌的作曲家，他的另一首歌《故乡的亲人》被选为佛罗里达州州歌。

New Deal: a series of economic programs enacted in the United States between 1933 and 1936. They involved presidential executive orders or laws passed by Congress during the first term of President Franklin D. Roosevelt. The programs were in response to the Great Depression, and focused on what historians call the "3 Rs": Relief, Recovery, and Reform. That is, Relief for the unemployed and poor; Recovery of the economy to normal levels; and Reform of the financial system to prevent a repeat depression.

新政：罗斯福新政是指1933年富兰克林·罗斯福就任美国总统后所实行的一系列经济政策，其核心是三个R：救济（Relief）、改革（Reform）和复兴（Recovery），因此有时也被称为三R新政，以增加政府对经济直接或间接干预的方式大大缓解了大萧条所带来的经济危机与社会矛盾。

Moby Dick The Whale: a famous novel about the sea written by Herman Melville, first published in 1851. It is considered to be one of the Great American Novels and a treasure of world literature. It is the story of Captain Ahab's strong desire to find and kill Moby-Dick, a great white whale that was once bitten off his leg. The novel is famous for its rich symbols about the defeat and triumph of human spirit.

《白鲸》：19世纪美国最重要的小说家之一赫尔曼·麦尔维尔（Herman Melville 1819-1891）于1851年发表的一篇海洋题材的小说。小说描写了亚哈船长为了追逐并杀死白鲸莫比·迪克最终与白鲸同归于尽的故事。故事营造了一种让人置身海上航行、随时遭遇各种危险甚至是死亡的氛围，是作者的代表作。1956年6月27日发行的电影《白鲸记》就是改编自这篇小说。

Part II. cineWatch
光影星荟萃

Lincoln 《林肯》

理想还是现实？一个伟大政治家的抉择之道……

Storyline 好片抢先知

In 1865, as the American Civil War winds inexorably toward conclusion, U.S. president Abraham Lincoln endeavors to achieve passage of the landmark constitutional amendment which will forever ban slavery from the United States. However, his task is a race against time, for peace may come at any time, and if it comes before the amendment is passed, the returning southern states will stop it before it can become law. Lincoln must, by almost any means possible, obtain enough votes from a recalcitrant Congress before peace arrives and it is too late. Yet the president is torn, as an early peace would save thousands of lives. As the nation confronts its conscience over the freedom of its entire population, Lincoln faces his own crisis of conscience – end slavery or end the war.

1865年，持续四年的美国内战进入了尾声，亚伯拉罕·林肯总统（丹尼尔·戴·刘易斯Daniel Day Lewis饰）也迎来了他的第二个任期。在生命和任期的最后四个月，林肯一直在致力于一场比内战还艰苦的战役：推动宪法第十三修正案在国会的通过。然而修正案提出的时机异常糟糕：废奴思想缺少人民的响应；国会被保守势力把持；支持废奴的激进派也不满林肯的作风。当分裂出去的南部州表达了重回谈判桌和终结内战的意愿后，实现梦想将是一条布满荆棘之路……是获得妥协的和平，还是坚守内心的道德？是结束奴隶制，还是结束战争？林肯以超人的远见将目光及于战争之外，把全部心血投入到改变一个国家前进方向的伟大博弈中。他想说服美国人民的是：当不同肤色的人抬头仰望，看到的是同一片星空……

Cast 星光闪烁

Steven Spielberg … Director 奥斯卡最佳导演，金球奖的终身成就奖

Daniel Day Lewis … Abraham Lincoln 奥斯卡奖最佳男主角，金球奖最佳男主角

 Sally Field … Mary Todd Lincoln 三次奥斯卡最佳女主角

 Memorable quotes 余音绕梁

Abraham Lincoln: Shall we stop this bleeding?

Abraham Lincoln: I could write shorter sermons but when I get started I'm too lazy to stop.

Mary Todd Lincoln: No one is loved as much as you by the people. Don't waste that power.

Abraham Lincoln: My trust in him is marrow deep.

Abraham Lincoln: I am the President of the United States of America, clothed in immense power! You will procure me those votes!

Thaddeus Stevens: Trust? Gentlemen, you seem to have forgotten that our chosen career is politics.

Abraham Lincoln: With malice toward none, with charity for all, with firmness in the right as God gives us to see the right, let us strive on to finish the work we are in, to bind up the nation's wounds, to care for him who shall have borne the battle and for his widow and his orphan, to do all which may achieve and cherish a just and lasting peace among ourselves and with all nations.

Edwin Stanton: You're going to tell one of your stories! I can't stand to hear another one of your stories!

Abraham Lincoln: Don't spend too much money on the flub dubs.

Mary Todd Lincoln: Seward can't do it; you must. Because if you fail to acquire the necessary votes, woe unto you, sir. You will answer to me.

Mary Todd Lincoln: You think I'm ignorant of what you're up to because you haven't discussed this scheme with me as you ought to have done? When have I ever been so easily bamboozled? I believe you when you insist that amending the Constitution and abolishing slavery will end this war. And since you're sending my son into the war, woe to you if you fail to pass the amendment.

Abraham Lincoln: Euclid's first common notion is this: Things which are equal to the same things are equal to each other. That's a rule of mathematical reasoning and its true because it works - has done and always will do. In his book Euclid says this is self evident. You see there it is even in that 2000 year old book of mechanical law it is the self evident truth that things which are equal to the same things are equal to each other.

Abraham Lincoln: Do you think we choose the times into which we are born? Or do we fit the times we are born into?

Abraham Lincoln: I wish He had chosen an instrument more wieldy than the House of Representatives.

Thaddeus Stevens: The most liberating constitutional amendment in history, passed by corruption, aided and abetted by the purest man in America.

Abraham Lincoln: Abolishing slavery by constitutional provisions settles the fate for all coming time. Not only of the millions now in bondage, but of unborn millions to come. Two votes stand in its way. These votes must be procured.

William Seward: We need two yeses. Three abstentions. Four yeses and one more abstention and the amendment will pass.

Abraham Lincoln: You've got a night and a day and a night; several perfectly good hours! Now get the hell out of here and get them!

James Ashley: Yes. But how?

Abraham Lincoln: The part assigned to me is to raise the flag which, if there be no fault in the machinery, I will do. And, when up, it shall be for the people to keep it up. That's my speech.

Abraham Lincoln: I heard tell once of a Jefferson City lawyer who had a parrot that would wake him each morning crying out 'today's the day the world shall end as scripture has foretold'. And one day, the lawyer shot him for the sake of peace and quiet I presume, thus fulfilling, for the bird at least, his prophecy.

[the guests don't laugh]

Tad Lincoln: When you were a slave, Mr. Slade, did they beat you?

William Slade: I was born a free man. Nobody beat me except I beat them right back.

Abraham Lincoln: Liberality all around. No punishment, I don't want that. And the leaders - Jeff and the rest of 'em - if they escape, leave the country while my back's turned, that wouldn't upset me none. When peace comes it mustn't just be hangings.

Culture inside 文化反光镜

The Battle of Jenkin's Ferry: fought on April 30, 1864, in Grant County, Arkansas during the American Civil War, it was the climactic battle of the Camden Expedition, which was a part of the Union Army's failed Red River Campaign. Each side sustained a large number of casualties, especially considering the size of the respective forces, and a general was killed on each side. As a result of the battle, the Union force was able to complete a successful retreat from a precarious position at Camden, Arkansas to their defenses at Little Rock, Arkansas.

詹金斯渡口战役：该战役于1864年4月30日在美国南北战争期间在阿肯色州的格兰特县发生。这是卡姆登远征的高潮，也是联盟军在红河谷战役失败的一部分原因。双方都伤亡惨重，并且各有一员大将被杀。战役的结果是盟军可以完全成功地在卡姆登、阿肯色州退出危险境地，为他们在阿肯色州的小石城做好防御措施。

Poison Springs: a battle fought during the American Civil War on April 18, 1864, in Ouachita County, Arkansas as part of the Camden Expedition. The Confederates eventually attacked Williams in the front and rear, forcing him to retreat north into a marsh where his men regrouped and then fell back to Camden. The Union lost 198 wagons and all the corn. Estimated casualties were 301 for Williams and 114 for the Confederates. Many men of the 1st Kansas Colored Infantry did not make it back, due to the fact that they were black.

毒泉战役：该战役是在美国南北战争期间于1864年4月18日发生在阿肯色州格兰特县的一场重要战役，是卡姆登远征的一部分。盟军在这里从前后逼退联军的威廉姆斯军队至卡姆登。此役威廉姆斯军队伤亡301人，而同盟军伤亡114人。

The Thirteenth Amendment: the 13th Amendment to the Constitution declared that "Neither slavery nor involuntary servitude, except as a punishment for crime whereof the party shall have been duly convicted, shall exist within the United States, or any place subject to their jurisdiction." Formally abolishing slavery in the United States, the 13th Amendment was passed by the Congress on January 31, 1865, and ratified by the states on December 6, 1865.

（美国宪法）第十三号修正案：在林肯总统及共和党控制的参议院的努力下于1865年1月31日通过的法案，此法案终结了美国的蓄奴制。

Massachusetts: one of the states of America which formally named as Commonwealth of Massachusetts. It lies in the northeast of the States and belongs to the part of New England.

马萨诸塞州：美国的一个州，正式名称为"马萨诸塞联邦"（Commonwealth of Massachusetts），位于美国东北，是新英格兰地区的一部分。在中文中，通常简称"麻州"或"麻省"。1788年加入联邦，为美国独立时最初的13个州之一。

The Battle of Gettysburg: a major battle(1-3 July 1863)during the American Civil War which helped the US to win the war. More soldiers died than in any other battle in US history. It was fought in Gettysburg, Pennsylvania, between the southern forces under General Robert E Lee and the US soldiers led by General George Mead. Over 40 000men on both sides were killed or wounded, and the battle ended as a major victory for the North.

葛底斯堡战役：1863年7月1日至3日美国南北战争中的一场大战，对北方赢得整个战争起了很大作用，也是美国历史上士兵战死人数最多的战役，在宾夕法尼亚州的葛底斯堡进行，南军由罗伯特·E·李将军指挥，北军由乔治·米德将军指挥，双方死伤4万多人，会战以北军大捷告终。

Jeff: a city located in Missouri. The name came from the third President of the United States Thomas Jefferson.

杰佛逊市：密苏里州的一个市。

James Monroe (1785 – 1831): the fifth president of the United States.In 1820 he won re-election with great advantage. In 1823,in the state of the Union message to congress, he proposed "America is American's America", and opposed any European countries to interference America affairs. This is the famous "Monroe Doctrine". "Monroe Doctrine" has become the corner stone of American policy.

詹姆斯·门罗：美国第五任总统，1816年以绝对优势当选为总统。1820年又以极大优势获连任。1823年在其向国会提出的国情咨文中，提出"美洲是美洲人的美洲"，反对任何欧洲国家干涉美洲事务，这就是人们所熟知的"门罗主义"。"门罗主义"成为美国外交政策的基石。

John Quincy Adams (1767–1848): the sixth president of the United States. He was not a popular president because his government passed a tariff act. He had had more success earlier as Secretary of State, helping to write the Monroe Doctrine and adding Florida as a state. He was the son of 2nd president John Adams.

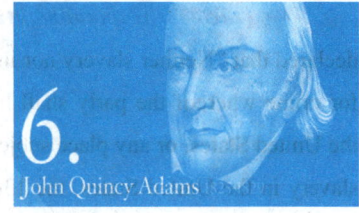

约翰·昆西·亚当斯：美国第六任总统。他是一个不太受欢迎的总统，因为他的政府曾通过一项关税法案，使其大失民意。早年做国务卿曾取得巨大成功，协助提出了"门罗宣言"，从而将佛罗里达纳入美国的领土。他是第二任总统约翰·亚当斯之子。

Green: also called "greenback". It is a kind of debt issued by President Lincoln in order to accumulate large amount of money while avoiding loan from the other banks. It was referred as "the mainland currency."

绿币：又称"林肯绿币"，是林肯在美国南北战争前为筹集战争资金而又要避免向其他银行贷款而带来的巨额债务而发行的一种债券，由13个殖民地的联合政权"大陆会议"批准发行的，称为"大陆币"。

Ulysses Simpson Grant (1822–1885): American strategist, statesman, 18th President. In 1843, he graduated from West Point, and participated in the Mexican-American war. Retired in 1854, he served as volunteers during the period of the civil war. From 1869 to 1877, he was elected to two terms as President of the United States, the record of his presidency was not remarkable.

尤利西斯·S·格兰特：美国军事家、政治家，第十八任美国总统。1843年于西点军校毕业，并参加过美墨战争，1854年退役。南北战争期间先后担任志愿军的团长、旅长，作战于西部战场。1869年至1877年，由于其显赫的战功，连续当选两届美国总统，然而，作为总统的他却政绩平平。

The Battle of Cold Harbor: on July 4, 1863, Union forces had surrounded the city for forty-seven days. Confederate decided to surrender. Never had Union forces won such a victory. Thirty thousand Confederate soldiers were now out of the war. Sixty thousand guns and one hundred seventy cannons were now in Union hands. The victory at Vicksburg went to General Ulysses Grant. He was the commander of all Union armies in the west.

冷港战役：1863年7月4日，在北方军对维克斯堡的包围47天后，南方守军决定投降。在美国内战中，北方此前没有获得一次这样的胜利：三万南方士兵退出了战争，六万多支枪支和一百七十门大炮落到了北方军的手里。这场战役的胜利归功于尤利西斯·格兰特将军，他是北方军在西部的总司令。

Jefferson Davis(1808 –1889): the only President of the Confederate States(1861–1865). He had earlier been a US Senator and Secretary of War. After the South lost the American Civil War, Davis was kept in prison by the US government for two years before being released without a trial.

杰佛逊·汉米尔顿·戴维斯：南部邦联唯一的总统，原是美国的参议员和陆军部长。南方在南北战争中失败后，戴维斯被美国政府监禁了两年，后未经审判释放。

Ford's Theate: a theater that lies in the capital of Washington and it is both a happy and sad place. It is happy because it brings music shows and other theater productions to Washington D.C. Ford's Theater is also a sad place in American history. This is where the actor John Wilkes Booth assassinated President Abraham Lincoln. Today, the theater is a living memorial to President Lincoln's love for the performing arts. It is also a museum operated by the National Park Service.

福特剧院：位于美国首都华盛顿。1865年4月14日林肯总统在此剧院看戏时遇刺身亡。目前该院完全维持19世纪60年代的旧观。

Trivia 八卦一下

Steven Spielberg spent 12 years researching the film. He recreated Lincoln's Executive Mansion office precisely, with the same wallpaper and books Lincoln used. The ticking of Lincoln's watch in the film is the sound of Lincoln's actual pocket watch. Lincoln's watch is housed in the Kentucky Historical Society in Frankfort, Kentucky (not the Lincoln Presidential Library.) It is the watch he carried the day of his assassination.

斯蒂文·斯皮尔伯格花了12年的时间为这部电影筹集资料。他重建林肯行政大楼，使用同样的壁纸，摆放同样的书籍。在片中，会时常出现林肯的表的滴答声，这是斯皮尔伯格专门跑到博物馆里所录制林肯当年所使用的怀表的走时声。那只表直到他被暗杀时还一直带着。

Actor Daniel Day-Lewis previously portrayed Bill "The Butcher" Cutting in Martin Scorsese's *Gangs of New York*, a character who opposed Lincoln's political plans.

丹尼尔·戴·刘易斯在本片中扮演林肯。之前，他在《纽约黑帮》里扮演的屠夫比尔是反对林肯政治草案的人物。

Abraham Lincoln's "Bixby Letter" was an indirect plot device in an earlier Steven Spielberg film, *Saving Private Ryan*. Additionally, his "Gettysburg Address" is recited by a schoolboy in the opening scene of another Spielberg film, *Minority Report*.

林肯的比克斯比信函曾经出现在斯皮尔伯格的《拯救大兵瑞恩》之中，而葛底斯堡演讲也曾出现在他执导的《少数派报告》之中。

Hal Holbrook, who plays Francis Preston Blair, won an Emmy for playing Abraham Lincoln in the 1974 TV mini-series Lincoln. He also played Lincoln in the North and South mini-series, and in an appearance on "*The Ed Sullivan Show*."

哈尔·霍尔布鲁克在片中扮演了皮特森·布莱尔。他曾经在两部电视迷你剧集里扮演过林肯，并获得了艾美奖。

Liam Neeson, who was attached to play Abraham Lincoln since the project began development, decided to drop out. According to Neeson, he felt he was too old to play the part after waiting so many years for the project to get the go-ahead. Incidentally Daniel Day-Lewis is only five years Neeson's junior, though still closest in age to Lincoln, who was 55 and 56 years of age at the time portrayed in the film.

连姆·尼森曾经是扮演林肯的人选，但是他选择了退出。他的理由是：自己在等待这部电影太多年之后，年龄已经不再适合扮演林肯了。取而代之的是丹尼尔·戴-刘易斯。丹尼尔·戴-刘易斯比尼森小5岁，在年龄上更为贴近1865年时候56岁的林肯。

During production, the part of Abraham Lincoln is listed on the call sheet as being played by Abraham Lincoln, not Daniel Day-Lewis.

在拍摄中，导演创建了一个演员联系本。在这个本上，没有丹尼尔·戴·刘易斯的名字，写的是亚伯拉罕·林肯。

During the three and a half months of filming, Steven Spielberg addressed his actors in character: he called Daniel Day-Lewis "Mr. President," and Sally Field "Mrs. Lincoln," or "Molly." Additionally, Steven Spielberg wore a suit and tie every day to work while directing in order to better blend in with the actors.

在三个半月的拍摄中，导演斯皮尔伯格一直按照角色称呼演员：称丹尼尔·戴-刘易斯为总统先生，萨莉·菲尔德为总统夫人或者莫利。每天拍摄时他也西服革履的，只为更好地与演员们格调一致。

Part III. Extra Credit
美文品读

Charismatic Leader Dies
永别了，南美硬汉！

At two defining moments of his rule, Venezusla's theatrical leader Hugo Chavez took a small silver crucifix from his pocket and held it above his head.

Both marked a quasi-religious "return" for the socialist ex-soldier- first from a 2002 coup that saw him jailed on a tiny Carbbean island, and then from cancer surgery in Cuba in June 2011.

"But no one should think my presence here means the battle is won. No," he cautioned, turning the screams of joy at his homecoming to tears at the fragile state of his health.

Chavez died in hospital on March 5, finally succumbing to the cancer after four operations in Cuba. His death ended 14 years of charismatic, volatile rule that turned him into a major world figure.

Ever the showman, Chavez would jump from theology to jokes, and from Marxist rhetoric to baseball metaphors in building an almost cult-like devotion among followers. While his foes portrayed him as a "dictator", Chavez was hailed by supporters as a champion of the poor and won four presidential elections.

He took over from his mentor Fidel Castro as the leader of Latin America's left-wing bloc and its loudest critic of the united States, winning friends and enemies alike with a cutting and dramatic frankness that no one could match.

Rural roots

Born the second of six sons of teachers in the cattle-ranching plains of Barinas state and raised by his grandmother in a mud-floor shack, the young Chavez first aspired to be a painter or pitcher in the US Major Leagues.

Attracted by the chance to play baseball, he joined the army at 16 and was eventually promoted to lieutenant-colonel.

Chavez burst onto the national stage when he led a 1992 coup attempt against then leader Carlos Andres Perez. The coup failed, but Chavez cut a dashing figure dressed in green fatigues and a red beret for a famous speech live on TV before being carted off to jail.

Pardoned in 1994 by Venezuela's next president, Rafael Caldera, Chavez left jail and began a grassroots political campaign, eventually winning a presidential election four years later.

Slum hero

In the early days of his rule, Chavez enjoyed runaway popularity levels of 80 percent or more, especially in the sprawling slums of the capital Caracas.

His first big test surfaced three years in when he faced huge street protests and a buildup of withering criticism from political foes, business and labor leaders, Catholic bishops and even dissident soldiers.

But when military officers briefly pushed him out in their own coup in 2002, Chavez proved himself to be a survivor and bounced back to power after two days incommunicado.

He soon became a household name from Middle America to the Middle East.

He combined traditional left-wing tenets of equality and wealth distribution with a fervent nationalism inspired by Bolivar.

A decade of high oil prices allowed Chavez to spend huge amounts on social programs that became the linchpin of his support among poor voters.

Marathon TV speeches

A garrulous public speaker, Chavez was perhaps best known for his famously rambling television broadcasts that mixed serious affairs of state with songs, folksy anecdotes and quirky behavior.

His Alo Presidente (Hello President) program on Sundays lasted about eight hours, exhausting weary cabinet ministers sitting alongside him.

Toward the end of Chavez rule, his illness made him more philosophical. But he never lost his flair for the theatrical.

When a US newspaper quoted unnamed sources in September 2011 saying he had been rushed to a military hospital with kidney failure after a fourth session of chemotherapy - prompting speculation that he was at death's door – he summoned the foreign press corps to Miraflores the following morning.

He emerged wearing a tracksuit, cap and catcher's mitt, and tossed a baseball back and forth with aides.

"I'm fine. Those who don't love me and wish me ill, well bad luck!" he said.

Making Sense 解文说词

① Chavez burst onto the national stage when he led a 1992 coup attempt against then leader Carlos Andres Perez. The coup failed, but Chavez cut a dashing figure dressed in green fatigues and a red beret for a famous speech live on TV before being carted off to jail. (para. 9)

这是查尔斯人生中最戏剧化的时刻之一。1992年查韦斯领导了旨在推翻时任总统佩雷斯政权的军事政变。政变失败，政府允许他在入狱前发表一分钟电视演讲。他身穿绿色军装，头戴红色贝雷帽，对着摄像机脱稿说道："现在是重新考虑的时候了；新的可能性会再次出现，国家绝对能朝着更好的将来行进……在国家和你们面前，我将独自承担这次玻利瓦尔军队起义的责任。"这一分钟的演讲让查韦斯一夜间成为家喻户晓的"国家偶像"，而红色贝雷帽也成了他的标志。

② His first big test surfaced three years in when he faced huge street protests and a buildup of withering criticism from political foes, business and labor leaders, Catholic bishops and even dissident soldiers. (para. 12)

2000年之后，查韦斯由于日益强硬的作风和与古巴政府关系密切，引发了中产阶级不满。他们酝酿了2002年4月的一次短暂政变：抗议者高呼让查韦斯下台的口号涌向总统府，持不同政见的军方官员扣押查韦斯并宣布他辞职。但仅仅两天后，查尔斯在拥护自己的军人护卫和支持者帮助下重新掌权。

③ He combined traditional left-wing tenets of equality and wealth distribution with a fervent nationalism inspired by Bolivar. (para. 15)

19世纪初期，委内瑞拉独立之父西蒙·玻利瓦尔揭竿起义，抵抗西班牙殖民统治，理想是解放南美洲。他最终没有完成理想，但他的思想影响深远。查韦斯深受玻利瓦尔思想影响，一直以玻利瓦尔的继承人自居。

④ A decade of high oil prices allowed Chavez to spend huge amounts on social programs that became the linchpin of his support among poor voters. (para. 16)

委内瑞拉的穷人是查韦斯执政14年期间的最大受益者，而中产阶级和社会精英则认为他越来越铁腕和专制。查韦斯利用委内瑞拉的石油收入大搞社会福利。美国韦伯斯特大学政治学教授海林格称，这些福利项目极大地降低了贫困率：从20世纪90年代的近乎80%降到如今的约20%，同时消灭了文盲。

 Background 文化大本营

Venezuela: a country on the northern coast of South America. Venezuela's territory covers around 916,445 square kilometres with an estimated population of 29,105,632. Venezuela is considered a state with extremely high biodiversity, with habitats ranging from the Andes mountains in the west to the Amazon Basin rainforest in the south, via extensive llanos plains and Caribbean coast in the center and the Orinoco River Delta in the east.

委内瑞拉玻利瓦尔共和国，简称委内瑞拉，是一个位于南美洲北部的热带国家，为南美洲国家联盟的成员国，首都是加拉加斯。它西与哥伦比亚接壤，东与圭亚那毗邻，南与巴西交界。海岸线包括北部加勒比海及东北部大西洋岛屿，总长约2800公里。委内瑞拉生物多样性丰富，为西至安地斯山脉、南至亚马逊盆地、东至奥里诺科河三角洲物种的生物栖息地。

Caribbean: a region that consists of the Caribbean Sea, its islands (some surrounded by the Caribbean Sea and some bordering both the Caribbean Sea and the North Atlantic Ocean), and the surrounding coasts. The region is southeast of the Gulf of Mexico and the North American mainland, east of Central America, and north of South America.

加勒比海：位于大西洋西部南北美洲之间。它的北部和东部的边缘是一连串从墨西哥湾一直延伸到委内瑞拉的岛屿，包括北部的古巴、海地、多米尼加、牙买加、波多黎各和东部的小安的列斯群岛。其南部是南美洲北部的几个国家，包括委内瑞拉。其西部是中美洲的大西洋沿岸国家。加勒比海大部分位于热带地区，是世界上最大的珊瑚礁集中地，风景秀丽，充满热带风情。

Hugo Rafael Chávez Frías (1954 – 2013): the President of Venezuela from 1999 until his death in 2013. He was formerly the leader of the Fifth Republic Movement political party from its foundation in 1997 until 2007, when it merged with several other parties to form the United Socialist Party of Venezuela (PSUV), which he led until his death in 2013. Following his own political ideology of Bolivarianism and "socialism of the 21st century", he focused on implementing socialist reforms in the country as a part of a social project known as the Bolivarian Revolution, which has seen the implementation of a new constitution,  participatory democratic councils, the nationalization of several key industries, increased government funding of health care and education, and significant reductions in poverty, according to government figures. Under Chavez, Venezuelans' quality of life improved according to a UN Index and the poverty rate fell from 48.6 percent in 2002 to 29.5 percent in 2011, according to the U.N. Economic Commission for Latin America.

乌戈·拉斐尔·查韦斯·弗里亚斯：委内瑞拉左翼政治人物，是委内瑞拉立国以来最年轻的总统。他执政十四年，是近当代全世界最具争议也最具影响力的政治人物之一。2013年3月5日下午，委内瑞拉副总统尼古拉斯·马杜罗在军事医院宣布，委内瑞拉总统查韦斯于当地时间16时25分去世，终年58岁。查韦斯遗体做防腐处理后被安置在革命博物馆，并以国葬形式举行了葬礼。

Fidel Alejandro Castro Ruz (1926 –): a Cuban communist revolutionary and politician who was Prime Minister of Cuba from 1959 to 1976, and President from 1976 to 2008. He also served as the Commander in Chief of the country's armed forces from 1959 to 2008, and as the First Secretary of the Communist Party of Cuba from 1961 until 2011. Politically a Marxist-Leninist, under his administration the Republic of Cuba became a one-party socialist state; industry and businesses were nationalized, and socialist reforms implemented in all areas  of society. Internationally, Castro was the Secretary-General of the Non-Aligned Movement, from 1979 to 1983 and from 2006 to 2008.

菲德尔·亚历杭德罗·卡斯特罗·鲁斯古巴共产党、古巴共和国和古巴革命武装力量的主要创立者和领导人，前任古巴共产党中央委员会第一书记，古巴共和国前国务委员会主席（国家元首）和部长会议主席（政府首脑）。2005年6月卡斯特罗因病住院，其弟——时任第一副主席的劳尔·卡斯特罗暂代国务委员会主席职务。后劳尔·卡斯特罗正式出任国务委员会主席兼部长会议主席职务。卡斯特罗于2008年2月19日公开表示不会再寻求担任古巴国务委员会主席的职务，2011年在公开文章中称五年前已经辞去所有职务。

Left-wing bloc: in politics, left-wing describes an outlook or specific position that accepts or supports social equality, often in opposition to social hierarchy and social inequality. It usually involves a concern for those in society who are disadvantaged relative to others and an assumption that there are unjustified inequalities (which right-wing politics views as natural or traditional) that need to be reduced or abolished. The political terms Left and Right were coined during the French Revolution (1789–1799), referring to the seating arrangement in the Estates General.

左翼阵营：又称左派，是指支持改变传统社会秩序，创造更为平等的财富和基本权利分配的阵营。这一名词来自法国大革命时期，在议会中坐在左侧，支持共和制、大众政治运动和世俗化的人。

Rafael Antonio Caldera Rodríguez（1916 – 2009）: President of Venezuela from 1969 to 1974 and again from 1994 to 1999. He was a founding member of COPEI, Venezuela's Christian Democratic Party. When he was sworn into office in 1969, it marked the first peaceful transfer of power from one party to another in Venezuela's history. During his first presidency, Caldera was able to pacify the country by granting an amnesty that allowed guerrilla fighters, who had been operating clandestinely for almost a decade, to reincorporate into society and participate in politics. In 1993, Caldera split from COPEI, the party he had founded, to form a new political party, Convergence, which, supported by a coalition of many small leftist parties as well as some centre-right parties, raised Caldera to the presidency in December 1993.

拉斐尔·卡尔德拉·罗德里格斯：第54任和第60任委内瑞拉总统。1946年1月与路易斯·埃雷拉一起创建委内瑞拉基督教社会党，1969–1974年，基督教社会党第一次执政，卡尔德拉出任总统。任内采取了一系列民族主义和缓和国内矛盾的措施，如提高石油价格、废除美委不平等的通商条约、积极推动拉美经济一体化运动、继续进行土地改革等。1993年因政见分歧被基督教社会党开除出党。卡尔德拉随后创建"全国同盟"，参加1993年12月的大选并获胜，1994年2月2日宣誓就职。

Simón Bolívar (1783–1830): a Venezuelan military and political leader. Bolívar played a key role in Latin America's successful struggle for independence from the Spanish Empire, and is today considered one of the most influential politicians in the history of the Americas. Following the triumph over the Spanish monarchy, Bolívar participated in the foundation of the first union of independent nations in Hispanic-America, a republic, which was named Gran Colombia, of which he was president from 1819 to 1830. Bolívar remains

regarded in Hispanic-America as a hero, visionary, revolutionary, and liberator. During his lifetime, he led Venezuela, Colombia, Ecuador, Peru, and Bolivia to independence, and helped lay the foundations for democratic ideology in much of Latin America.

西蒙·玻利瓦尔：拉丁美洲革命家、军事家、政治家、思想家，他与圣马丁遥相呼应，为南美洲脱离西班牙帝国统治而独立发挥了关键作用。在与西班牙君主的斗争中取胜后，玻利瓦尔参与建立了拉丁美洲第一个独立国家联盟，即大哥伦比亚，并于1819年至1830年任该国总统。西蒙·玻利瓦尔在西班牙语中被公认为英雄、革命者与解放者。在他有生之年，他领导玻利维亚、哥伦比亚、厄瓜多尔、巴拿马、秘鲁和委内瑞拉取得独立，并促进民主意识形态在这些国家的发展。

 Writing Tips 写作秘笈

人物具有多面性和复杂性，只有抓住其突出特征，重点刻画，才能使得人物形象个性鲜明。切忌面面俱到，笔墨均沾。

这是一篇回顾委内瑞拉传奇人物查韦斯生平的文章，作者重点刻画了他"戏剧化的表演家个性"，在文中运用多个例子来印证这一个性特征：如1992年戴着红色贝雷帽发表的一分钟电视演讲，亲自主持连续几小时的电视节目，大玩棒球驳斥病危报道等。

参考文献

[1] Corbett, M. Politics and Religion in the United State. New York: Garland Pub, 1999.

[2] Santino, Jack. All around the year: Holiday and Celebrations in American Life. Urbana: University of Illinois Press,1994.

[3] Santino, Jack: New Old-fashioned Ways: Holidays and Popular Culture. Knoxville: University of Tennessee Press, 1996.

[4] Litwicki,Ellen M. America's Public Holidays, 1865-1920. Washington, D. C.: Smithsonian Institute Press, 2000.

[5] Wikipedia. http://www. wikipedia.org/.

[6] Queen, E. L. Encyclopedia of American Religious History. New York: Facts on File,2008.

[7] Encyclopedia. http://encyclopedia.thefreedictionary.com.

[8] Economy of the United States. http://en. wikipedia. Org/wiki/Economy_of_the_United_States.

[9] The New World Encyclopedia. http://www.newworldencyclopedia.org/.

[10] Mobile Encyclopedia. http://wapedia.mobi/en/.

[11] http://www.sonofthesouth. Net/revolutionary-war/explorers/discovering-america-columbus.htm.

[12] 邓炎昌. 现代美国社会与文化[M]. 北京：高等教育出版社，1989.

[13] 徐志英. 英语电影视听说[M]. 北京：外语教学与研究出版社，2009.

[14] 刘澎. 当代美国宗教[M]. 北京：科学文献出版社，2001.

[15] 梅仁毅. 美国文化读本[M]. 北京：外语教学与研究出版社，2002.

[16] 卫玲. 英语影视欣赏[M]. 苏州：苏州大学出版社，2009.

[17] 王恩铭. 美国文化与社会[M]. 上海：上海外语教育出版社，2003.

[18] 周静琼. 当代美国概况[M]. 上海：上海外语教育出版社，2004.

[19] 姜欣，姜怡. 文化交流英语[M]. 北京，高等教育出版社，2006.

[20] 冒兮. 文化英语视听说[M]. 重庆：重庆大学出版社，2010.

[21] 范悦. 美国历史概况[M]. 北京：对外经济贸易大学出版社，2006.

[22] 谢福之. 英语国家概况[M]. 北京：外语教学与研究出版社，2007.

[23] 温洪瑞，李雪珍. 英美概况[M]. 济南：山东大学出版社，2008.

[24] 李景琦. 英美文化[M]. 天津：天津大学出版社，2010.

[25] 范建华，毛启红. 新编英美国家社会与文化（美国篇）[M]. 苏州：苏州大学出版社，2010.